Franc-w

Richard Binns

Chiltern House

To
Mike
for his invaluable inspection help

If you have a copy of *French Leave Encore* please delete the following entries – for varying reasons: Epinal p37; Gérardmer (Réserve) p42; Mittelwihr p43; Dinan p64; St-Malo p70; Gimel p133; Claix p142; Varces (Matitis) p147; Echallon p173; Huisseau p210; Montreuil p211; Onzain p212; Tours (Groison) p213; Artemare p226; Donzère p249; Domfront p275; Goupillières p275; Arras (Faisanderie) p289; Bourcefranc p304; Challans p305; Montmorillon p307; Pons p307; Castillon p324; Biddarray p363; Grenade p364.

© Richard Binns 1995 (Text and Maps)
Published in February 1995 by Richard & Anne Binns – trading as Chiltern House Publishers, Honeywood House, Avon Dassett, Leamington Spa, Warwickshire CV33 0AH

ISBN 0-9516930-5-0

The contents of the guide are believed correct at the time of printing. Nevertheless Chiltern House Publishers cannot accept responsibility for errors or omissions, or for changes in details given. The prices indicated in the guide were supplied to us during the summer of 1994.

Maps drawn by the author
Typeset in Concorde (text) and Gill (maps) by Art Photoset Limited, 64 London End, Beaconsfield, Bucks HP9 2JD
Printed by Butler & Tanner Limited, The Selwood Printing Works, Caxton Road, Frome, Somerset BA11 1NF

Abbreviations

Few abbreviations are used in *Franc-wise France* (*FWF*). Each entry has an introductory summary of the main facilities provided and a concluding section where essential information is shown as follows:

Menus   range of cost of fixed-price menus (*prix-fixe*) or, if not available, the minimum cost of three courses from the à la carte menu; see price bands listed below

Rooms   number of bedrooms (in brackets) and price band range (for the bedroom). The word "Disabled" indicates that some bedrooms are accessible to guests in wheelchairs

Cards   accepted: Access (also MasterCard and Eurocard); AE American Express; DC Diners Club; Visa. Always check ahead

Closed   annual holidays (if any) and days of the week closed. Always check ahead, as changes are often made. If no details provided then the establishment is open all the year

Post   post code, village or town name, *département*

Region   for details of both regional cuisine and regional specialities see the region(s) indicated at the back of *Franc-wise France*

Tel   telephone number

Fax   fax number, where available

Mich   page number and grid square on which the entry is located in the spiral-bound *Michelin Motoring Atlas France*

Map   map number (1 to 6 – these follow the four introductory pages) on which the entry is located

Prices

		(Bands D to G: see notes below)	
A	under 100 Francs	D	165 to 250 Francs
B	100 to 135 Francs	E	250 to 350 Francs
C	135 to 165 Francs	F	350 to 500 Francs
		G	over 500 Francs

(a) (b) etc: menus not available at weekends or on public holidays.
G2: multiply G by figure indicated. Price bands include service and taxes but not wines and breakfasts. Agree *pension* terms in advance.

All recommendations in *FWF* offer one or more menus in price bands A, B or C. At least one qualifying menu should also be available at weekends and on public holidays. More expensive menus (price bands D to G) may also be available. Bedroom prices will probably be outside the price bands A, B and C.

If you would like a pocket-sized version (19 x 10cm) of the *Glossary of Menu Terms* (featured in *FWF*) send your name, address and **two** 2nd-class stamps to the Avon Dassett address on page 2. One copy per reader.

Introduction

Franc-wise France has one objective: to identify quality cooking for the fewest francs possible. ("Fine fare for few francs" would make an apt alternative title.) The French have the ideal label to summarise exactly what I mean: *rapport qualité-prix* (*RQP*). *Rapport*, a precise word, emphasises the all-important balance between quality and price.

"Good-value", "value-for-money" and "bargain-price" cooking are inadequate English labels. Not one of them stresses the importance of "quality". There has never been any difficulty nosing out low-cost menus in France. The only snag is you eat many a disappointing meal along the way; cheap menus save francs but often quality is non-existent.

To qualify for inclusion in *Franc-wise France* (*FWF*) all recommended hotels and restaurants must offer clients quality cooking in **one or more menus** within three price bands: **A** (under 100 francs); **B** (between 100 and 135 francs); and **C** (between 135 and 165 francs). At current exchange rates that means a range covering from about £10 ($15) to a ceiling of £20 ($30). One onerous additional condition of entry is that at least one qualifying menu must be available at all times – including weekends and public holidays. Many prospective candidates fail on this count. (All French menu prices include both service and taxes.)

Michelin multi-starred chefs fail to meet my price criteria. However, many one-star chefs do offer a *RQP* menu – and several are included. Starred restaurants have had a tough time in recent years but those lower down the ambition scale, guided by the lifesaving *RQP* culinary lighthouse, have had fewer problems and continue to flourish.

Your hard-earned cash is better spent when you seek out the hotels and restaurants in this guide. Any rough edges here and there matter not one iota. You are not paying for a theatrical extravaganza; what counts is the food on the plate. Owners are *in situ* and the enjoyment factor is high. As a bonus, value-for-money prices stretch your francs further.

Three caveats. First, like all my guides, *FWF* is for the independent motorist. **I deliberately do not direct you into the centres of cities and the largest towns** – where noise, traffic, thefts from cars, parking and navigation are all nightmares. Visit them during the day to admire their architectural glories but, come the evening, look elsewhere for a meal and a place to lay your head. (I've provided an overnight hotel recommendation for every restaurant *sans chambres*.) Second, when I use the word **basic** to describe bedrooms, that's exactly what I mean. Third, standards at Michelin *"Repas"* (*"R"*) restaurants vary wildly; many have been excluded from *FWF*.

Of the 351 recommendations in *Franc-wise France* approximately one-third have been "inspected" by 22 of my readers – all of whom have long understood what I mean by *rapport qualité-prix*. My very special thanks go to Mike Millbourn who checked out 30 of the entries.

For campers and caravanners I recommend *The Alan Rogers' Good Camps Guide France*. Another indispensable travelling companion is Alastair Sawday's *Guide to French Bed & Breakfast*.

Culinary Comments

Let me tell you how I categorise cooking standards – a system which has taken years to evolve and which I first used in *French Leave Encore* (*FLE*). I use five ratings – but with four important variations which allow me to solve the problem where, from day to day or even from course to course, standards can vary up or down. I know of no better system.

Cooking 1 Simple, straightforward cooking which, more often than not, will consist of *cuisine Bourgeoise* specialities. Many readers could do as well, or better, at home. This rating is not considered adequate enough to gain an entry in *Franc-wise France* (*FWF*).

Cooking 2 Good, competent cooking – Gault-Millau one *toque* and most Michelin "*Repas*" ("*R*") restaurants. When standards vary, up or down, I use **Cooking 2-3** or **Cooking 1-2** as a rating.

Cooking 3 Very good level of cooking. Some faults but close or equal to a Michelin one-star restaurant standard. If standards are sometimes higher I use **Cooking 3-4** as a rating (awarded to several *FWF* chefs).

Cooking 4 Excellent cooking, often innovative and ambitious and rarely flawed. (No chef in *FWF* wins either this or a **Cooking 4-5** rating.)

Cooking 5 Superb, flawless cooking. (No *FWF* chef wins this rating.)

(Most entries in *FWF* have a **Cooking 2** or **2-3** rating. The place names of 39 recommendations with a **Cooking 3** or **3-4** rating are highlighted on the maps which follow in this way: **Belcastel***)

Finally, some comments on culinary terms. I have included the Glossary of Menu Terms and all the Regional Cuisine/Specialities notes and lists from *FLE* (see the last section of *FWF*). I would also like to provide you with thumbnail-sized descriptions of the different French cooking styles – key terms which I refer to constantly in the guide.

La cuisine Bourgeoise. Simple, family, home cooking using good produce and invariably done well. The repertoire often seems to revolve around 20 to 30 dishes – wherever you are in France: *terrine, escalope, jambon, côte de veau, côte d'agneau, entrecôte, gigot, poulet* and so on.

La cuisine Régionale. Self-explanatory. Alas, authentic regional cooking continues to wither away at an alarming rate. (*Cuisine terroir*: cooking of the local area, including both produce and ancient recipes.)

La haute cuisine (classical cooking). A repertoire of hundreds of rich sauces and garnishes combined with carved-in-stone recipes, techniques and preparation, developed over the last 200 years, make this style of cooking France's greatest contribution to the culinary arts. Many chefs have worked hard to bring a lighter touch to classical cuisine – described in this guide as neo-classical cooking.

La cuisine moderne. Dishes prepared to preserve natural flavours and with the simplest of sauces. Simplicity, and the quality and purity of produce, are essential keys. Improvisation, too, plays a vital part.

Specimen Letters of Reservation

To reserve bedrooms; options on right (in brackets)

1 Would you please reserve a room	(2 rooms, etc.,)
2 with a double bed	(with 2 single beds)
	(one room with) (each room with)
3 and bathroom/WC	(and shower/WC)
4 for one night	(2 nights, etc.,)
5 (*indicate day, date, month*)	
6	(We would like *pension* (half-*pension*) terms for our stay)
7 Please confirm the reservation as soon as possible and please indicate the cost of the rooms	(your *pension* terms for each person)
8 An International Reply Coupon is enclosed	
9 Yours faithfully	
1 Pouvez-vous, s'il vous plaît, me réserver une chambre	**(2 chambres, etc.,)**
2 avec un grand lit	**(avec les lits jumeaux)**
	(une chambre avec)
	(chaque chambre avec)
3 avec salle de bains/WC	**(et douche/WC)**
4 pour une nuit	**(2 nuits, etc.,)**
5 le (*indicate day, date, month*)	
6	**(Nous voudrions pension complète (demi-pension) pour notre séjour)**
7 Veuillez confirmer la réservation dès que possible, et indiquer le tarif des chambres	**(le tarif de pension par personne)**
8 Ci-joint un coupon-réponse international	
9 Je vous prie, Monsieur, d'accepter l'expression de mes salutations distinguées	

If appropriate: Can I have a room/table overlooking the water
Puis-je avoir une chambre/une table qui donne sur l'eau

To reserve tables; options (in brackets)

Would you please reserve a table for ___ persons for lunch (dinner) on (*indicate day, date, month*). We will arrive at the restaurant at ___ hours (*use 24-hour clock*). (We would like a table on the terrace.) Please confirm the reservation. An International Reply Coupon is enclosed. Yours faithfully
Pouvez-vous me réserver une table pour ___ personnes pour déjeuner (dîner) le (*indicate day, date, month*). **Nous arriverons au restaurant à ___ heures** (*use 24-hour clock*). **(Nous aimerons une table sur la terrasse.) Veuillez confirmer la réservation. Ci-joint etc.,** (see 8 above). **Je vous prie, etc.,** (see 9 above)

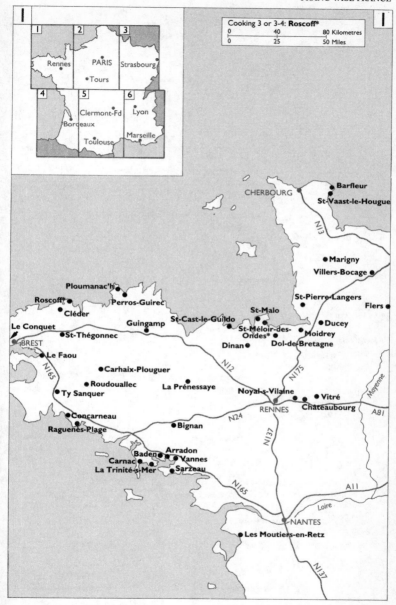

Cooking 3 or 3-4: **Roscoff***

| 0 | 40 | 80 Kilometres |
| 0 | 25 | 50 Miles |

1

2

3

Rennes

PARIS

•Tours

Strasbourg

4

5

6

Clermont-Fd

Bordeaux

•Lyon

Toulouse

Marseille

CHERBOURG

•Barfleur

St-Vaast-le-Hougue

N13

•Marigny

Villers-Bocage•

Ploumanac'h•

St-Pierre-Langers

Flers •

Roscoff*•

Perros-Guirec•

Cléder•

Le Conquet

Guingamp•

St-Cast-le-Guildo•

•St-Malo

•Ducey

St-Thégonnec•

St-Méloir-des-Ondes*•

•Moidrey

BREST

Dinan•

Dol-de-Bretagne

•Le Faou

N165

•Carhaix-Plouguer

N12

N175

Moyenne

•Roudouallec

La Prénessaye•

Noyal-s-Vilaine•

•Vitré

Ty Sanquer•

Châteaubourg

A81

RENNES

•Concarneau

•Bignan

N24

N137

Raguenès-Plage

Baden•

•Arradon

Carnac•

•Vannes

La Trinité-s-Mer

•Sarzeau

N165

A11

Loire

•NANTES

•Les Moutiers-en-Retz

N137

7

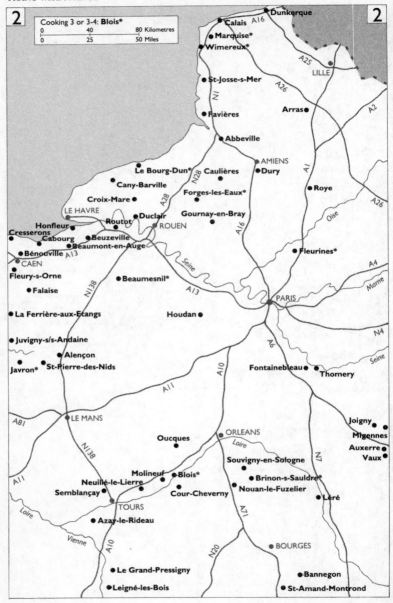

2 2

Cooking 3 or 3-4: **Blois***

0   40   80 Kilometres
0   25   50 Miles

Dunkerque
Calais A16
Marquise*
Wimereux*
LILLE
St-Josse-s-Mer
A26
Arras
N1
Favières
Abbeville
AMIENS
Le Bourg-Dun* **Caulières**
Dury
Cany-Barville
Roye
Croix-Mare
A28
Forges-les-Eaux*
LE HAVRE
Routot **Duclair**
Gournay-en-Bray
Honfleur
Cresserons ROUEN
Oise
Cabourg **Beuzeville**
Beaumont-en-Auge
Seine
Bénouville A13
Fleurines*
A4
CAEN
Fleury-s-Orne
Marne
Beaumesnil* A13
Falaise
PARIS
La Ferrière-aux-Etangs
Houdan
N4
Juvigny-s/s-Andaine
A6
Seine
Alençon
Fontainebleau **Thomery**
Javron* **St-Pierre-des-Nids**
A11
A10
LE MANS
Joigny
A81
Migennes
Oucques
ORLEANS
Auxerre
Loire
Vaux
N138
Souvigny-en-Sologne
Molineuf
N7
Neuillé-le-Lierre **Blois***
Brinon-s-Sauldre*
Semblançay
Cour-Cheverny
Nouan-le-Fuzelier
Léré
TOURS
A71
Azay-le-Rideau
A10
Vienne
Loire
BOURGES
N20
Le Grand-Pressigny
Bannegon
Leigné-les-Bois
St-Amand-Montrond
A2
A1
A26
A16

8

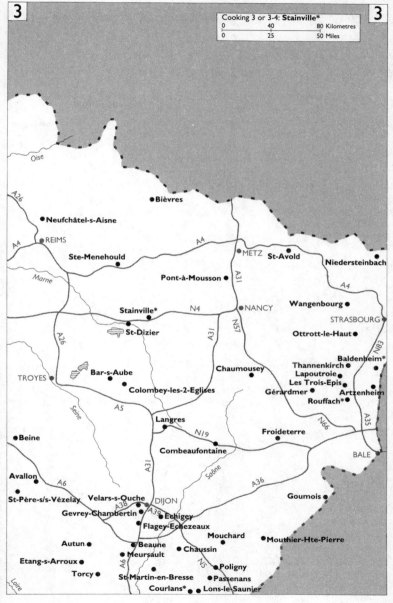

Cooking 3 or 3-4: **Stainville***

| 0 | 40 | 80 Kilometres |
| 0 | 25 | 50 Miles |

Oise

A26

A4

● Bièvres

● Neufchâtel-s-Aisne

● REIMS

A4

METZ ● St-Avold ●

● Niedersteinbach

● Ste-Menehould

Marne

● Pont-à-Mousson ●

A31

A4

N4

● NANCY

● Wangenbourg ●

● Stainville*

N57

STRASBOURG ●

● St-Dizier

● Ottrott-le-Haut ●

A26

N83

● Baldenheim*

● Chaumousey

Thannenkirch ●

● Bar-s-Aube

Lapoutroie ●

TROYES ●

Les Trois-Epis ●

● Colombey-les-2-Eglises

Gérardmer ● ● Artzenheim

Seine

A5

Rouffach*●

● Langres

N19

● Froideterre

N66

A35

● Beine

● Combeaufontaine

BALE

Saône

● Avallon

A6

A36

● St-Père-s/s-Vézelay   ● Velars-s-Ouche

● Goumois ●

A38

● DIJON

● Gevrey-Chambertin

A39

● Echigey

● Flagey-Echezeaux

● Mouchard

● Mouthier-Hte-Pierre

● Autun ●

● Beaune

● Chaussin

● Etang-s-Arroux ●

A6

● Meursault

● Torcy ●

N5

● Poligny

● St-Martin-en-Bresse

● Passenans

Loire

● Courlans*   ● Lons-le-Saunier

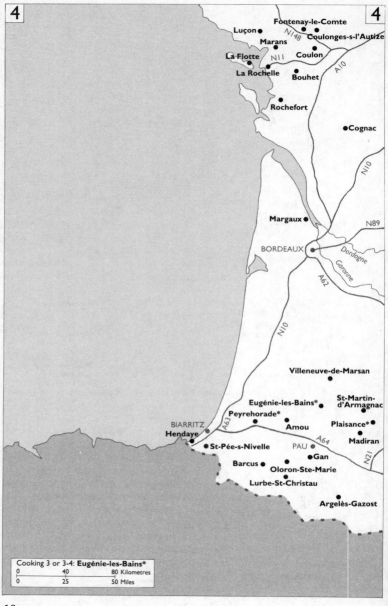

4   **4**

Fontenay-le-Comte
Luçon ●   ● N148   ● Coulonges-s-l'Autize
Marans ●
●   Coulon ●
La Flotte ● N11
La Rochelle ●   ● Bouhet

● Rochefort

● Cognac

N10

Margaux ●

N89

BORDEAUX ●   Dordogne

A62   Garonne

N10

Villeneuve-de-Marsan
●

Eugénie-les-Bains*   St-Martin-
●   d'Armagnac ●
Peyrehorade*
A63 ●   Plaisance* ●
BIARRITZ   Amou ●   A64   Madiran ●
Hendaye ●   PAU ●
● St-Pée-s-Nivelle   ● Gan   N21
Barcus ●   ● Oloron-Ste-Marie
Lurbe-St-Christau ●

● Argelès-Gazost

Cooking 3 or 3-4: **Eugénie-les-Bains***
0   40   80 Kilometres
0   25   50 Miles

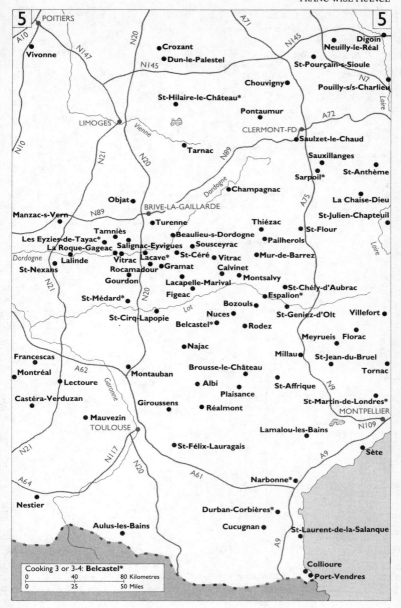

5 POITIERS

Vivonne

Crozant
Dun-le-Palestel

Digoin
Neuilly-le-Réal

St-Pourçain-s-Sioule

Chouvigny

Pouilly-s/s-Charlieu

St-Hilaire-le-Château*

Pontaumur

LIMOGES

CLERMONT-FD

Saulzet-le-Chaud

Tarnac

Sauxillanges

St-Anthème

Sarpoil*

La Chaise-Dieu

Objat

Champagnac

St-Julien-Chapteuil

Manzac-s-Vern

BRIVE-LA-GAILLARDE

Turenne

Thiézac
St-Flour

Beaulieu-s-Dordogne
Pailherols

Tamniès

Les Eyzies-de-Tayac*
Salignac-Eyvigues   Sousceyrac

La Roque-Gageac
Vitrac   Lacave*   St-Céré   Vitrac
Mur-de-Barrez

Lalinde
Rocamadour   Gramat   Calvinet

St-Nexans
Gourdon
Lacapelle-Marival   Montsalvy

St-Médard*
Figeac
St-Chély-d'Aubrac

Bozouls   Espalion*

St-Cirq-Lapopie
Nuces   St-Geniez-d'Olt   Villefort

Belcastel*
Rodez

Meyrueis   Florac

Najac

Francescas
Millau   St-Jean-du-Bruel

Brousse-le-Château   Tornac

Montréal
Lectoure   Montauban
Albi
St-Affrique

Castéra-Verduzan
Giroussens   Plaisance
St-Martin-de-Londres*

Réalmont
MONTPELLIER

Mauvezin
TOULOUSE

Lamalou-les-Bains

St-Félix-Lauragais
Sète

Nestier

A61

Narbonne*

Durban-Corbières*

Aulus-les-Bains
Cucugnan
St-Laurent-de-la-Salanque

Collioure
Port-Vendres

Cooking 3 or 3-4: **Belcastel***
0   40   80 Kilometres
0   25   50 Miles

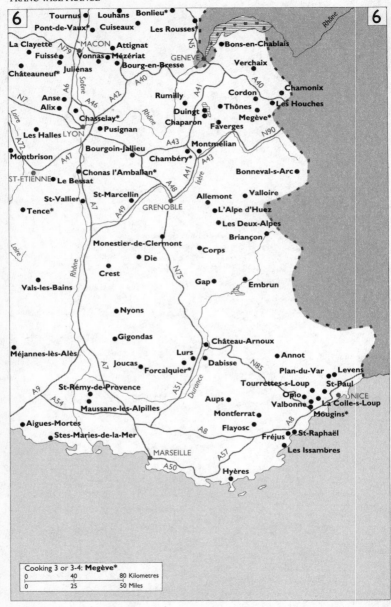

Cooking 3 or 3-4: **Megève***

| 0 | 40 | 80 Kilometres |
| 0 | 25 | 50 Miles |

ABBEVILLE

Auberge de la Corne

Comfortable restaurant/Cooking 2

Two dining rooms: one described as *anglo-normande*; the other a warm, panelled *salle*. There's an equally warm welcome from English-speaking *patronne*, Maryse Lematelot. Her husband, Yves, walks a classical path and is competently adept with alternative specialities ranging from *morue fraîche, fondue et poireaux* to a hearty *faux filet de sauce échalote*. One regional must is a filling *ficelle picarde*.
Menus ACDE. Cards All. (Rooms: nearby Relais Vauban – 100 m walk E.)
Closed 19 Feb to 9 Mar. Sun evg. Mon. (W of station, parking and N1.)
Post 32 chaussée du Bois, 80100 Abbeville, Somme. Region North.
Tel 22 24 06 34. Fax 22 24 03 65. Mich 6/C3. Map 2.

AIGUES-MORTES

Arcades

Comfortable restaurant with rooms/Cooking 2
Terrace

A 16th-century house with a stone, beamed and flower-filled dining room; an arcade; tiny patio garden; and stylish bedrooms. Classical fare: savour home-made *soupe de poissons*, flavoursome *rable de lapin farci sauce à la sauge*, and simple *fraises au sucre*. Enter the fortified town by the gate halfway along the north wall (bd Gambetta).
Menus BCD. Rooms (6) FG. Cards All. (Cheaper rooms: Croisades.)
Closed Feb. Rest: Mon (not July/Aug). Region Languedoc-Roussillon.
Post 23 bd Gambetta, 30220 Aigues-Mortes, Gard.
Tel 66 53 81 13. Fax 66 53 75 46. Mich 157/D3. Map 6.

ALBI

Jardin des Quatre Saisons

Comfortable restaurant/Cooking 2-3

Georges Bermond, after an absence of 20 years, has returned to his *pays*. The inventive, modern *cuisinier*, together with his blond wife Martine, weave a *RQP* cloth of gold. No less than seven starters, a dozen main courses (divided equally between fish and meat offerings) and nine scrumptious desserts. In addition, a limited choice menu C includes a half-bottle of Gaillac. Right bank, near river and town bridge.
Menus BC. Cards Access, AE, Visa. (Rooms: Cantepau, 150 m E; parking.)
Closed Mon (not public hols).
Post 19 bd Strasbourg, 81000 Albi, Tarn. Region Languedoc-Roussillon.
Tel 63 60 77 76. Fax 63 60 77 77. Mich 154/A1. Map 5.

A100frs & under. B100–135. C135–165. D165–250. E250–350. F350–500. G500+

ALENCON   Au Petit Vatel

Very comfortable restaurant/Cooking 2-3

The town's most famous restaurant – rightly so, as the window-boxed exterior provides an attractive *entrée* to the culinary patterns so delicately woven by classicist, Michel Lerat. (The restaurant is almost next door to the Musée des Beaux-Arts with its fine lace collection.) Precision *plats* like *délice de cèpes, duo de sole et saumon sauce cardinal, coq au vin à la Solognotte* and super *sorbets et glaces*.
Menus BCD. Cards All. (Rooms: Ibis, 300 metre-walk away to E.)
Closed Feb school hols. 1-23 Aug. Sun evg. Wed.
Post 72 pl. Cdt Desmeulles, 61000 Alençon, Orne. Region Normandy.
Tel 33 26 23 78. Mich 51/D2. Map 2. (Plenty of parking nearby.)

ALIX   Le Vieux Moulin

Simple restaurant/Cooking 1-2
Terrace/Parking

Annie and Gérard Umhauer's mill shines with pride – literally, as the *moulin* is constructed from the local golden stone (*pierres dorées*). Gérard's cooking is Lyonnais fare at its most Pavlovian: temptations tagged *terrine maison, grenouilles, poulet à la crème, andouillette de "Chez Besson" sauce moutarde, fromage blanc* and *sorbet vigneron*.
Menus BCD. Cards Access, Visa. (Rooms: A6 *autoroute* hotels Limonest.)
Closed 7 Aug to 5 Sept. Mon and Tues (not pub hols). (See *FLE* p222.)
Post 69380 Alix, Rhône. Region Lyonnais. (Limonest is SE of Alix.)
Tel 78 43 91 66. Fax 78 47 98 46. Mich 115/F1. Map 6.

ALLEMONT   Giniès

Simple hotel/Cooking 1-2
Quiet/Terrace/Gardens/Parking

A colourful, shady garden is one big bonus; a second is the enterprising Giniès family – Robert and Gilberte, their chef son, Philippe, and his wife, Isabelle. Run-of-the-mill *Bourgeoise* and classical cuisine – of the *terrine maison, truite meunière, escalope de veau* variety. Order *râclette* and *fondue* (regional winners) at least two hours in advance.
Menus aBCD. Rooms (28) DE. Cards Access, Visa.
Closed Rest: 10 Apl to 2 May; mid Sept to Jan.
Post 38114 Allemont, Isère. Regions Hautes-Alpes/Savoie.
Tel 76 80 70 03. Fax 76 80 73 13. Mich 132/B2. Map 6.

A100frs & under. B100–135. C135–165. D165–250. E250–350. F350–500. G500+

L'ALPE D'HUEZ
Le Lyonnais

Comfortable restaurant/Cooking 2-3

As you drive the 3000-ft climb with two dozen *lacets* think of the Tour de France cyclists using only pedal power to reach the top. Your car-aided efforts are well rewarded by Gérard Astic's classical and Lyonnais *plats: carpaccio de thon frais à la coriandre, quenelle de brochet soufflé au coulis crustacés* (what memories) and *cervelle de Canut (fromage frais aux herbes)* are typical. Closed at lunchtime.
Menus bCD. Cards Access, Visa. (Rooms: Alp'Azur, 500m-walk away to NE.)
Closed Lunch. May-June. Sept-Nov. Regions Htes-Alpes/Savoie/Lyonnais.
Post rte du Coulet, 38750 L'Alpe d'Huez, Isère.
Tel 76 80 68 92. Mich 132/B2. Map 6.

AMOU
Commerce

Simple hotel/Cooking 2
Terrace/Garage/Parking

As colourful an exterior as you'll find in France: window boxes, blinds, awnings and creeping vines. The Darracq family enterprise is geared up for entertaining individuals and large gatherings. Classical, *Bourgeois* and regional repasts: *terrine maison, quenelles d'oie, confit de porc* and *gâteau Basque* (from wide-choice menu B) will quench any appetite.
Menus aBCD. Rooms (20) DE. Cards All.
Closed 14-28 Feb. 11-30 Nov. Mon (not high season).
Post 40330 Amou, Landes. Region Southwest.
Tel 58 89 02 28. Fax 58 89 24 45. Mich 149/E3. Map 4.

ANNOT
Avenue

Simple hotel/Cooking 2

A warm welcome at this much-liked *FLE* favourite (now "discovered" by Michelin) – ideally placed to explore the mountains to the north. Enterprising *Bourgeoise* and classical cooking with Italian touches from *chef/patron* Jean-Louis Genovesi: starters such as *cannellonis de homard au coulis de crustacés* and *millefeuille de truites rosées*; and welcome main courses like *daube légère de pigeon en couronne de fettucine*.
Menus AB. Rooms (12) DE. Cards Access, Visa.
Closed Nov to March. Regions Côte d'Azur/Hautes-Alpes.
Post 04240 Annot, Alpes-de-Haute-Provcence.
Tel 92 83 22 07. Fax 92 83 34 07. Mich 147/E4. Map 6.

A100frs & under. B100–135. C135–165. D165–250. E250–350. F350–500. G500+

ANSE
St-Romain

Comfortable hotel/Cooking 2
Quiet/Terrace/Gardens/Parking

Easily found if you have my *En Route* (p58). A quiet site, sunny terrace, beamed and flower-filled *salle* and smiling *patronne* are all pluses. So, too, is the classical cuisine of Bruno Levet: try perhaps a *melon glacé aux 4 fruits rouges* or a well-executed *truite de mer en crépinette*, *crème ciboulette*. Alas, only "so-so" sweets from the trolley.
Menus aBCDE. Rooms (24) DE. Cards All.
Closed 27 Nov to 4 Dec. Sun evg (Nov to Apl).
Post rte Graves, 69480 Anse, Rhône. Region Lyonnais.
Tel 74 60 24 46. Fax 74 67 12 85. Mich 116/A1. Map 6.

ARGELES-GAZOST
Hostellerie Le Relais

Comfortable hotel/Cooking 2
Terrace/Lift (being installed)/Parking

Jeannette Hourtal's flowers on the shady terrace and in the main rooms are colourful eye-catchers. Husband Jean's copious classical, regional, and *Bourgeoise* fare is not prissy stuff. Highly satisfying grub of the *flan de cèpes*, *pâté de lièvre confiture d'oignons*, *tranche de gigot de mouton poêlée* and *coupe aux myrtilles flambées* variety.
Menus abCD. Rooms (23) DE. Cards Access, Visa.
Closed 10 Oct to 8 Feb. Region Southwest.
Post 25 r. Mar. Foch, 65400 Argelès-Gazost, Hautes-Pyrénées.
Tel 62 97 01 27. Mich 168/B3. Map 4.

ARRADON
L'Arlequin

Comfortable restaurant/Cooking 2
Terrace/Gardens/Parking

On the D101, at the spot marked Boloré on the map. Prices have remained the same for four years – a remarkable record. Fine *cave* (many halves). Lunch under umbrellas on the terrace. Modern, classical and regional touches: witness *millefeuille de saumon*, *crème d'agrumes*; *tournedos de rumsteack*; and *petit far minute aux pommes et calvados*.
Menus aBCD, Cards All. (Rooms: Le Logis de Parc er Gréo; off D101 to W.)
Closed Sun evg. (Above is *sans rest*, secluded and has swimming pool.)
Post Parc Botquelen, 56610 Arradon, Morbihan. Region Brittany.
Tel 97 40 41 41. Fax 97 40 52 93. Mich 62/C2. Map 1.

A 100frs & under. B 100–135. C 135–165. D 165–250. E 250–350. F 350–500. G 500+

FRANC-WISE FRANCE

ARRAS
Ambassadeur

Very comfortable restaurant/Cooking 2-3

A posh name for a swish show. But, for all railway nuts, this is the ultimate *buffet de gare* – a real "stop" *par excellence. Haute cuisine* TGV classics share the line with regional, anything but punk, puffers: the latter could include *tarte aux maroilles, ficelles à la Picarde and andouillette d'Arras*; the former may number *escalope de saumon à la crème d'aneth* and *rable lapin à la crème de moutarde de Meaux.*
Menus BCD. Cards All. (Rooms: Les 3 Luppars – a brisk 5 m walk to N.)
Closed Sun evg. (Parking for restaurant adjacent to station.)
Post gare, pl. Foch, 62000 Arras, Pas-de-Calais. Region North.
Tel 21 23 29 80. Fax 21 71 17 07. Mich 8/A2. Map 2.

ARTZENHEIM
Auberge d'Artzenheim

Comfortable restaurant with rooms/Cooking 2
Quiet/Terrace/Gardens/Parking

A colourful mix of old and new – with, in true Alsace fashion, flowers everywhere. Some bedrooms smallish. Chef Edgar Husser, who trained at the nearby three-star Aub. de l'Ill, mixes regional and both old and new: a filling *assiette des terrines et crudités*, tasty *mignons de porc aux choux rouges* and a heady finale, a smooth *mousse au kirsch.*
Menus b(lunch)CDE. Rooms (10) E. Cards Access, Visa.
Closed Mid Feb to mid Mar. Mon evg. Tues.
Post 68320 Artzenheim, Haut-Rhin. Region Alsace.
Tel 89 71 60 51. Fax 89 71 68 21. Mich 61/E3. Map 3.

ATTIGNAT
Dominique Marcepoil

Very comfortable restaurant with rooms/Cooking 2-3
Terrace/Gardens/Parking

A perfect lunch: a covered terrace with a retina-piercing tapestry and vast colourful mural; and, better still, eye-catching cooking from *chef/patron*, the bubbly DM. A well-balanced *repas* of *saumon* marinaded in olive oil and dill, a *quiche de ris de veau au Côtes de Jura*, a fresh goat's cheese *quenelle* and strawberry tart. Perfection?
Menus bCDE. Rooms (9) EF. Cards Access, AE, Visa. (On D975.)
Closed 11-17 Sept. 13-19 Nov. Sun evg. Mon.
Post 01340 Attignat, Ain. Region Lyonnais.
Tel 74 30 92 24. Fax 74 25 93 48. Mich 103/D3. Map 6.

A100frs & under. B100–135. C135–165. D165–250. E250–350. F350–500. G500+

17

AULUS-LES-BAINS

Terrasse

Simple hotel/Cooking 2
Terrace

Step over the bridge and travel back in time 30 years – furnishings, service and cooking as they used to be; so, too, is Madame, Rose Amiel, a headmistress martinet. No modern frills here. Chef Jean-François Maurette is a true-blue classics/regional fan: savour rich dishes like *tourte de foie gras de canard* and *cuisse de canard confite du Gers*.
Menus b(lunch)CDE. Rooms (19) DE. Cards Access, Visa (cash preferred!).
Closed Oct to Apl (but not school hols). (Essential to book ahead.)
Post 09140 Aulus-les-Bains, Ariège. Region Southwest.
Tel 61 96 00 98. Mich 170/C4. Map 5.

AUPS

Le Chalet

Very simple restaurant/Cooking 2
Terrace & Gardens (newly-created)

Philippe La Montagne, in his mid-30s, is a classical chef, a self-confessed disciple of Escoffier. Wife Béatrice is a welcoming *patronne*. A flurry of rich, tasty specialities: *pièce de boeuf grillée à l'essence de truffe et au foie gras* is just one memorable example. Mouthwatering sweets, especially an irresistible hot *soufflé au Grand Marnier*.
Menus ABC. Cards None. (Rooms: hotels at Tourtour & Moustiers-Ste-M.)
Closed Mon evg & Wed evg (out of seas). (Best: Le Colombier, Moustiers.)
Post 3 r. Maréchal Foch, 83630 Aups, Var. Region Côte d'Azur.
Tel 94 70 04 22. Mich 162/C2. Map 6.

AUTUN

Chalet Bleu

Comfortable restaurant/Cooking 2

Papa Bouché, Georges, was once the chef at the French Embassy in London. Here he runs the front of house and his son, Philippe, is the chef. Regional, classical and neo-classical alternatives: *saupiquet de jambon vieux Morvan, jambon persillé à la Bourguignonne, pièce de boeuf rôtie au fumet de Bourgogne* and *fondant de crabe océan* are a representative quartet. Terrific old-time desserts. (Near *mairie* – town hall.)
Menus aBCD. Cards Access, AE, Visa. (Rooms: Arcades – 5 min walk to NW.)
Closed 5-20 Feb. Mon evg. Tues.
Post 3 r. Jeannin, 71400 Autun, Saône-et-Loire. Region Burgundy.
Tel 85 86 27 30. Mich 87/E3. Map 3.

A 100frs & under. B 100–135. C 135–165. D 165–250. E 250–350. F 350–500. G 500+

AUXERRE
Le Moulin

Comfortable restaurant/Cooking 2
Terrace/Parking

Just north of the Auxerre-Sud A6 exit (follow signs). Jean-Pierre Vaury is highly thought of by his regional peers. A mainly classical repertoire confirms their opinions: a rarely seen *pied de veau, sauce ravigote*; a smooth and full-of-flavour *saumon grillée beurre blanc*; a cheese chariot (regional varieties); and drooling *tarte aux pommes*.
Menus bCDEF. Cards Access, Visa. (Rooms: Ibis near A6 exit.)
Closed 15-31 Jan. 19-30 Aug. Sun evg. Mon.
Post La Coudre, 89290 Venoy, Yonne. Region Burgundy.
Tel 86 40 23 79. Fax 86 40 23 55. Mich 72/A2. Map 2.

AVALLON
Le Morvan

Very comfortable restaurant/Cooking 2
Terrace/Gardens/Parking

Step back to France as she used to be; not for those influenced by lightness and brightness cooking and served on black octagonal plates. Jean, the chef, and Marinette Breton are loyal regional and classical troopers: dig into a meaty *duo de terrine, jambon sec de pays, saucisson chaud au canard fumé* and *filets de lapin farcis Bourguignonne*.
Menus BD. Cards All. (Rooms: Avallon-Vauban – a 5 min walk to SE.)
Closed Jan. Feb. Sun evg. Mon (not public hols).
Post 7 rte de Paris (N6), 89200 Avallon, Yonne. Region Burgundy.
Tel 86 34 18 20. Mich 72/B3. Map 3.

AZAY-LE-RIDEAU
Aigle d'Or

Comfortable restaurant/Cooking 2-3
Terrace

A pleasure in every sense: a pastel-shaded dining room with flowers on each table; a garden terrace for eating out; an attractive hostess, Ghislaine Fèvre; and traditional cooking from her husband, Jean-Luc. *Crème d'oseille et quenelles de brochet, jambonnette de volaille à la crème de morilles* and *craquant aux fraises* are lip-smacking memories.
Menus a(lunch)CDE. Cards Access, Visa. (Rooms: De Biencourt.) Closed 6 Feb-2 Mar. 4-10 Sept. 15-25 Dec. Sun evg. Tues evg (Oct-mid May). Wed.
Post 37190 Azay-le-Rideau, Indre-et-Loire. Region Loire.
Tel 47 45 24 58. Fax 47 45 90 18. Mich 82/A1. Map 2.

A 100frs & under. B 100–135. C 135–165. D 165–250. E 250–350. F 350–500. G 500+

BADEN   Le Gavrinis

Comfortable hotel/Cooking 2
Terrace/Gardens/Parking

A sparkling, multi-faceted family affair. Alain Justum and sons, Olivier
and Frédéric, man the stoves; mum, Michèle, and daughter Sybille run
the front of house. English-speaking Sybille is a knowledgeable delight.
Modern and neo-classical *plats* excecuted with flair, harmony and good
taste. Modern, spick and span hotel with flower-bedecked terrace.
Menus CDE. Rooms (19) DEF. Cards All.
Closed Dec. Jan. Mon (not evg from June to Sept).
Post Toulbroch, 56870 Baden, Morbihan. Region Brittany.
Tel 97 57 00 82. Fax 97 57 09 47. Mich 62/C2. Map 1.

BALDENHEIM   La Couronne

Very comfortable restaurant/Cooking 3

Chefs Argèle Trébis and her son-in-law, Daniel Rubiné, marry regional
and classical in their culinary offerings. Marcel Trébis and his pretty
daughter, Chantal, watch over their flower-filled, panelled dining rooms
with courtesy and flair. Typical qualifying menu: *amuse bouche*, *filet de
hareng mariné*, gutsy *civet de chevreuil* and sumptuous *sorbets*.
Champion *matelote de Ried* (the name for the marshy Rhine plain).
Menus CDE. Cards Access, AE, Visa. (Rooms: several hotels N of Colmar.)
Closed 3-10 Jan. 25 July to 5 Aug. Sun evg. Mon (not public hols).
Post 67600 Baldenheim, Bas-Rhin. Region Alsace.
Tel 88 85 32 22. Fax 88 85 36 27. Mich 61/E2. Map 3.

BANNEGON   Auberge Moulin de Chaméron

Comfortable restaurant with rooms/Cooking 2-3
Secluded/Terrace/Gardens/Swimming pool/Parking

English-speaking Jacques and Annie Candoré are the informed *patrons* at
the 18thC mill (with milling museum). Son-in-law, chef Jean Mérilleau,
conjures up neo-classical and modern tricks: a *flan de langoustines au
vin blanc de Sancerre* and a *feuillantine de framboises* are examples of
his skills. Drink Menetou, Quincy, Reuilly and St-Pourçain wines.
Menus CD. Rooms (12) EF. Disabled. Cards Access, AE, Visa.
Closed Mid Nov to end Feb. Tues (out of season).
Post 18210 Bannegon, Cher. Region Berry-Bourbonnais. Map 2.
Tel (R) 48 61 84 48. (H) 48 61 83 80. Fax 48 61 84 92. Mich 85/D4.

A 100frs & under. B 100–135. C 135–165. D 165–250. E 250–350. F 350–500. G 500+

BARCUS

Chez Chilo

**Very comfortable restaurant with rooms/Cooking 2
Terrace/Gardens/Parking**

Pierre and Martine Chilo are the third generation *patrons* (a family renowned locally for their rugby links). Scrum down for Pierre's classical and regional culinary balls – among them bright *piments "piquillos" farcis à la morue*, hearty *civet de marcassin* and yummy *gâteau Basque au coulis de cerises noires*. Eight super new bedrooms.
Menus aC. Rooms (14) BDEF. Cards Access, AE, Visa.
Closed 15-31 March. Sun evg and Mon (not high season).
Post 64130 Barcus, Pyrénées-Atlantiques. Region Southwest.
Tel 59 28 90 79. Fax 59 28 93 10. Mich 167/E2. Map 4.

BARFLEUR

Moderne

Comfortable restaurant with rooms/Cooking 2

A small pepperpot tower is an unusual man-made exterior feature. Mme Le Roulier is a friendly, helpful *patronne*. Her husband, chef Evrard, steams a classical course and capitalises on the nearby ocean's piscatorial harvests: *soupe de poisson*, oysters and a *choucroute de poisson au beurre blanc* are typical treats. Patterned plates reflect the rather busy cooking style. Home-made breads/pasta. Many half-bottles.
Menus aBD. Rooms (8) BD. Cards Access, Visa.
Closed Mid Jan to 20 Mar. Tues and Wed (mid Sept to mid Jan).
Post 50760 Barfleur, Manche. Region Normandy.
Tel 33 23 12 44. Fax 33 23 91 58. Mich 12/C1. Map 1.

BAR-SUR-AUBE

Relais des Gouverneurs

**Comfortable restaurant with rooms/Cooking 2
Garage/Parking**

A dour-looking *relais* at the heart of Bar-s-Aube. A small flower-filled courtyard provides limited off-the-road parking. Modern creations from the 23-year-old chef son of Mme Guilleminot. Examples include a colourful *levée de rougets aux haricots* and a *sorbet à la framboise avec fruits* (served, intelligently, with a glass of Coteaux Champenois).
Menus aBC. Rooms (15) E. Cards All.
Closed Sat midday. Sun evg. Mon midday (not public hols).
Post 38 r. Nationale, 10200 Bar-s-Aube, Aube. Region Champagne-Ardenne.
Tel 25 27 08 76. Fax 25 27 20 80. Mich 57/E3. Map 3.

A100frs & under. B100–135. C135–165. D165–250. E250–350. F350–500. G500+

BEAULIEU-SUR-DORDOGNE

Central Hôtel Fournié

Simple hotel/Cooking 1-2
Terrace/Parking

A fairly modern, brown-shuttered *logis* with easy parking in the large *place* opposite. An all-fish menu (how welcome) is only just outside the C price range ceiling. Menu B includes a *pillau de calmar d'encre, foie gras de canard frais en terrine* and a middling only *navarin d'agneau et ses pâtes fraîches*. Overall, enjoyable grub from Bernard Bessière.
Menus aBCDE. Rooms (27) CDE. Cards Access, Visa.
Closed Nov to Mar. Region Dordogne.
Post 4 pl. Champ-de-Mars, 19120 Beaulieu-sur-Dordogne, Corrèze.
Tel 55 91 01 34. Fax 55 91 23 57. Mich 125/D3. Map 5.

BEAUMESNIL

L'Etape Louis XIII

Comfortable restaurant/Cooking 3
Terrace/Gardens/Parking

A line of evocative 17th-century half-timbered Normandy cottages is the initial eye-tickler. Next the welcome from Françoise Sureau. Only one qualifying menu (top-end A) – but what palette-tickling classical largesse from chef Philippe Sureau: *fricassée de légumes aux herbes, choux farci de sa pintade au romarin*, cheese and *mousse au chocolat*.
Menus ADE. Cards Access, AE, Visa. (Rooms: Acropole to SW of Bernay.)
Closed 18 Jan to 9 Feb. 21 June to 12 July. Sun evg. Mon. Tues.
Post 27410 Beaumesnil, Eure. Region Normandy.
Tel 32 44 44 72. Mich 33/F2. Map 2.

BEAUMONT-EN-AUGE

La Haie Tondue

Comfortable restaurant/Cooking 1-2
Parking

Chef Dominique Tolmais is a champion menu changer; every three weeks a new version appears. Menus B&C provide a choice of five starters, five main courses, followed by many cheeses and even more puds. Appetite-quenching classical and *Bourgeoise* grub: like *terrine campagnarde, terrine de poisson verte* and *faux-filet grillé maître d'hôtel*.
Menus BCD. Cards Access, Visa. (Rooms: Climat de France, Pont-l'Evêque.)
Closed 1-15 Mar. 19 June-4 July. 2-17 Oct. Mon evg (not Aug). Tues.
Post 14130 La Haie Tondue, Beaumont-en-Auge, Calvados. Region Normandy.
Tel 31 64 85 00. Fax 31 64 69 34. Mich 32/C1. Map 2. (2 km to S.)

A 100frs & under. B 100–135. C 135–165. D 165–250. E 250–350. F 350–500. G 500+

BEAUNE

Central

Comfortable hotel/Cooking 2

At the heart of the flower-covered town, a tennis court length from the multi-hued Hôtel-Dieu patterned roof. Bright, pretty patterns also grace the Central plates: menu B includes *petites salades mélangées au blanc de volaille fumé maison* and *saumon cuit sur peau à l'encre de seiche, gnocchi de moelle*. Regional classics – *jambon persillé fait maison* and *véritable coq au vin à l'ancienne mode* – are on menu C.
Menus a(lunch)BCD. Rooms (20) EFG. Cards Access, Visa.
Closed 21 Nov to 22 Dec. Sun evg (Nov to Mar). Wed (Nov to June).
Post 2 r. V. Millot, 21200 Beaune, Côte-d'Or. Region Burgundy.
Tel 80 24 77 24. Fax 80 22 30 40. Mich 88/A2. Map 3.

BEINE

Le Vaulignot

Comfortable restaurant/Cooking 1-2

Alongside the D965, six km west of Chablis, six km from an A6 exit and in the thick of vineyard terrain. Jean-Claude Dubois believes in choice and seems to have a low opinion of all slimmers. *Bourgeoise*, classical and regional grub. Forget your diet, loosen your belts and tuck into a nostalgic *saucisson chaud du Beaujolais pommes à l'huile; sole meunière; fromage blanc*; and *baba au rhum et sa crème anglaise*.
Menus aCD. Cards Access, Visa. (Rooms: Les Lys, Chablis; Ibis, A6 exit.)
Closed Feb. 2nd half Oct. Sun evg. Mon.
Post Beine, 89800 Chablis, Yonne. Region Burgundy.
Tel 86 42 48 48. Mich 72/B2. Map 3.

BELCASTEL

Vieux Pont

Comfortable restaurant with rooms/Cooking 3
Quiet/Gardens

A sumptuously scenic spot and a seductive modern, natural style of cooking from self-taught *cuisinière*, Nicole Fagegaltier-Rouquier; sister Michèle runs the front of house. Extensive use of oil (olive, walnut and hazelnut) and light cooking reductions: examples are *essence de morilles* and *lait d'amandes*. New bedroom annexe on opposite bank of the river.
Menus BDE. Rooms (7) EF. Cards Access, Visa.
Closed Jan. Feb. Sun evg (not July/Aug). Mon (but not midday July/Aug).
Post 12390 Belcastel, Aveyron. Region Massif Central (Cevénnes).
Tel 65 64 52 29. Fax 65 64 44 32. Mich 140/B1-B2. Map 5.

A100frs & under. B100–135. C135–165. D165–250. E250–350. F350–500. G500+

BENOUVILLE Manoir d'Hastings et la Pommeraie

Very comfortable restaurant with rooms/Cooking 2-3
Quiet/Gardens/Parking

New owners, Carole and José Aparicio, praised by readers, have injected a new lease of life into the 17thC priory. Classical/regional cooking and a wide choice for each course is a plus. Faultless technique with specialities such as *terrine de foie gras au vieux porto*, *ris de veau aux morilles*, *goujonnettes de soles poêlées* and *tarte chaude Normande*.
Menus b(lunch)CDEF. Rooms (11) G. Cards All.
Closed Feb school hols. 15-30 Nov. Rest: Sun evg and Mon (not July/Aug).
Post 14970 Bénouville, Calvados. Region Normandy.
Tel 31 44 62 43. Fax 31 44 76 18. Mich 32/B1. Map 2.

Le BESSAT La Fondue

Comfortable restaurant with rooms/Cooking 1-2
Garage

The over 3800 ft-high village is at the heart of the Pilat Regional Park, a green lung for industrial St-Etienne, 18 km to the NW. La Fondue comes in a wedge-shaped stone building. Enjoy *Bourgeois* and classical basics like mussels and leeks in a cream sauce, *venison à l'ancienne*, stuffed *lapereau*, goat's cheese and desserts from a trolley.
Menus aBCDE. Rooms (9) CDE. Cards All.
Closed Dec to Feb.
Post 42660 Le Bessat, Loire. Region Massif Central (Ardèche).
Tel 77 20 40 09. Fax 77 20 45 20. Mich 115/E4. Map 6.

BEUZEVILLE Petit Castel/Aub. Cochon d'Or

Comfortable hotel (annexe) & restaurant with rooms/Cooking 2
Gardens (hotel)

A much-liked family show: Charles and Monique Folleau, aided by their English-speaking daughter, Catherine, and her husband, Olivier Martin. Classical and regional delights: spiky *safranée de truite aux champignons*, stylish *gâteau de pleurotes au beurre échalotes* and saucy *faux-filet grillé Béarnaise*. Annexe (Petit Castel) across the road.
Menus aCD. Rooms (21 of which 16 in annexe) CDE. Cards Access, Visa.
Closed Mid Dec to mid Jan. Mon. (Park in large *place*.)
Post 27210 Beuzeville, Eure. Region Normandy. Map 2.
Tel (R) 32 57 70 46. (H) 32 57 76 08. Fax 32 42 25 70. Mich 15/D4.

A100frs & under. B100–135. C135–165. D165–250. E250–350. F350–500. G500+

BIEVRES

Relais de St-Walfroy

Comfortable restaurant/Cooking 1-2
Parking

A hidden hamlet, north-west of Montmédy and south of the N43. Michel Vignol is the mayor and *directeur* of the small, rustic *relais*. Chef Jean-Noël Vignol treads *Bourgeois* and regional paths: *truite belle meunière*, *quiche Ardennaise*, *jambon d'Ardenne*, *faux-filet maître d'hôtel*, *sorbets* and similar. Franc-wise is the Vignol motto.
Menus ABC. Cards Access, Visa. (Rooms: Le Mady at Montmédy to SE.)
Closed Tuesday.
Post Bièvres, 08370 Margut, Ardennes. Region Champagne-Ardenne.
Tel 24 22 61 62. Mich 22/B3. Map 3.

BIGNAN

Auberge La Chouannière

Comfortable restaurant/Cooking 2

Jean Luc and Anne-Marie Simon opened their restaurant, with a Louis XVI-style dining room, almost 25 years ago. A typical menu C could include a silky *mousse de foie gras de volaille au porto*, a crunchy and moist *croustillant de saumon à l'oseille* (or, loosen the belts, a *pièce de boeuf grillée*, *sauce verte* with a robust *galette de pomme de terre*), *Brie de Meaux* and *nougat maison glacé*. Champion classical fare.
Menus aCD. Cards Access, AE, Visa. (Rooms: L'Argoat at Locminé, 5 km.)
Closed Feb school hols. 2-13 Oct. Sun evg. Mon. (Rest. SE of Locminé.)
Post 56500 Bignan, Morbihan. Region Brittany.
Tel 97 60 00 96. Fax 97 44 24 58. Mich 62/C1. Map 1.

BLOIS

Rendez-vous des Pêcheurs

Comfortable restaurant/Cooking 3

Menu C (low-end) at the tiny home of young master chef Eric Reithler does not appear in written form. Ask the waitress to get Eric to explain the daily-changing menu – in French or English. The three courses which follow are modern gems, bursting with flavours: examples are *rouelles de cabillaud aux pommes de terre en anchoïade* and a consummate *nougat glacé sur beurre d'oranges*. (Rooms: many hotels within walking distance.)
Menus C(menu)DE(à la carte). Cards Access, AE, Visa. (S of château.)
Closed Feb school hols. 1st 3 wks Aug. Sun. Mon midday. Public hols.
Post 27 r. Foix, 41000 Blois, Loir-et-Cher. Region Loire.
Tel 54 74 67 48. Fax 54 74 47 67. Mich 68/C3. Map 2.

A 100frs & under. B 100–135. C 135–165. D 165–250. E 250–350. F 350–500. G 500+

BONLIEU   La Poutre

Comfortable restaurant with rooms/Cooking 3
Parking

Don't judge a restaurant by a dismal exterior – as at least one reader has done here (he drove on). Inside the well-named "beamed" home of Denis Moureaux lurks an able chef and his delicious regional/classical dishes. Menu B could include *tête de veau, crêpes Jurassiennes; filet de poisson aux petits légumes*; *pintade aux champignons*; and *sorbets*.
Menus BDEF. Rooms (10) DE. Cards Access, Visa.
Closed Mid Oct to mid Feb.
Post 39130 Bonlieu, Jura. Region Jura.
Tel 84 25 57 77. Mich 89/F4. Map 6.

BONNEVAL-SUR-ARC   Auberge Le Pré Catin

Simple restaurant/Cooking 1-2
Terrace

Alpine from boots to helmet: a stone-built chalet; mountain flowers and decorations; and filling *Bourgeoise* and regional fare. Daniel Delaplace, a Parisian, and his wife, Josiane, from Normandy, serve up gutsy grub: mainly grills (*feu de bois*) – like *entrecôte* and *agneau*; tasty cheeses, *jambon de Savoie*, locally-dried meats and *ravioles de Royans*.
Menus ABC. Cards Access, Visa. (Rooms: A la Pastourelle.)
Closed 3 May to 16 June. 18 Sept to 15 Dec. Mon. (Above *sans rest*.)
Post 73480 Bonneval-sur-Arc, Savoie. Region Savoie.
Tel 79 05 95 07. Mich 119/F4. Map 6.

BONS-EN-CHABLAIS   Progrès

Comfortable hotel/Cooking 2
Lift/Parking

The dining room is alongside the main road; the modern bedrooms in an annexe behind the restaurant (note the lift). Brigitte Colly is an obliging *patronne*. Her husband, Charles, is a champion classicist: reference an excellently executed *filet de féra au Crépy* (a local white wine) and an intense *suprême de pintade à la crème d'échalottes*.
Menus a(Tues-Thurs)BCE. Rooms (10) E. Disabled. Cards Access, Visa.
Closed 2-22 Jan. Last wk June. Sun evg & Mon (not 15 July-15 Aug).
Post 74890 Bons-en-Chablais, Haute-Savoie. Region Savoie.
Tel 50 36 11 09. Fax 50 39 44 16. Mich 104/C2. Map 6.

A100frs & under. B100–135. C135–165. D165–250. E250–350. F350–500. G500+

BOUHET   Auberge du Vieux Moulin

Comfortable restaurant with rooms/Cooking 2
Terrace/Parking

Nelly and Stéphane Jacob have won the hearts of many readers at their
working mill (the wheel and grinding mechanism still turn). Both worked
in the UK and speak good English. Neo-classical *plats* with idiosyncratic
touches – *terrine de poisson sauce Tyrolienne* – and a flavoursome
fricassée de volaille au thym et à la sarriette. Good breakfasts.
Menus BD. Rooms (6) DE. Cards Access, Visa.
Closed Rest: Sun evg and Mon (not public hols). Rooms: out of season.
Post 17540 Bouhet, Charente-Maritime. Region Poitou-Charentes.
Tel 46 68 20 86. Mich 93/E3. Map 4.

Le BOURG-DUN   Auberge du Dun

Comfortable restaurant/Cooking 3
Parking

What a classy restaurant: Pierre Chrétien is as smart a chef as his dining
rooms are stylish. Menu B (perhaps low-end C by publication)
epitomised *RQP* at its most exhilarating: *aumonière de coquillages,
paupiettes de saumon aux épinards*, a selection of creamy regional
cheeses and *sable au citron meringué* was a masterly neo-classical feast.
Menus BDE. Cards Acc, Visa. (Rooms: Altea, St-Valery-en-Caux to W.)
Closed 9-27 Feb. 24 Aug to 9 Sept. Sun evg and Mon (not public hols).
Post 76740 Le Bourg-Dun, Seine-Maritime. Region Normandy.
Tel 35 83 05 84. Mich 15/F1. Map 2.

BOURG-EN-BRESSE   La Galerie

Comfortable restaurant/Cooking 2

A modest, shop-fronted look about La Galerie but, when added to the
Mail and Jacques Guy (both in *FLE*), you have a redoubtable Bourg *RQP*
trio to choose from. Here Michel, the chef, and Dominique Chanteloup
beguile with regional, neo-classical and classical treats – reference *persillé
de tête de veau, crépinette de sanglier aux châtaignes, noisettes de
lièvre au genièvre* and *fromage frais de Bresse à la crème*.
Menus BCD. Cards Access, Visa. (Rooms: Logis de Brou, 800 m walk to SE.)
Closed Sat midday. Sun. (La Galerie is SW of Notre-Dame church.)
Post 4 r. Th. Riboud, 01000 Bourg-en-Bresse, Ain. Region Lyonnais.
Tel 74 45 16 43. Mich 103/D3. Map 6. (Logis is *sans rest*, parking.)

A100frs & under. B100–135. C135–165. D165–250. E250–350. F350–500. G500+

BOURGOIN-JALLIEU   Chavancy

Very comfortable restaurant/Cooking 2

An air-conditioned, orange-hued oasis in bustling Bourgoin-Jallieu (400 metres north of the N6, near the hospital and close to parking). Bruno Chavancy drives all carriageways. Menu C (low-end) offers a chance to try a Bresse culinary landmark – *petit pâté chaud*, followed by a light *saumon beurre aux herbes*. Another regional treat comes in the chance to savour a Bresse *suprême de volaille* (mated to *curry, riz sauvage*).
Menus CDE. Cards All. (Rooms: Ibis & Climat de France to W of town.)
Closed 24 July to 22 Aug. Sun evg. Mon.
Post av. Tixier, 38300 Bourgoin-Jallieu, Isère. Region Lyonnais.
Tel 74 93 63 88. Fax 74 28 42 44. Mich 116/C3. Map 6.

BOZOULS   Le Belvédère

Comfortable restaurant with rooms/Cooking 1-2
Quiet/Terrace

Overlooking the Trou de Bozouls (a small, wooded, meandering *cirque* – and the plus of a handsome *église*), Marcel Girbelle keeps matters plain and simple in his rustic dining room. The chimney's roaring fire provides grills for the main courses (*boeuf* or *magret de canard*); *Roquefort* cheese features in tasty first and second courses.
Menus aBC. Rooms (11) DE. Cards Access, Visa.
Closed Dec. Sat and Sun evg (out of season).
Post 12340 Bozouls, Aveyron. Regions MC (Auvergne/Cévennes).
Tel 65 44 92 66. Fax 65 48 87 33. Mich 140/C2. Map 5.

BRIANCON   Le Péché Gourmand

Very comfortable restaurant/Cooking 2
Parking

A modern dining room and stylish neo-classical cooking from 22-year-old Sandrine Bellet. Emphatic full-of-flavour dishes: witness the *confit de lapin aux endives* or the *velouté de lentilles et canard fumé*; the enlightened *papillote de pintade de citron*; and silky-smooth *marquise aux deux chocolats*. Some wines sold by the glass: just ask.
Menus BCDE. Cards Access, AE, Visa. (Rooms: Mont-Brison; 2 min walk E.)
Closed 4-24 Jan. Sun evg and Mon (mid Sept to June). (Above *sans rest.*)
Post 2 rte Gap, 05100 Briançon, Hautes-Alpes. Regions Htes-Alpes/Savoie.
Tel 92 20 11 02. Mich 133/D3. Map 6.

A100frs & under. B100–135. C135–165. D165–250. E250–350. F350–500. G500+

BRIANCON

Comfortable hotel/Cooking 2
Gardens/Lift/Parking

A striking apricot and cream façade ensures you can't miss the Semiond family hotel in the lower town. Utterly straightforward classical and *Bourgeoises* specialities: *quenelles aux fruits de mer, canard à l'orange, tarte Tatin* and *soufflé au Grand Marnier* – all well executed and precisely cooked. André Semiond speaks fluent English.
Menus BD. Rooms (44) EF. Cards Access, Visa.
Closed 5 Nov to 18 Dec. Regions Hautes-Alpes/Savoie.
Post 13 av. Gén. de Gaulle, 05100 Briançon, Hautes-Alpes.
Tel 92 21 12 11. Fax 92 20 58 20. Mich 133/D3. Map 6.

BRINON-SUR-SAULDRE

Comfortable hotel/Cooking 3
Quiet/Gardens/Parking

Andrée Girard is a warm-hearted, smiling *patronne*; husband Dominique is a classical specialist, capitalising on his *pays* and its rich larder. Beamed dining rooms in old red-brick Sologne cottages; bedrooms in modern extension at rear. Menu C *plats* such as *feuilleté de lotte au fenouil* and earthy *joues de porc braisées au Menetou rouge*.
Menus CDE. Rooms (13) EF. Cards Access, Visa.
Closed 15 Feb-15 Mar. Last wk May. 12-22 Sept. Tues evg (Oct-June). Wed.
Post 18410 Brinon-sur-Sauldre, Cher. Region Loire.
Tel 48 58 50 29. Fax 48 58 56 00. Mich 69/F3. Map 2.

BROUSSE-LE-CHATEAU

Simple hotel/Cooking 1-2
Quiet/Parking

An endearing riverside village pleases the eye; and the efforts of young English-speaking Sybile and Philippe Senegas please both the spirits and taste buds at their unfussy home. Copious regional, *Bourgeois* and classical offerings: *canard aux olives* and *filet de truite à la mer à la crème de Roquefort* most certainly pleased us. Modernised bedrooms.
Menus ACD. Rooms (12) D. Cards Access, Visa.
Closed 19 Dec to 19 Jan. Fri evg and Sat midday (Oct to Apl).
Post 12480 Brousse-le-Château, Aveyron. Region MC (Cévennes).
Tel 65 99 40 15. Mich 140/C4. Map 5.

A100frs & under. B100–135. C135–165. D165–250. E250–350. F350–500. G500+

CABOURG   Pied de Cochon

Comfortable restaurant/Cooking 1-2

You'll nose out the pig's trotter on the D514, just inland from the beach at Le Hôme, 2 km W of Cabourg. Jacqueline and Claude Renard are crafty *patrons*, living up to their surname. Choose from his fish dishes – *moules à la créme crue, soupe de poisson* or fresh-as-daisies filets of fish; or from spit-roasted grills (turned in the dining room fireplace). One highlight: *pied de cochon* with *frites et cresson – bien sûr*.
Menus BDE. Cards Access, Visa. (Rooms: Le Cottage, 2 km to E on D514.)
Closed 16 Jan to 1 Feb. 28 Nov to 14 Dec. Mon evg. Tues.
Post Le Hôme, 14390 Cabourg, Calvados. Region Normandy.
Tel 31 91 27 55. Mich 32/B1. Map 2.

CALAIS   Au Côte d'Argent

Comfortable restaurant/Cooking 2

For many readers Bertrand Lefebvre is the best chef in the busy Channel port. His modern restaurant, overlooking both the Channel and the bustling port entrance – plus the bonus of a huge public car park at the door – is a classical haven. The Menu Douceur (A) keeps wallets full: a filling *caudière*, a fresh-from-the-sea filet of cod in a tangy, perfectly executed *beurre blanc* sauce and a knockout sweet to finish.
Menus ACDE. Cards All. (Rooms: Richelieu & Windsor; both 5 min walk.)
Closed Sun evg. Mon. (Both above *sans rest*; Windsor has garage.)
Post 1 digue G. Berthe, 62100 Calais, Pas-de-Calais. Region North.
Tel 21 34 68 07. Fax 21 96 42 10. Mich 2/B1. Map 2.

CALAIS   Le Channel

Comfortable restaurant/Cooking 2

José (Jo) and Monique Crespo do a great job but don't call with excessive expectations as they can't match the over-the-top sycophancy of some British food writers. Monique speaks English and Jo digs a classical tunnel with, not surprisingly, a significant reliance on fish delights: from *langoustines* to *turbotin*. A channel-wide choice for all courses on menu C (low-end). Cellar? 600 wines and 60,000 bottles.
Menus aCDE. Cards All. (Rooms: Richelieu & Windsor; both 3 min walk.)
Closed 19 Dec to 16 Jan. 5-14 June. Sun evg. Tues. (See previous entry.)
Post 3 bd Résistance, 62100 Calais, Pas-de-Calais. Region North.
Tel 21 34 42 30. Fax 21 97 42 43. Mich 2/B1. Map 2.

A 100frs & under. B 100–135. C 135–165. D 165–250. E 250–350. F 350–500. G 500+

CALVINET
Beauséjour

Comfortable restaurant with rooms/Cooking 2
Terrace/Parking

Louis-Bernard Puech is an unsmiling host – which matches the style of
the renovated, whitewashed interior. His cooking has a brighter face (*la
cuisine d'hier et d'aujourd-hui*) using both local produce and fish and
shellfish from distant oceans; examples are a punchy *filet de boeuf rôti
sauce Béarnaise* and *chartreuse de tourteaux au jus de crustacés*.
Menus ACE. Rooms (12) DE. Cards Access, Visa.
Closed Mid Jan-mid Feb. 2-9 Oct. Sun evg & Mon (mid Sept-mid June).
Post 15340 Calvinet, Cantal. Region Massif Central (Auvergne).
Tel 71 49 91 68. Fax 71 49 98 63. Mich 126/A4. Map 5.

CANY-BARVILLE
Manoir de Barville

Very comfortable restaurant with rooms/Cooking 2
Secluded/Gardens/Parking

A gorgeous spot, south of the town at the marked *gué* (ford); to avoid the
latter approach from the D131. Magnificent trees, the River Durdent,
colourful gardens and a handsome house – plus Lionel Morin's classical
cooking: a menu of *brouillade d'oeuf aux champignons des bois et
avocat, filet de truite de la Durdent* (the delectable river which forms the
ford mentioned earlier), cheese and strawberry tart was most enjoyable.
Menus CDE. Rooms (4) DF. Cards Access, Visa.
Post 76450 Cany-Barville, Seine-Maritime. Region Normandy.
Tel 35 97 79 30. Fax 35 57 03 55. Mich 15/E1-E2. Map 2.

CARHAIX-PLOUGUER
Auberge du Poher

Comfortable restaurant/Cooking 1-2
Gardens/Parking

Robert Le Roux's modern *auberge* is at Port de Carhaix, south of the
Nantes-Brest Canal. An austere dining room, attractive gardens, stream
and views. Classical and *Bourgeoise* grub with a wide choice for each
course. Loosen your belts for homely *soupe de poisson, terrine de chef,
faux filet grillée, boeuf en daube, truite au Roquefort* and similar.
Menus ABCD. Cards Acc, Visa. (Rooms: D'Ahès, Carhaix-Plouguer.)
Closed 1-21 Feb. 5-18 Sept. Mon.
Post 29270 Carhaix-Plouguer, Finistère. Region Brittany. (SW of town.)
Tel 98 99 51 18. Mich 46/A1. Map 1.

A100frs & under. B100–135. C135–165. D165–250. E250–350. F350–500. G500+

CARNAC   Alignements

Comfortable hotel/Cooking 2
Lift

An all-modern, three-storey hotel with every room having its own minuscule terrace. (On D781 Lorient road.) Menu C offers choice, quality and quantity: a wholesome *assiette de fruits de mer*, an entire *canette de Challans aux épices* (for two) and a calorie-boosting *gâteau aux deux chocolats* will test readers with even the most whopping appetites.
Menus ACD. Rooms (27) EF. Cards Access, Visa.
Closed Hotel: Oct to Easter. Rest: Oct to Apl. Fri midday. Mon. Tues.
Post 45 r. St-Cornély, 56340 Carnac, Morbihan. Region Brittany.
Tel 97 52 06 30. Fax 97 52 76 56. Mich 62/B2. Map 1.

CASTERA-VERDUZAN   Hôtel Ténarèze/Rest. Florida

Simple restaurant with rooms/Cooking 2
Terrace

The stone-built Florida is in a tiny thermal spa. Bernard Ramounéda, a third-generation chef (his grandmother kicked off in 1935), mixes classical, regional and *Bourgeoise*: a typical filling menu C could be *potage, poule farci Henri IV, épaule d'agneau rôtie aux herbes* and *trois chocolates (marquise, mousse, glace)*. Hotel run as separate business.
Menus a(lunch)CD. Rooms (24) CD. Cards All.
Closed Feb. Sun evg & Mon (Oct to Mar). Rest: Wed (Apl to Sept).
Post 32410 Castéra-Verduzan, Gers. Region Southwest. Map 5.
Tel (R) 62 68 13 22. (H) 62 68 10 22. Fax 62 68 14 69. Mich 151/E2.

CAULIERES   Auberge de la Forge

Very comfortable restaurant/Cooking 2

Once the village *café/tabac/épicerie* and facing the forge which, in times past, must have been kept busy shoeing horses whilst their riders fed *en face*. Alan, the *cuisinier*, and Michele Mauconduit make you welcome at their rustic dining room. Regional and classical fare: from *cuisse de lapin au cidre* (a Normandy tempter) and *ficelle Picarde* (a northern teaser) to *saumon à l'oseille*. (Bedroom annexe planned.)
Menus aBCDE. Cards Access, Visa. (Rooms: Le Cardinal, Poix-de-Picardie.)
Closed Feb school hols. 7-20 Aug. (7 km W of Poix-de-Picardie.)
Post 80590 Caulières, Somme. Regions Normandy/North.
Tel 22 38 00 91. Fax 22 38 08 48. Mich 17/E2. Map 2.

A100frs & under. B100–135. C135–165. D165–250. E250–350. F350–500. G500+

La CHAISE-DIEU
Au Tremblant

Simple hotel/Cooking 1-2
Gardens/Garage/Parking

Jean and Josette Boyer are the third generation at this family *logis*, first opened in 1902. Josette has a beaming smile. Jean's menus are beaming classical and *Bourgeois* with a sofa-wide range of choice: *soufflé de foies de volailles forestières, truite belle meunière, pâté de brochet, loup farci au safran* and *coquelet au vin* are typical.
Menus ABD. Rooms (27) CDE. Cards Access, Visa.
Closed Nov to Apl. (On D906.)
Post 43160 La Chaise-Dieu, Haute-Loire. Region MC (Auvergne).
Tel 71 00 01 85. Mich 128/B1. Map 5.

CHAMBERY
L'Essentiel

Very comfortable restaurant/Cooking 3

As good as any *RQP* cooking in the French Alps. Young Jean-Michel Bouvier, trained by Guérard and Senderens, is a modern cooking addict: a *filet de rouget poêlé à la tapenade dans son jus acidulé aux herbes fraîches* is the Med on a plate; and a *moëlleux au chocolat chaud, glace pistache aux zestes d'orange confits* is an intense, yummy sweet. (On the ground floor of the Hôtel Mercure – which has its own garage.)
Menus a(lunch)CD. Cards Access, AE, Visa. (Rooms: see Mercure above.)
Closed Sat midday. (Opposite station.)
Post 183 pl. Gare, 73000 Chambéry, Savoie. Region Savoie.
Tel 79 96 97 27. Fax 79 96 17 78. Mich 117/F3. Map 6.

CHAMONIX
Eden

Comfortable restaurant with rooms/Cooking 2
Parking

A blue and white exterior and a stylish, light interior. Odette Lesage is the elegant *patronne*; husband Gérard skis the classical cooking *piste*. Relish the majestic views and also the restrained mastery of accomplished specialities like *terrine de poisson à la croûte d'algues* (in the Alps!) and a tasty *contre filet de boeuf marchand de vin*.
Menus bCDE. Rooms (10) EF. Cards All. (Les Praz is NE of Chamonix.)
Closed 1-15 June. Nov. 1st wk Dec. Tues (not high season).
Post Les Praz, 74400 Chamonix, Haute-Savoie. Region Savoie.
Tel 50 53 06 40. Fax 50 53 51 50. Mich 105/F4. Map 6.

A100frs & under. B100–135. C135–165. D165–250. E250–350. F350–500. G500+

CHAMPAGNAC   Le Lavendès

Comfortable hotel/Cooking 2
Secluded/Gardens/Swimming pool/Parking

The hotel, a handsome old manor house, is gorgeously situated – between the high Auvergne and green Périgord. Louisette Gimmig is the hostess; husband Gérard, a prize-winning desserts champ, paddles classical and regional courses: a *chartreuse de canard confit vinaigrette de pied de porc* and *fondant et sa glace au miel de pays* confirm the latter.
Menus b(lunch)CDE. Rooms (8) FG. Cards Access, Visa.
Closed 15 Nov-Feb. Rest: Sun evg (Oct-15 May). Mon (not evg 15 May-Oct).
Post 15350 Champagnac, Cantal. Regions Dordogne/MC (Auvergne).
Tel 71 69 62 79. Fax 71 69 65 33. Mich 112/A4. Map 5.

CHAPARON   La Châtaigneraie

Comfortable hotel/Cooking 1-2
Secluded/Terrace/Gardens/Tennis/Parking

An alluring setting for a family hotel, led by English-speaking Martine Millet and her husband Robert – a friendly, helpful duo. Competent classical and *Bourgeoise* cooking with a repertoire ranging from *terrine maison* and *filet de haddock fumé sur lit de salade* to a more ambitious, thumpingly good *jambonette de volaille farcie sauce poivre vert.*
Menus a(lunch)BCDE. Rooms (25) F. Cards All. (S of Brédannaz.)
Closed 20 Oct to end Jan. Sun evg and Mon (Oct to Apl).
Post Chaparon, 74210 Faverges, Haute-Savoie. Region Savoie.
Tel 50 44 30 67. Fax 50 44 83 71. Map 118/B1. Map 6.

CHASSELAY   Guy Lassausaie

Comfortable restaurant/Cooking 3
Parking

Brilliant is the word which sums up the efforts of Guy Lassausaie – an imaginative modern master chef. Menu C is culinary largesse: four exuberant courses with two *petites surprises* at start and finish (melon balls in a cream sauce; and a small *crème brûlée*). Of the four courses a *cuisse de lapin braisée à la coriandre et basilic* was scented heaven.
Menus CDEF. Cards All. (Rooms: A6 *autoroute* hotels; Limonest 9 km SW.)
Closed Aug. Tues evg. Wed. (See *FLE* p222 for details of above hotels.)
Post r. Belle-Cize, 69380 Chasselay, Rhône. Region Lyonnais.
Tel 78 47 62 59. Fax 78 47 06 19. Mich 116/A1. Map 6.

A100frs & under. B100–135. C135–165. D165–250. E250–350. F350–500. G500+

CHATEAU-ARNOUX   L'Oustaou de la Foun

Comfortable restaurant/Cooking 2-3
Terrace/Parking

Young Natalie and Gérald Jourdan (the chef) have moved from Digne to
a gorgeous old farm with cool, stylish, spacious rooms and a pleasing
central courtyard. Great emphasis on regional produce and specialities.
Gérald's claims that the tastes and perfumes of Haute-Provence dominate
his cooking are vividly demonstrated. (2 km N, on N85; near A51 exit.)
Menus BCD. Cards Access, AE, Visa. (Rooms: Ibis, Sisteron; end of A51.)
Closed Wed (out of season). Regions Hautes-Alpes/Provence.
Post Rte Napoléon, 04160 Château-Arnoux, Alpes-de-Haute-Provence.
Tel 92 62 65 30 (and 31). Fax 92 62 65 32. Mich 146/B4. Map 6.

CHATEAUBOURG   Pen'Roc

Comfortable hotel/Cooking 2
Terrace/Gardens/Swimming pool/Lift/Parking

Top marks on all counts for this modern hotel, next door to the Eglise
Notre Dame at La Peinière, 6 km east of the town. Colour and
brightness dominate both Mireille Froc's rooms and husbands Joseph's
cuisine. Clever choice formula. Highlights: an assertive *gelée de
lapereau et sa confiture d'oignons* and filling *choucroute du pêcheur*.
Menus bCDE. Rooms (33) EF. Cards All. Regions Brittany/Normandy.
Closed School hols Feb and Nov. Rest: Sun evg (mid Sept to Apl).
Post La Peinière, 35220 Châteaubourg, Ille-et-Vilaine.
Tel 99 00 33 02. Fax 99 62 30 89. Mich 49/D3. Map 1.

CHATEAUNEUF   La Fontaine

Simple restaurant/Cooking 3
Parking

Yves and Anne Jury's tiny home is a touch odd-ball. But there's nowt odd-
ball about his modern and neo-classical cooking. Menu C is a superlative
RQP bargain: perhaps a *salade de saumon fumé au vinaigre balsamique*;
some *noix d'agneau au coulis d'olive*; a *fromage du charolais chaud en
salade*; and brilliant sweets tagged *délices de la Fontaine*.
Menus bCDE. Cards Access, Visa. (Rooms: Relais de l'Abbaye, Charlieu.)
Closed 22 Jan to 16 Feb. 2-12 Oct. Tues evg. Wed. (Above 10 km to SW.)
Post 71740 Châteauneuf, Saône-et-Loire. Region Lyonnais.
Tel 85 26 26 87. Mich 101/E3. Map 6.

A100frs & under. B100–135. C135–165. D165–250. E250–350. F350–500. G500+

CHAUMOUSEY

Le Calmosien

Comfortable restaurant/Cooking 2
Terrace

On the D460, west of Epinal. A whitewashed, window-boxed exterior hides a *belle époque* interior. Chef Jean-Marc Béati paddles all streams: *huîtres de Cancale aux épinards, julienne de citrons au sel*; a thumpingly tasty *saucisson de canard au foie gras* with *chutney de pommes vertes*; and *gratin de poires aux amandes* are the proof.

Menus BCDE. Cards All. (Rooms: Epinal; Mercure, Ibis, Ariane & Europe.)
Closed Sun evg. (10 km SW of Epinal.)
Post 37 r. d'Epinal, 88390 Chaumousey, Vosges. Region Alsace.
Tel 29 66 80 77. Fax 29 66 89 41. Mich 59/F3. Map 3.

CHAUSSIN

Voyageurs Chez Bach

Comfortable hotel/Cooking 2
Quiet/Parking

Near *la gare*: don't take ear plugs – there's no line now. Modern *logis* with forests of greenery in the cool dining room. A cascade of menus from young Christophe Vernay who plays Bach's Jura tunes adroitly: a robust *assiette Jurassienne* (mountain ham, *brési, terrine*, etc.); and *feuilleté de quenelles de volaille au vin jaune* – a polished melody.

Menus BCDE. Rooms (22) DE. Cards Access, Visa.
Closed 1st 3 wks Jan. Fri evg and Sun evg (not July to Sept).
Post pl. Ancienne Gare, 39120 Chaussin, Jura. Region Jura.
Tel 84 81 80 38. Fax 84 81 83 80. Mich 89/D2. Map 3.

CHONAS L'AMBALLAN

Domaine de Clairefontaine

Comfortable hotel/Cooking 3
Quiet/Terrace/Gardens/Tennis/Parking

Mme Girardon and her chef sons, Philippe (ex-Michel Roux student) and Hervé, have injected new life into this ideally-situated hotel. Menu B (top-end) is a good excuse for a visit: *velouté de moules aux fins légumes, cuissot de volaille farci Grande-mère, fromage blanc* and caramelised *gratin de poires William* is impressive neo-classical fare.

Menus BDEF. Rooms (14) DEF. Cards All. Regions Lyonnais/MC (Ardèche). Closed Dec. Jan. Rest: Sat midday (July/Aug). Sun evg. Mon (not evg July/Aug). Post 38121 Chonas l'Amballan, Isere. (9 km S of Vienne.)
Tel 74 58 81 52. Fax 74 58 80 93. Mich 116/A4. Map 6.

A100frs & under. B100–135. C135–165. D165–250. E250–350. F350–500. G500+

CHOUVIGNY
Gorges de Chouvigny

Simple restaurant with rooms/Cooking 1-2
Secluded/Terrace/Parking

West of Ebreuil and the A71 junction 12 – in a riverside setting on the Sioule's north bank. Bedrooms are in an ivy-covered house across the road. Young Eric and Sylvie Fleury do a sound job. *Cuisine Bourgeoise*: *terrine de saumon, truite menunière, filet de boeuf Fleury, petite friture* and *jambon sec d'Auvergne* – all plain, homely cooking.
Menus ABCD. Rooms (8) DE. Cards Access, Visa.
Closed 19 Dec to end Feb. Tues evg and Wed (mid Sept to May).
Post 03450 Chouvigny, Allier. Regions Berry-Bourbonnais/MC (Auvergne).
Tel 70 90 42 11. Mich 99/F4. Map 5.

La CLAYETTE
Gare

Comfortable restaurant with rooms/Cooking 2
Terrace/Gardens/Swimming pool/Garage/Parking

The well-kitted out *logis* is in the capable hands of Simone Thoral and her classicist *cuisinier* husband Michel. Even menu A is a humdinger: perhaps a *dodine de colvert aux noisettes, confiture d'oignons* to start; then *cuisse de pain farcie à l'ail et aux olives noires, sauce au romorain*; finishing with *fromage blanc à la crème*. Beat that for RQP.
Menus ABCDE. Rooms (8) DEF. Cards Access, Visa. (S entrance to town.)
Closed 25 Dec to 15 Jan. Sun evg (not July/Aug). Mon.
Post av. Gare, 71800 La Clayette, Saône-et-Loire. Region Lyonnais.
Tel 85 28 01 65. Fax 85 28 03 13. Mich 101/E3. Map 6.

CLEDER
Le Baladin

Comfortable restaurant/Cooking 2

In a quiet side street, east of the church. One welcome innovation is that you can try different wines by the glass: just ask. Monsieur Queffelec's dining room is spartan but his cooking is most certainly not. Modern and classical: an aromatic *fricassée de rable de lapin et tabac forestière* with the counterpoint of a spicy *jambonette de canard aux poivres vertes*. (For rooms use Roscoff's *sans rest* hotels.)
Menus ACD. Cards Access, Visa. (Rooms: several hotels at Roscoff to NE.)
Closed Mon and Tues evg (not July and Aug).
Post 9 r. Armorique, 29233 Cléder, Finistère. Region Brittany.
Tel 98 69 42 48. Mich 27D1. Map 1.

A100frs & under. B100–135. C135–165. D165–250. E250–350. F350–500. G500+

COGNAC   Pigeons Blancs

Very comfortable restaurant with rooms/Cooking 2-3
Terrace/Gardens/Parking

A young family trio: Jacques Tachet is *le cuisinier*; brother Jean-Michel is *le sommelier*; and sister Catherine is *la patronne*. Elegance radiates in all areas: in the 17thC *relais de poste*; in the furnishings; and in the neo-classical dishes. Menu C, Le Nez du Marché, is a spontaneous affair: *⅓ produits extra frais, ⅓ savoir, ⅓ d'amitié*.
Menus BCD. Rooms (7) EF. Cards All. (On D731 Poitiers road.)
Closed Rest: 6-19 Jan. Sun evg.
Post 110 r. J.-Brisson, 16100 Cognac, Charente. Region Poitou-Charentes.
Tel 45 82 16 36. Fax 45 82 29 29. Mich 107/E2. Map 4.

La COLLE-SUR-LOUP   La Belle Epoque

Comfortable restaurant/Cooking 2
Terrace/Gardens/Parking

The clue to the décor is in the restaurant name: old-world charm, a seductive terrace and clever lighting come darkness. Michelle Frédéric is a seductive hostess; husband Jean-Pierre is happy with both classical and Provençal plats. Home-made *assiette de ravioli*, *daube d'agneau à l'Avignonnaise* and all the chef's desserts have won readers' praise.
Menus BCD. Cards All. (Rooms: nearby Marc Hély.). Closed 5 Jan-5 Feb. Tues *midi* & Wed *midi* (July/Aug). Mon evg & Tues (Sept-June).
Post 06480 La Colle-sur-Loup, Alpes-Maritimes. Region Côte d'Azur.
Tel 93 20 10 92. Fax 93 20 29 66. Mich 165/D4. Map 6. (On D6 to SE.)

La COLLE-SUR-LOUP   La Stréga

Comfortable restaurant/Cooking 2
Terrace/Parking

An unprepossessing exterior (easily missed) but a pretty Provençal interior. A light, neo-classical and modern approach from chef Gilbert Stella. *Fleurs de courgette farcies à la mousseline de rascasse* can be so fresh you may even see the flowers being delivered. Wine and coffee included on cheapest menu; and *Brie* cheese on more expensive version.
Menus CD. Cards Access, Visa. (Rooms: nearby Marc Hély. Both on D6.)
Closed Jan. Feb. Sun evg (out of season). Mon. Tues *midi* (July/Aug).
Post 06480 La Colle-sur-Loup, Alpes-Maritimes. Region Côte d'Azur.
Tel 93 22 62 37. Mich 165/D4. Map 6. (On D6 to SE of village.)

A100frs & under. B100–135. C135–165. D165–250. E250–350. F350–500. G500+

COLLIOURE La Frégate

Comfortable hotel/Cooking 2
Terrace/Lift

A fiery, English-speaking maverick, Yves Costa has managed to fall out with both the main French guides. Short-fuse Catalan he may be – but he's a cracking chef, capable of creative fireworks. A wide choice of *Catalane*, classical and modern: *anchois de Collioure à l'escalivade*, *moules à la "Sang et Or"*, *riz Frégate* (a *paella* filler), *filet de boeuf sauce Béarnaise* and *crème Catalane* are typical sparklers.
Menus BCD. Rooms (24) EFG. Cards Access, Visa. Region Languedoc-Rouss.
Post 24 bd Camille-Pelletan, 66190 Collioure, Pyrénées-Orientales.
Tel 68 82 06 05. Fax 68 82 55 00. Mich 177/F3. Map 5. (NW of château.)

COLLIOURE Nouvelle Vague

Comfortable restaurant/Cooking 2
Terrace

Claude Nourtier, the young owner, is a passionate champion of both *Catalane* cuisine and Roussillon wines. The Menu Catalan (low-end C) could include *les rillettes de pain à la fleur de thym*, *les figues au vinaigre* (two flavours not quite jelling); *"paupilles" d'agneau aux pignons et à la Soubressade*; and a luscious *crème Catalane*.
Menus ACE. Cards Access, Visa. (Rooms: Casa Païral and Madeloc.)
Closed 1-18 Mar. 1-18 Dec. Sun evg (out of season). Mon (not evgs high season). Post 7 r. Voltaire, 66190 Collioure, Pyrénées-Orientales.
Tel 68 82 23 88. Mich 177/F3. Map 5. Region Lang-Rouss. (S of château.)

COLOMBEY-LES-DEUX-EGLISES Auberge Montagne

Comfortable restaurant with rooms/Cooking 2
Quiet/Gardens/Parking

A hatful of pluses here: away from the busy N19; Arlette Natali is an attentive *patronne*; and her extrovert husband Gérard is a competent chef. Appetite-quenching *plats*: a duo of *hures – sanglier et lapereau* composed of one slice of each in jelly; and several rounds of tasty *noix de veau aux pleurottes*. Debits? Small bedrooms; moody waitress.
Menus bCDE. Rooms (7) DE. Cards Access, Visa.
Closed Mid Jan to mid Feb. Mon evg. Tues. Region Champagne-Ard.
Post 52330 Colombey-les-deux-Eglises, Haute-Marne.
Tel 25 01 51 69. Fax 25 01 53 20. Mich 57/F3. Map 3.

A100frs & under. B100–135. C135–165. D165–250. E250–350. F350–500. G500+

COMBEAUFONTAINE   Balcon

Comfortable hotel/Cooking 2
Garage

Yvette & Christian Parnet (Oye-et-Pallet: Jura *FLE* p175) gave me the nod about their *copains* – Claudine, *la patronne*, and chef Gérard Gauthier. He's a classical/neo-classical fan but also finds room for exemplary Jura gems: *petite salade de brési au vinaigre de Xérès* and *poulet au vin jaune et morilles* are two examples. Super passion fruit *bavarois*.
Menus CDEF. Rooms (18) CDEF. Cards All.
Closed 27 Dec to 12 Jan. 25 June to 3 July. Sun evg. Mon.
Post 70120 Combeaufontaine, Haute-Saône. Regions Jura/Champagne-Ard.
Tel 84 92 11 13. Fax 84 92 15 89. Mich 75/E2. Map 3.

CONCARNEAU   Les Sables Blancs

Comfortable hotel/Cooking 1-2
Terrace

The aptly-labelled Chabrier family *logis*, north-west of the port, has its toes in the beach and sea. Dishes are artistically presented. Aromatic *soupe de poissons maison*, *moules à la crème* (60 no less), melt-in-the-mouth *magret de canard*, *riz au curry* as a vegetable, and flashy *galette Concarnoise flambée*. Plenty of half-bottles of wine.
Menus ABC. Rooms (48) E. Cards Access, DC, Visa.
Closed November to March. Region Brittany.
Post Plage Sables Blancs, 29182 Concarneau, Finistère. Mich 45/D3.
Tel 98 97 01 39 (98 97 86 93 – out of season). Fax 98 50 65 88. Map 1.

Le CONQUET   Pointe Ste-Barbe

Comfortable hotel/Cooking 1-2
Lift/Parking

An ugly, ultra-modern concrete and glass structure with a spectacular site on rocks above the sea – west of Brest. Great views. Menu C has vast choice with fish specialities predominating. Classical sauces – *Béarnaise*, *hollandaise*, *beurre blanc* and *mayonnaise* – served with salmon, white fish and crab as examples. Also various meat dishes.
Menus aCDF. Rooms (49) CEFG. Disabled. Cards All.
Closed 11 Nov to 16 Dec. Mon (mid Sept to June).
Post 29217 Le Conquet, Finistère. Region Brittany.
Tel 98 89 00 26. Fax 98 89 14 81. Mich 26/A3. Map 1.

A100frs & under. B100–135. C135–165. D165–250. E250–350. F350–500. G500+

CORDON   Le Cordonant

Comfortable hotel/Cooking 1-2
Secluded/Terrace/Parking

A flower-bedecked chalet with the most friendly of owners in the shape
of Gisèle Pugnat. Stand on the flower-filled terrace, turn your eyes south-
east and revel in the superb view of the Mont Blanc *massif*. Alain
Pugnat keeps his fare simple: *fera au beurre blanc, gigot d'agneau rôti,
osso bucco* and similar temptations. Utterly enjoyable in every sense.
Menus bCD. Rooms (16) E. Cards Access, Visa.
Closed 1st 2 wks May. 24 Sept to 18 Dec.
Post 74700 Cordon, Haute-Savoie. Region Savoie.
Tel 50 58 34 56. Mich 105/E4. Map 6.

CORPS   Poste

Comfortable restaurant with rooms/Cooking 2
Terrace/Garage

Young Gilbert and Christiane Delas are steaming ahead. Their extrovert
N85 outpost is a huge success. Now they've also opened the swish Ch.
des Herbeys at St-Firmin (to the SE; pool and calm). A classical course
at the Poste from Gilbert, once chef on the liner *France*. Even the
cheapest menu offers wide-choice, four-course, appetite-scuttling grub.
Menus bCD. Rooms (20) DEF. Cards Access, Visa.
Closed Dec to 20 Jan.
Post 38970 Corps, Isère. Regions Hautes-Alpes/Savoie.
Tel 76 30 00 03. Fax 76 30 02 73. Mich 132/A3. Map 6.

COULON   Central

Comfortable restaurant/Cooking 1-2
Terrace

The name is spot on; central it is. Anny Monnet is the *cuisinière* at this
smart *logis*; husband Jean is the attentive front-of-house boss. Be sure to
make a reservation if you want to punt with classical treats such as
daube de joue de boeuf à l'ancienne and *oeufs à la neige*. Lots of local
produce: *mogettes* (small pulse beans) for example.
Menus aCD. Cards Access, Visa. (Rooms: Espace; N11, 5 km SW of Niort.)
Closed 8 Jan to 1 Feb. 18 Sept to 12 Oct. Sun evg. Mon.
Post 79510 Coulon, Deux-Sèvres. Region Poitou-Charentes.
Tel 49 35 90 20. Fax 49 35 81 07. Mich 93/F2. Map 4.

A100frs & under. B100–135. C135–165. D165–250. E250–350. F350–500. G500+

COULONGES-SUR-L'AUTIZE   Citronnelle

Simple restaurant/Cooking 1-2
Terrace

An airy dining room with a sun-trap terrace for warm days. *Chef/patron* Eddy Zefner is mad keen on red cars (note the Ferrari models); his own runabout is an Alfa. Colourful cooking covering the spectrum of culinary styles: *salade multicolore à la hure de langue, omble chevalier fourré à la crème de St-Jacques aux pistaches* and *mouclade au curry*.
Menus ABCD. Cards Access, AE, Visa. (Rooms: St-Nicolas, Maillezais.)
Closed Sun evg. Mon. (Above *sans rest* hotel easy drive to SW.)
Post 79160 Coulonges-sur-l'Autize, Deux-Sèvres.
Tel 49 06 17 67. Mich 93/F1. Map 4. Region Poitou-Charentes.

COUR-CHEVERNY   Trois Marchands

Comfortable hotel/Cooking 1-2
Parking

The Bricault family, from father to son, have owned the hotel since 1865. Classical cooking from the past, too, with some Sologne flavours: among them *fricassée de girolles, cuisse de grenouilles fraîches*, asparagus and chicken breast in a cream sauce. Jean-Jacques, the latest Bricault, is an uncommunicative *patron*. Readers dislike annexe rooms.
Menus bCDE. Rooms (37) CDE. Cards All.
Closed Feb to mid March. Mon (Oct to Easter).
Post 41700 Cour-Cheverny, Loir-et-Cher. Region Loire.
Tel 54 79 96 44. Fax 54 79 25 60. Mich 68/C3. Map 2.

COURLANS   Auberge de Chavannes

Very comfortable restaurant/Cooking 3-4
Terrace/Gardens/Parking

Taste is everything to chef Pierre Carpentier. Flavours dominate his modern, classical and neo-classical repertoire. Menu C (top-end) is a steal (choice for each course). How about a luscious *terrine fondante de pigeon*, a *poupeton de volaille de Bresse rôti* and *chariot de desserts*. Monique Carpentier is an elegant, knowledgeable *patronne/sommelière*.
Menus CE. Cards Access, Visa. (Rooms: Comfort Inn Primevère, N of Lons.)
Closed Feb. 26 June to 3 July. Sun evg. Mon. Region Jura.
Post 39570 Courlans, Jura. (On N78, 6 km W of Lons-le-Saunier.)
Tel 84 47 05 52. Mich 89/D4. Map 3.

A100frs & under. B100–135. C135–165. D165–250. E250–350. F350–500. G500+

CRESSERONS   La Valise Gourmande

Very comfortable restaurant/Cooking 2-3
Terrace/Gardens/Parking

A wisteria-clad, 18thC *maison Bourgeoise*. Jean-Jacques Hélie's culinary
valise includes classical and regional tricks. From menu B (low-end)
choose from *moules marinières, soupe de poissons* or *terrine de foies
de volaille*; next *coq au vin, pavé aux poivres* or *poisson*; then *tartes
aux fruits, glaces* or *teurgoule (terrine de riz au lait à la cannelle)*.
Menus BDE. Cards Access, AE, Visa. (Rooms: Novotel, Ibis, etc. at Caen.)
Closed Xmas to New Year. Sun evg. Mon. (All above hotels N side Caen.)
Post rte Lion-sur-Mer, 14440 Cresserons, Calvados. Region Normandy.
Tel 31 37 39 10. Mich 32/B1. Map 2.

CREST   Grand Hôtel

Simple hotel/Cooking 2

Danielle and René Lattiers' *logis* is 200 metres or so from the Tour de Crest,
a formidable medieval dungeon reckoned to have the highest walls in
France. Chef René's cooking is no less formidable with classical and
Bourgeois plats in each of the multi-choice menus. Step back in time to
*terrine de foies, truite meunière, faux filet marchand de vin, gigot
d'agneau au thym, crème caramel* and *pêche Melba* (an ubiquitous dame).
Menus aBD. Rooms (22) CDE. Cards Access, Visa. Closed 22 Dec to 20
Jan. School hols Feb. Sun evg (Sept to mid June). Mon (not evg Apl to Oct).
Post 60 r. Hôtel de Ville, 26400 Crest, Drôme. Regions Hte-Alpes/Savoie.
Tel 75 25 08 17. Fax 75 25 46 42. Mich 130/B4. Map 6.

CROIX-MARE   Auberge de la Forge

Comfortable restaurant/Cooking 2
Parking

Don't be put off by the run-down, decrepit exterior. Three immaculate
rustic dining rooms (once separate cottages) will cheer you up no end. A
mix of styles from Christian Truttmann: *oeufs cocotte crème de haddock,
escalope de saumon frais crème de courgettes au curry* and *pièce de
boeuf sauce marinade* are a typical filling, flavoursome trio. (Park at rear.)
Menus ACE. Cards Acc, AE, Visa. (Rooms: Havre at nearby Yvetot to NW.)
Closed Tues evg and Wed (not public hols).
Post N15, Croix-Mare, 76190 Yvetot, Seine-Maritime. Region Normandy.
Tel 35 91 25 94. Mich 15/F3. Map 2.

A100frs & under. B100–135. C135–165. D165–250. E250–350. F350–500. G500+

CROZANT
Auberge de la Vallée

Comfortable restaurant/Cooking 1-2

I've had mixed reports on the *auberge* (hence the low rating) -- with waitresses dressed in Marchois folk costumes. Françoise Guilleminot and daughter Béatrice are *les patronnes*; and husband Jean turns classical, regional and *Bourgeoises* pedals in the kitchen. *Jambon demi sel au porto*; *aloyau* (sirloin) *Limousin rôti* (famed beef); and *magret de canard aux cèpes* (equally acclaimed local mushrooms) are three examples.
Menus aBCE. Cards Access, DC, Visa. (Rooms: nearby Lac – *sans rest.*)
Closed Jan. Mon evg and Tues (not July/Aug).
Post 23160 Crozant, Creuse. Region Poitou-Charentes.
Tel 55 89 80 03. Mich 97/E2. Map 5.

CUCUGNAN
Auberge de Cucugnan

Simple restaurant/Cooking 1-2
Parking

Climb the stepped lanes to reach the *auberge*, once a barn. The village is within sight of two of the famous Cathar castles. Menu A is not for the diet squeamish: start with either a plate of *crudités* or a *charcuterie* assortment; then *coq au vin*, *lapin au saupiquet* or *pintadeau en salmis*; vegetables; cheese; dessert. Surely you are not still peckish?
Menus ACD. Cards Access, Visa. (Rooms: Alta Riba at Rivesaltes to ESE.)
Closed Wed (Jan to March.) (Above has lift, garage and parking.)
Post 11350 Cucugnan, Aude. Region Languedoc-Roussillon.
Tel 68 45 40 84. Fax 68 45 01 52. Mich 175/F2. Map 5.

CUISEAUX
Commerce

Comfortable restaurant with rooms/Cooking 2
Swimming pool/Garage/Parking

A stone-built *logis* in an evocative village, bypassed by the very busy N83. Jean and Viviane Vuillot are regional addicts, *naturellement* – but we chose the oh-so-welcome, light Menu Pêcheur: a *rosace de langoustines au beurre de safran* (choice of 3 courses); *filet de sandre à l'oseille* (choice of 2); *fromage blanc à la crème*; and strawberry ice-cream.
Menus ABCDE. Rooms (16) DE. Cards Access, Visa.
Closed 20 June-4 July. 30 Sept-8 Oct. Mon (not bedrooms in season).
Post 71480 Cuiseaux, Saône-et-Loire. Regions Jura/Lyonnais.
Tel 85 72 71 79. Fax 85 72 54 22. Mich 103/E1. Map 6.

A100frs & under. B100–135. C135–165. D165–250. E250–350. F350–500. G500+

DABISSE   Vieux Colombier

Comfortable restaurant/Cooking 2-3
Terrace/Parking

An old farm and once a *relais de poste*. A rustic dining room with a
handsome terrace, shaded by two proud trees. Sylvain Nowak is an
inventive modern cook, doing a remarkable job in an out-of-the-way
spot. Worth a detour for tomatoes stuffed with *ratatouille* and *chèvre,
sauce basilic*; and *pintadeau poêlée aux gousses d'ail en chemise*.
Menus CD. Cards Access, Visa. (Rooms: Villiard at St-Auban to N.)
Closed 2-8 Jan. Sun evg (Oct to May). Wed. Regions Htes-Alpes/Provence.
Post Dabisse, 04190 Les Mées, Alpes-de-Haute-Provence.
Tel 92 34 32 32. Fax 92 34 34 26. Mich 146/A4. Map 6. (S of village.)

Les DEUX-ALPES   Chalet Mounier

Comfortable hotel/Cooking 2
Gardens/Swimming pools (indoor & outdoor)/Tennis/Lift/Parking

Great facilities (see above) and a heart-stopping view from the cliff at the
end of the gardens – over Venosc and the Véneon Valley. The chalet is
busy; some details need polishing up. Menu C could include a starter,
then spicy *meurson en brioche* (a tasty pork sausage), *filet de flétan à la
creme de ciboulette* and an absolutely top-notch dessert.
Menus bCD. Rooms (48) EFG. Cards Access, Visa.
Closed May. June. 4 Sept to 17 Dec.
Post 38860 Les Deux-Alpes, Isère. Regions Hautes-Alpes/Savoie.
Tel 76 80 56 90. Fax 76 79 56 51. Mich 132/B2. Map 6.

DIE   La Petite Auberge

Comfortable restaurant with rooms/Cooking 2
Terrace/Parking

No wonder readers have enthused over the years about Maryse Montero
and her warm welcome and the classical cooking of her husband Patrick.
The chef, now 45, once worked for three-star gods Bocuse and Outhier in
his 20s; the couple settled in Die in 1979. Culinary fireworks could
include *le meilleur du boeuf poêlé à la moelle* – lip-smackingly good.
Menus aBD. Rooms (11) CDE. Cards Access, Visa. Closed 15 Dec-
15 Jan. 17-24 Sept. Sun evg & Wed (not July/Aug). Mon (July/Aug).
Post av. Sadi-Carnot, 26150 Die, Drôme. Regions Hautes-Alpes/Savoie.
Tel 75 22 05 91. Fax 75 22 24 60. Mich 131/D4. Map 6. (Opposite *gare*.)

A100frs & under. B100–135. C135–165. D165–250. E250–350. F350–500. G500+

DIGOIN   Gare

Comfortable restaurant with rooms/Cooking 2-3
Gardens/Parking

Jean-Pierre and Jacqueline Mathieu have won praise from readers since
they bought the Gare – after Billoux moved to Dijon. Jean-Pierre paints a
classical canvas. Menu C has a palette of brights colours: *feuilletés
chauds de lièvre sur son lit de verdure* and *panaché de poissons de
mer aux baies roses* are invigorating *plats*. (Some rooms noisy.)
Menus bCDE. Rooms (13) EF. Cards Access, Visa.
Closed Mid Jan to mid Feb. Wed (not July & Aug). Region Berry-Bourb.
Post 79 av. Gén. de Gaulle, 71160 Digoin, Saône-et-Loire.
Tel 85 53 03 04. Fax 85 53 14 70. Mich 101/D2. Map 5.

DINAN   Caravelle

Comfortable restaurant/Cooking 2-3

Menu B is a wide-choice *RQP* stunner. Consider the evidence: to start
perhaps a *lapereau en gelée, crépinette aux herbes, marmalade
d'oignons et de primeurs* – intense and colourful; then a *tranche de lieu
doré au paprika* – pretty and punchy; next pungent cheeses; and, finally,
an unabashedly sweety treat – *crêpes soufflé aux cerises à la verveine
de jardin*. Bravo Jean-Claude (the chef) and Christiane Marmion.
Menus BDEF. Cards All. (Rooms: Arvor – 5 min walk SE; parking.)
Closed 14-23 Mar. 11 Nov to 3 Dec. Sun evg. Wed (Oct to mid June).
Post 14 pl. Duclos, 22100 Dinan, Côtes d'Armor. Region Brittany.
Tel 96 39 00 11. Mich 29/F3. Map 1.

DINAN   Les Grands Fossés

Comfortable restaurant/Cooking 2
Parking

The bespectacled duo, Alain and Jacqueline Colas, opened their *maison
Bourgeoise*, opposite the ramparts (NW corner), in 1990. Relish Alain's
neo-classical offerings in two handsome dining rooms: an ace *terrine de
ris de veau à l'hydromel*; melting *ballotin de julienne* (fish), *sauce à
l'oseille*; and a pretty-as-a-picture *palette des sorbets*.
Menus ACE. Cards Access, Visa. (Rooms: du Bas Frêne, 2 km to W.)
Closed 25-31 Jan. Thurs.
Post 2 pl. Gén. Leclerc, 22100 Dinan, Côtes d'Armor. Region Brittany.
Tel 96 39 21 50. Mich 29/F3. Map 1.

A 100frs & under. B 100–135. C 135–165. D 165–250. E 250–350. F 350–500. G 500+

DOL-DE-BRETAGNE
La Bresche Arthur

Comfortable restaurant with rooms/Cooking 2
Gardens/Parking

Philippe Martel's refurbished *logis* (fire damaged shortly after he bought the property) is liked by readers. Revitalised, pick-me-up, modern fare (he's well named): *carpaccio de saumon à la vinaigrette de concombre, escalopes de barbue en vapeur d'algues et petits oignons nouveaux* and a *crème brûlée à la vanille* remain Cognac-clear memories.
Menus ABD. Rooms (24) DE. Cards Access, Visa.
Closed 2nd half Jan. Rest: Wed (Oct to June). Region Brittany.
Post 36 bd Deminiac, 35120 Dol-de-Bretagne, Ille-et-Vilaine.
Tel 99 48 01 44. Fax 99 48 16 32. Mich 48/B1. Map 1.

DUCEY
Auberge de la Sélune

Comfortable hotel/Cooking 2
Gardens

The small, weed-choked gardens have a view of the Sélune, a famed salmon river. Chef Jean-Pierre Girres and his wife Josette offer classical catches such as *terrine d'aubergine, paupiettes de saumon, pie au crabe* (soup with a pastry topper), *truite soufflée à la ducéene* and, alas, an absolutely comatose *tarte aux pommes* (cooking rating of zero).
Menus aBCD. Rooms (19) E. Cards All.
Closed Mid Jan to mid Feb. Mon (Oct to Feb).
Post 50220 Ducey, Manche. Regions Brittany/Normandy.
Tel 33 48 53 62. Fax 33 48 90 30. Mich 30/C4. Map 1.

DUCLAIR
Poste

Comfortable restaurant with rooms/Cooking 2
Lift

A busy site beside the Seine. The restaurant is on the first floor and the bustling river traffic and ferry ensure there's never a dull visual moment. Eric Montier does the same with his classical dishes: *terrine de canard au porto, filet de lotte sauce Nantua, fromage blanc* and a *tarte Normande* makes a great lunch. (Also separate cheaper "Grill".)
Menus aBCD. Rooms (19) DE. Cards All.
Closed School hols in Feb, Nov and at Xmas. Sun evg. Mon.
Post 76480 Duclair, Seine-Maritime. Region Normandy.
Tel 35 37 50 04. Fax 35 37 39 19. Mich 15/F3. Map 2.

A 100frs & under. B 100–135. C 135–165. D 165–250. E 250–350. F 350–500. G 500+

DUINGT   Lac

Comfortable hotel/Cooking 2
Terrace/Gardens/Lake swimming/Lift/Parking

An exquisite setting: gorgeous views and the modernised hotel's toes literally in Lac d'Annecy. Thierry and Anne Borsoi are justifiably proud of their tonic hotel. Chef Marc Catellani treads water in the modern cooking pool: delight in exuberant catches like *bisquit de truite rose au curry* and *carpaccio de volaille en marinière de sauce vierge*.
Menus BCD. Rooms (23) EF. Cards Access, Visa.
Closed Hotel: Nov to 8 Feb. Sun (not May to Sept). Rest: Oct to Apl.
Post 74410 Duingt, Haute-Savoie. Region Savoie. Map 6.
Tel (R) 50 68 95 87. (H) 50 68 90 90. Fax 50 68 50 18. Mich 118/B1.

DUNKERQUE   Le Soubise

Very comfortable restaurant/Cooking 2
Gardens/Parking

Well clear of Dunkerque – at Coudekerque-Branche, south of the A16 and on W side of D916. Don't be put off by the scruffy frontage. Michel Hazebroucq is a creative classicist. His *saumon et canard* menu C has six starters and seven main courses. How about *carpaccio de canard*, *cotelettes de saumon grillées Béarnaise* and a *chocolat/nougat* dessert?
Menus ACD. Cards All. (Rooms: Campanile & Hôtel du Lac, 5 km W, Lac d'Armbouts-Cappel.) Closed Sat midday. Sun evg.
Post 49 rte Bergues, 59210 Coudekerque-Branche, Nord. Region North.
Tel 28 64 66 00. Fax 28 25 12 19. Mich 3/D1. Map 2.

DUN-LE-PALESTEL   Joly

Simple hotel/Cooking 2

The Creuse *département* is ideal walking and cycling *pays*. No wonder then that Claude Monceaux is happy to welcome walkers and cyclists to his *logis*; he's well equipped to give you sound advice on the best terrain. Step back in time at Joly: to Jacqueline's dining room; and to her husband's classical treats. A *faux-filet de Limousin mousseline de cèpes* is a local *terroir* joy. Also a welcome Special Poissons Menu (A).
Menus ACD. Rooms (26) DE. Cards Access, Visa.
Closed 1st 3 wks Mar. 4-24 Oct. Sun evg. Mon midday.
Post 23800 Dun-le-Palestel, Creuse. Region Poitou-Charentes.
Tel 55 89 00 23. Fax 55 89 15 89. Mich 97/E3. Map 5.

A 100frs & under. B 100–135. C 135–165. D 165–250. E 250–350. F 350–500. G 500+

DURBAN-CORBIERES

Le Moulin

Very comfortable restaurant/Cooking 3-4
Swimming pool/Parking

What a stunning show. All the staff, led by Corinne Moreno, speak English. The dining room is semi-circular with panoramic windows. Chef David Moreno, a Spaniard, lives and breathes good taste. Menu C could be a *tarte fine de tomate et anchois* – clearcut simplicity; a fish creation; a choice of 40 cheeses; and a sumptuous *crème brûlée*.
Menus CDE. Cards Acc, Visa. (Rooms: *autoroute* hotels S Narbonne.)
Closed 15 Oct-15 Mar. Sun evg & Mon (not July/Aug). (Above easy drive.)
Post 11360 Durban-Corbières, Aude. Region Languedoc-Roussillon.
Tel 68 45 81 03. Fax 68 45 83 31. Mich 172/C3. Map 5.

DURY

La Bonne Auberge

Comfortable restaurant/Cooking 2
Parking

A retina-searing, flower-covered exterior with a touch forced rustic interior. Nowt forced or prissy about Raoul Beaussire's regional and classical juggling. Menu C has a good range of choice: a typical meal could start with *ficelles Picardes*, move on to *pintade crème de champignon* and finish with a copious *fruits de jour Melba*.
Menus CD. Cards Access, AE, Visa. (Rooms: Novotel to E; N of Boves.)
Closed Sun evg and Mon. (Above hotel near junction N29/D934.)
Post 63 rte National (N1), 80480 Dury, Somme. Region North.
Tel 22 95 03 33. Mich 17/F1. Map 2.

ECHIGEY

Place (Rey)

Comfortable restaurant with basic rooms/Cooking 1-2
Gardens/Parking

A quiet village, south-east of Dijon. The *logis* is well-appointed and has basic but adequate bedrooms. Chef Dany Rey offers a good choice for each course. Nothing flashy with *plats* such as a shrimp and avocado cocktail; gutsy *pièce de boeuf* – touch spoiled by veg overpowered with nutmeg; top-notch cheese chariot; and dessert trolley. All on menu a.
Menus aCD. Rooms (13) BCD. Cards Access, DC, Visa.
Closed Jan. 1st wk Aug. Sun evg. Mon (not public hols).
Post Echigey, 21110 Genlis, Côte-d'Or. Region Burgundy.
Tel 80 29 74 00. Fax 80 29 79 55. Mich 88/C1. Map 3.

A100frs & under. B100–135. C135–165. D165–250. E250–350. F350–500. G500+

EMBRUN   Mairie

Simple hotel/Cooking 1-2
Terrace

The *logis* is at the heart of Embrun, opposite the Fontaine St-Pierre (follow signs for Centre Ville/Hôtel de Ville). Jean-Pierre François is from the Southwest, hence his fondness for *foie gras de canard* and *magret de canard fumé*. Menu A represents great *RQP* with a good choice (extra for *foie gras, bien sûr*). Classical and *Bourgeoise* grub.
Menus A. Rooms (22) DE. Cards All.
Closed 10-29 May. Oct. Nov. Sun and Mon (Oct to May but not sch. hols).
Post pl. Mairie, 05200 Embrun, Hautes-Alpes. Regions Htes-Alpes/Savoie.
Tel 92 43 20 65. Fax 92 43 47 02. Mich 147/D1. Map 6.

ESPALION   Le Méjane

Comfortable restaurant/Cooking 3-4

The cooking rating gives the clue to how impressed we were at this most beguiling of *Franc-wise France* recommendations; we can't wait to return. A young couple going places: Régine Caralp, a vibrant, vivacious hostess; and husband Philippe, a confident, modern master with an eye for technique, presentation and good taste. One dish, a *jambonette de pintade rôtie, jus reduit au vin rouge* was a superb showpiece.
Menus BCD. Cards All. (Rooms: Moderne or simpler Central—20 m away.)
Closed Feb school hols. 26 June to 1 July. Sun evg (not Aug). Wed.
Post r. Méjane, 12500 Espalion, Aveyron. Regions MC (Auvergne/Cévennes).
Tel 65 48 22 37. Mich 140/C1. Map 5. (South of Lot, E of D920.)

ETANG-SUR-ARROUX   Hostellerie du Gourmet

Comfortable restaurant with basic rooms/Cooking 1-2

The geranium-edged frontage is a bright and welcome sight at the Caboche *hostellerie* on the southern main road (D994) entrance to the village. Copious and anything but dull could describe a lunch of *salade de noix de pétoncles au vinaigre de framboise*; followed by, first, a *filet de julienne sauce crustacé* and, next, a *contrefilet vigneronne*; then *fromage* and, to finish, a large slice of *tarte aux pommes*.
Menus aCD. Rooms (12) CD. Cards Access, Visa.
Closed January.
Post 71190 Etang-sur-Arroux, Saône-et-Loire. Region Burgundy.
Tel 85 82 20 88. Mich 87/D3-E3. Map 3.

A100frs & under. B100–135. C135–165. D165–250. E250–350. F350–500. G500+

EUGÉNIE-LES-BAINS

La Ferme aux Grives

Simple restaurant/Cooking 3
Terrace

Enterprise 4 in the growing *"Village Minceur"* Eugénie empire of 3-star chef Michel Guérard. Rustic conversion and *la cuisine rustique* – using local produce and old recipes. Vast choice: a suckling pig turning on the spit in the huge fireplace, superb soups, Landes *terrines*, black puddings, *cochon de lait*, roast duck, meringues and *tartes*. First-class service.
Menus C. Cards Access, Visa. (Rooms: Maison Rose or Adour at Aire to E.)
Closed Dec/Jan (not Xmas/New Yr). Mon evg & Tues (10 July-10 Sept).
Public hols. Post 40320 Eugénie-les-Bains, Landes. Region Southwest.
Tel 58 51 19 08. Fax 58 51 13 59. Mich 150/A2. Map 4.

Les EYZIES-DE-TAYAC

Cro-Magnon

Very comfortable hotel/Cooking 3
Terrace/Gardens/Swimming pool/Parking

Anne and I have loved the vine-covered hotel and the genuine, caring owners, Jacques and Christiane Leyssales, for almost 35 years. Menu C (low-end) gives you the chance to understand another one of the reasons why you should visit: a subtle tasting *morue fraîche à l'anchoïade*; *fricassée de pintadeau aux Xérès*; and strawberries and cream.
Menus CDEF. Rooms (18) FG. Cards All.
Closed 10 Oct to end April. Rest: Wed midday.
Post 24620 Les Eyzies-de-Tayac, Dordogne. Region Dordogne.
Tel 53 06 97 06. Fax 53 06 95 45. Mich 123/F3. Map 5.

FALAISE

Poste

Comfortable hotel/Cooking 1-2
Parking

The only debit at the Poste is the main road site. Everything else is a credit: an informative *patronne*, Simone Collias, is one pleasing plus; another is her judo-loving husband Michel's classical repertoire. (He's also a pilot: take an aerial tour.) Limited choice: *tête de veau ravigote* and *entrecôte grillée sauce moelle* are typical dishes.
Menus aBCD. Rooms (21) DEF. Cards Access, AE, Visa.
Closed 17-23 Oct. 20 Dec to 20 Jan. Sun evg. Mon (not hotel).
Post 38 r. G. Clemenceau, 14700 Falaise, Calvados. Region Normandy.
Tel 31 90 13 14. Fax 31 90 01 81. Mich 32/B3. Map 2.

A100frs & under. B100–135. C135–165. D165–250. E250–350. F350–500. G500+

Le FAOU   **Vieille Renommée**

Comfortable hotel/Cooking 1-2
Lift

Readers usually give their vote to Mme Philippe's modern hotel, rather than Michelin's favourite, the Relais de la Place. Chef Daniel Bourhis' repertoire is a lengthy roll call of *Bretonne* and *Bourgeoise* fare with highlights like *truite saumonée au coulis de crustacés* and a gutsy *pot-au-feu de la mer*. Park in the football pitch-sized *place*.

Menus aCD. Rooms (38) E. Cards Access, Visa.
Closed Sun evg and Mon (not July/Aug).
Post pl. Mairie, 29580 Le Faou, Finistère. Region Brittany.
Tel 98 81 90 31. Fax 98 81 92 93. Mich 26/C4. Map 1.

FAVERGES   **Florimont**

Comfortable hotel/Cooking 2
Terrace/Gardens/Lift/Parking

Jacques and Marie-Josèphe Goubot (as unsmiling as ever) let their son, Jean-Christophe, run the kitchen show in their new home, north-east of Faverges. Classical and *Bourgeoise* fare: *cuisse de canard aux olives, omble chevalier rôti, magret de canard poêlé et sa sauce aux mûres* and similar. Marie-Claire, J-C's wife, provides a happier, warmer welcome.

Menus bCDF. Rooms (27) EF. Disabled. Cards All.
Closed Rest: Sun evg (Oct to June).
Post 74210 Faverges, Haute-Savoie. Region Savoie.
Tel 50 44 50 05. Fax 50 44 43 20. Mich 118/C2. Map 6.

FAVERGES   **Gay Séjour**

Simple hotel/Cooking 2-3
Secluded/Terrace/Parking

A cascade of pluses have made this a readers' top favourite: a 17thC *Savoyarde* farmhouse; a captivating site – near mountains, Lac d'Annecy and Tamié Abbey; and the caring family Gay – led by Bernard, a likeable dynamo of a chef. Neo-classical and *Savoyards plats* with great emphasis on fish dishes (from the lake and oceans). Superb regional cheeses.

Menus CDE. Rooms (12) F. Cards All. (Take D12 S from Faverges.)
Closed 27 Dec to 27 Jan. Sun evg and Mon (not school hols).
Post Tertenoz, 74210 Faverges, Haute-Savoie. Region Savoie.
Tel 50 44 52 52. Fax 50 44 49 52. Mich 118/C2. Map 6.

A 100frs & under. B 100–135. C 135–165. D 165–250. E 250–350. F 350–500. G 500+

FAVIERES   La Clé des Champs

Comfortable restaurant/Cooking 2
Parking

"The key" leads you to blue and white cottages and a rustic interior with
plenty of flowers – at the heart of a hamlet in the Somme estuary. Isabelle
and Bruno Flasque charm clients in many ways: a warm welcome,
competent service, sensible wines and appetising neo-classical dishes:
terrine de poissons aux 3 couleurs and *filet de turbotin* were champion.
Menus aBC. Cards Access, DC, Visa. (Rooms: Lion d'Or at Rue 3 km to N.)
Closed 2 Jan to 4 Feb. 28 Aug to 16 Sept. Sun evg. Mon.
Post 80120 Favières, Somme. Region North.
Tel 22 27 88 00. Mich 6/C2. Map 2.

La FERRIERE-AUX-ETANGS   Auberge de la Mine

Comfortable restaurant/Cooking 2-3

What an off-putting name; but please don't bypass this colourful oasis. A
talented young couple – Catherine and Hubert Nobis – have an eye for
detail. A bright-as-a-button dining room is the first eye-catcher; followed
by Hubert's inventive, modern repertoire: full-of-verve dishes such as
pavé de brochet rôti au gingembre frais; *filet de rascasse en nage de
coriandre*; and *pudding chocolat, creme de réglisse*.
Menus aBC. Cards Access/AE/Visa. (Rooms: Ermitage, Bagnoles-de-l'Orne.)
Closed 4-25 Jan. 1-15 Sept. Tues evg. Wed. (Above easy drive to SE.)
Post Le Gué-Plat, 61450 La Ferrière-aux-Etangs, Orne. Region Normandy.
Tel 33 66 91 10. Mich 32/A4. Map 2. (2 km S, via D21 and D825.)

FIGEAC   des Carmes

Very comfortable hotel/Cooking 2-3
Terrace/Swimming pool/Tennis/Lift/Parking

A capable *directeur*, Jean-Louis Tillet, and an equally able chef, Daniel
Raynaud, ensure that standards are kept high. Classical and regional
specialities: from many worthy alternatives choose delights such as an
earthy-scented *brouillade d'oeufs aux truffes*; a punchy *noix d'agneau
à la crème d'ail* and a voluptuous *trilogie de chocolat*.
Menus BDE. Rooms (40) EF. Cards All.
Closed Xmas to New Year. Sat (Oct to Apl). Sun evg.
Post Enclos des Carmes, 46100 Figeac, Lot. Region Dordogne.
Tel 65 34 20 78. Fax 65 34 22 39. Mich 139/E1. Map 5.

A100frs & under. B100–135. C135–165. D165–250. E250–350. F350–500. G500+

FLAGEY-ECHEZEAUX

Robert Losset

Simple restaurant/Cooking 2

What a disarming surprise. You'll see no signs – just "Bar" and "Tabac" in the small *place* north of the church. No airs and graces here – just emphatic, exemplary classics: an intense *terrine de caille*; a light, restrained *mousseline de saumon*; an unabashed *lapin farci façon chasse* or a hit-in-the-mouth *rognon veau à la moutarde*; finishing with a flourish – a *vacherin*. An endearing experience – in every way.
Menus a(lunch)BCD. Cards Access, Visa. (Rooms: St-Georges, Nuits.)
Closed Wed. (St-Georges hotel at A31 exit 1; see *FLE* p80 for details.)
Post Flagey-Echezeaux, 21640 Vougeot, Côte-d'Or. Region Burgundy.
Tel 80 62 88 10. Mich 88/B1. Map 3.

FLAYOSC

L'Oustaou

Comfortable restaurant/Cooking 1-2
Terrace

Pleasant village square setting; lovely out of doors on terrace, a touch confined inside. Provençale cuisine with several hunky dory *Bourgeois* tummy fillers: *pâté, boeuf en daube, coq au vin, pieds et paquets, magrets grillés*, goat's milk cheeses and above average sweets. One nice touch: help yourself from copper pans brought to the table.
Menus BCD. Cards Access, AE, Visa. (Rooms: Les Oliviers, 3 km to E.)
Closed 13-20 Mar. 13 Nov to 11 Dec. Sun evg. Mon.
Post 83780 Flayosc, Var. Region Côte d'Azur. (7 km W of Draguignan.)
Tel 94 70 42 69. Mich 162/C3. Map 6.

FLERS

Au Bout de la Rue

Comfortable restaurant/Cooking 2

The smile-forcing name is a happy start; the cascade of flowers over the shop-front façade is even better. Marie-Noël Lebouleux is a warm-hearted hostess and husband Jacky a classical/neo-classical chef. Huge choice on menu C (low-end) including *salade terre-mer en vapeur de poissons tiède, saumon d'Ecosse rôti aux graines de sésame, rognons de veau à la moutarde* and 10 cracking desserts. Also cheaper bistro.
Menus A(bistro)C. Cards Acc, Visa. (Rooms: Galion; *sans rest*, parking.)
Closed Sunday. Pub hols. (Above hotel 2 minute-walk to NE, same road.)
Post 60 r. Gare, 61100 Flers, Orne. Region Normandy.
Tel 33 65 31 53. Fax 33 65 46 81. Mich 32/A4. Map 1.

A100frs & under. B100–135. C135–165. D165–250. E250–350. F350–500. G500+

FLEURINES   Vieux Logis

Very comfortable restaurant/Cooking 3
Terrace/Gardens

North of Senlis (and A1 exit 8) and at the heart of the Forêt d'Halatte. Yann
and Valérie Nivet have assembled a knockout formula – which pleases both
the eyes and taste buds. Faultless classical and regional fare. Some autumn
examples: pungent *gibier, champignons, cul de lapin à la bière Picarde*
and a Normandy marvel, *douillon aux poires sauce caramel.*
Menus CDF. Cards All. (Rooms: Ibis, just W of A1 exit 8.)
Closed 1st 3 wks Aug. Sun evg. Mon. Regions Normandy/North
Post 105 av. Gén. de Gaulle, 60700 Fleurines, Oise.
Tel 44 54 10 13. Fax 44 54 12 47. Mich 36/B1. Map 2.

FLEURY-SUR-ORNE   L'Ile Enchantée

Comfortable restaurant/Cooking 2

Well-named: a pretty, wooded setting, across the road from the River Orne
and adjacent to an easily accessible riverside "green". Luscious classical
food with a varied choice of tastes: light *gourmandise de saumon à la
crème d'herbettes* and *minute de saumon aux huîtres, sauce lie de vin*;
or loosen-your-belts *médaillon de veau a l'anglaise, crème Vallée d'Auge*
and *fine tarte aux pommes chaudes, sauce caramel.*
Menus BCDE. Cards Access, Visa. (Rooms: Novotel & Ibis – N of Caen.)
Closed Feb sch hols. 1-8 Aug. Sun evg. Mon. (Use E bypass for above.)
Post 14123 Fleury-sur-Orne, Orne. (4 km S of Caen.) Region Normandy.
Tel 31 52 15 52. Mich 32/A1-B1. Map 2.

FLORAC   Grand Hôtel Parc

Comfortable hotel/Cooking 1-2
Gardens/Swimming pool/Lift/Parking

The large hotel is a mixture of modern and old, overlooking a large, shady
garden with an almost hidden, cool swimming pool. Claude Gleize,
chef/patron, rows in regional and classical boats: put your oars into
gutsy, filling grub – including *charcuteries Cévenoles, salade Cévenole,
tripoux Lozèriens, civet de caneton* and *côtes d'agneau grillées.*
Menus aCD. Rooms (66) CD. Cards All.
Closed Dec to mid March. Sun evg (not hotel). Mon (not high season).
Post 48400 Florac, Lozère. Region Massif Central (Cévennes).
Tel 66 45 03 05. Fax 66 45 11 81. Mich 142/B2. Map 5.

A100frs & under. B100–135. C135–165. D165–250. E250–350. F350–500. G500+

La FLOTTE (Ile de Ré)   Le Lavardin

Comfortable restaurant/Cooking 2-3

Georges and Patricia Barbet, the owners, look after the front of house while young chef William Donny, not yet 30, mixes neo-classical, *Charentaises* and Danish culinary cocktails. Refreshing, salty and sweet cocktails of flavours they are too: try a shaker mix of *harengs marinés Baltique*, *saumon grillé à la fleur de sel de Ré*, *bavette d'aloyau* (sirloin) *aux échalotes* and what else but *Ile Flottaise*!

Menus b(lunch)CDE. Cards Access, Visa. (Rooms: Hippocampe.)
Closed 10 Jan-10 Feb. 13 Nov-13 Dec. Mon evg & Tues (out of season).
Post r. H.Lainé, 17630 La Flotte, Charente-Maritime. Region Poitou-Char.
Tel 46 09 68 32. Mich 92/C3. Map 4.

FONTAINEBLEAU   Napoléon/Rest. La Table des Marcéchaux

Very comfortable hotel/Cooking 2
Terrace/Lift

Opposite the palace. Bedroom prices are as elevated as the emperor's ego. (The Ibis, 200 m away, has a garage and cheaper rooms.) The menu is *RQP* plus in the expensive Ile de France. Enjoy classical *plats* with a view of the interior garden – a real bonus: *agneau grillée*, *sauce Béarnaise*; *brandade de morue fraîche*; and superb *Bries* are typical.

Menus B. Rooms (56) G-G2. Cards All.
Closed 18 Dec to 2 Jan. Regions Ile de France/Champagne-Ardenne.
Post 9 r. Grande, 77300 Fontainebleau, Seine-et-Marne.
Tel (1) 64 22 20 39. Fax (1) 64 22 20 87. Mich 54/C2. Map 2.

FONTENAY-LE-COMTE   Chouans Gourmets

Comfortable restaurant/Cooking 2

Alongside the Vendée's right bank and at the heart of handsome Fontenay. Stone features overpoweringly in the main dining room; a smaller *salle* overlooks the dull river view. Madame is an eagle-eyed *patronne*. *Chef/patron* Robert Vrignon weaves a mix of culinary patterns: witness *emincé de porc Cantonnaise*, succulent *canette rôtie au miel et coriandre* and tender, pink *brochette de gigot d'agneau grillée aux herbes*.

Menus ABCD. Cards All. (Rooms: Rabelais or St-Nicolas at Maillezais.)
Closed 2-17 Jan. 4-11 July. Sun evg. Mon. (Maillezais easy 12 km to SE.)
Post 6 r. Halles, 85200 Fontenay-le-Comte, Vendée. Region Poitou-Char.
Tel 51 69 55 92. Mich 93/E2. Map 4.

A 100frs & under. B 100–135. C 135–165. D 165–250. E 250–350. F 350–500. G 500+

FORCALQUIER
Host. des Deux Lions

Comfortable hotel/Cooking 3
Garage

Old France in a time warp: gentle, caring hosts, Robert & Claude Audier and Michel Montdor-Florent, a classical/regional chef. No-choice menu B (top-end) confirms his old-fashioned skills: dishes like *oeuf brouillé au crabe et aux crevettes en aumônière croustillante*; *poitrine d'agneau mitonnée puis grillée aux herbes*; and *mousse au chocolat noir*.
Menus BDE. Rooms (17) EF. Cards Access, Visa.
Closed Jan. Feb. Mid Nov to 18 Dec. Region Provence.
Post 11 pl. Bourguet, 04300 Forcalquier, Alpes-de-Hte-Provence.
Tel 92 75 25 30. Fax 92 75 06 41. Mich 145/F4. Map 6.

FORGES-LES-EAUX
Auberge du Beau Lieu

Comfortable restaurant with basic rooms/Cooking 3
Terrace/Parking

Marie-France Ramelet is a *petite*, attentive *patronne* and *sommelière* – proud of her *cave* (with 40 halves) and beamed dining room (with many paintings by local artist, William Gantier). Patrick Ramelet is an inventive modern master: *gâteau d'andouille aux pommes confites* and *millefeuille de haddock mariné et salade* are two *RQP* treats.
Menus CDE. Rooms (3) E. Cards All. (2 km SE, alongside D915.)
Closed 23 Jan to 8 Feb. Tues (not school hols). Region Normandy.
Post Le Fosse, 76440 Forges-les-Eaux, Seine-Maritime.
Tel 35 90 50 36. Fax 35 90 35 98. Mich 16/C2-C3. Map 2.

FORGES-LES-EAUX
Paix

Comfortable restaurant with basic rooms/Cooking 1-2
Gardens/Parking

Régine and Rémy Michel claim that their culinary philosophy is to uphold *tradition et terroir*. They do just that at their modest town-centre *logis* with beamed dining rooms. Examples of regional *plats* using *terroir* produce: *andouillete à la Normande, terrine de canard à la Rouennaise, filets de sole Dieppoise, Bray* cheeses and hot apple tart.
Menus ABC. Rooms (5) BC. Cards All. Region Normandy.
Closed 20 Dec-15 Jan. Sun evg (not high seas). Mon (not evg high seas).
Post 15 r. Neufchâtel, 76440 Forges-les-Eaux, Seine-Maritime.
Tel 35 90 51 22. Fax 35 09 83 62. Mich 16/C2-C3. Map 2.

A100frs & under. B100–135. C135–165. D165–250. E250–350. F350–500. G500+

FRANCESCAS   Relais de la Hire

Very comfortable restaurant/Cooking 2-3
Terrace/Gardens

A high-ceilinged *salle* in an 18thC house with a *parc ombragé* – all at
the door of heart-stirring Gascony. Jean-Noël Prabonne adds his own
brand of musketeer bravura. Tuck into two menus – l'Ecuyer (a) and
Chevalier (C) – and savour classical largesse like *cromesquis de Ste-
Maure* and *petit salé de saumon à la crème de lentilles.*
Menus aCD. Cards All. (Rooms: Trois Lys & Logis des Cordeliers, Condom.)
Closed Sun evg (not July and Aug). Mon. (Both *sans rest*; 15 km to SW.)
Post 47600 Francescas, Lot-et-Garonne. Region Southwest.
Tel 53 65 41 59. Fax 53 65 86 42. Mich 136/C4. Map 5.

FREJUS   La Toque Blanche

Very comfortable restaurant/Cooking 2

At east end of Fréjus-Plage, as you enter St-Raphaël. Stylish, service *sous
cloches* and goldfish-bowl glasses. Jacky Collin is a classicist with a light
hand: *gratin de moules et huîtres, cervelles beurre noir, tournedos
sauté forestière* and *sorbets* are menu B possibilities. (Prices in francs &
écus – a horrible reminder that an EU single currency may be forced
upon us one day. Please – no; let's pull out of the EU now.)
Menus BDE. Cards All. (Rooms: L'Oasis, quiet, parking – 1 km away to W.)
Closed 9 June to 9 July. Mon. (See *FLE* – p111 – for details of above.)
Post 394 av. V.Hugo, 83600 Fréjus-Plage, Var. Region Côte d'Azur.
Tel 94 52 06 14. Mich 163/E3. Map 6.

FROIDETERRE   Hostellerie des Sources

Comfortable restaurant/Cooking 2
Terrace/Parking

Well-named with springs and pools – the latter used to breed *écrevisses.*
Marcel Brocard is a savvy wine buff and son Valéry an able young chef.
In the beamed dining room dig into eclectic French dishes: *soupe de
poisson à la Provençale*; *gras-double à la Lyonnaise*; *gigot des
Pyrénées*; and the ubiquitous *crème brûlée à la vanille* (hot or cold).
Menus ABDE. Cards Access, Visa. (Rooms: Eric Hôtel, Lure – 3 km to SW.)
Closed 1st wk Feb. Last wk July. 1st 2 wks Aug. Sat midday. Mon.
Post 4 r. du Grand Bois, 70200 Froideterre, Haute-Saône. Region Alsace.
Tel 84 30 13 91. Fax 84 30 29 87. Mich 76/B2. Map 3.

A100frs & under. B100–135. C135–165. D165–250. E250–350. F350–500. G500+

FUISSE
Pouilly Fuissé

Comfortable restaurant/Cooking 2
Terrace

Eric and Dominique Point (she's the fourth generation owner) entice with lick-your-lips *RQP* classical, *Bressane* and *Lyonnaise* cuisine. From an avalanche of five menus dig into the likes of *saladier Lyonnais*, *filet de perche sauce Duglérée* (sic), *grenouilles poëlées à la persillade* and the encore-please *crêpes Parmentier sucrées* (potato pancakes).
Menus aBCD. Cards Access, Visa. (Rooms: Ibis; SE at A6 Mâcon-Sud exit.)
Closed Mid Feb to mid Mar. 1st wk Aug. Sun evg. Tues evg. Wed.
Post 71960 Fuissé, Saône-et-Loire. Region Lyonnais.
Tel 83 35 60 68. Mich 102/B3. Map 6.

GAN
Le Tucq

Simple restaurant/Cooking 1-2
Terrace/Parking

If pennies count and if you would like to lose yourself in the exquisite foothills of the Pyrénées – and if you relish down-to-earth *Béarnaise* and *Bourgeoise* grub – then nose out Michel and Simone Rances. Take an appetite: *garbure Béarnaise*, *assiette de charcuterie*, *truite meunière*, *confit de canard* and six desserts all appear on the low-end menu B.
Menus aB. (Rooms: Bilaa, quiet, 6 km NW of Pau. Pau is 8 km N of Gan.)
Closed Oct. Mon evg, Tues and Wed (but not Aug). Region Southwest.
Post rte de Laruns, 64290 Gan, Pyrénées-Atlantiques. (4 km S – on D934.)
Tel 59 21 61 26. Mich 168/A1. Map 4.

GAP (also see next page)
Carré Long

Comfortable restaurant/Cooking 2-3

There are no gaps in Gap on the *RQP* front. Bernard Fiore-Rappelin is a modern *maître* with a sense of humour (read his menus carefully) and a taste for extrovert marriages: a *craquant de dorade aux petits légumes*, *sauce à la fleur d'aubépine* (hawthorn) is a tasty pastry-wallet treat. Monique, Bernard's wife, is an interesting, intelligent hostess. (Try, too, a Vin des Hautes-Alpes. A Vin de Théus no less! New to you?)
Menus BDE. Cards All. (Rooms: Ibis with garage – 5 min walk to E.)
Closed 1-15 May. Sun. Mon.
Post 32 r. Pasteur, 05000 Gap, Hautes-Alpes. Regions Htes-Alpes/Savoie.
Tel 92 51 13 10. Mich 146/B1. Map 6.

A100frs & under. B100–135. C135–165. D165–250. E250–350. F350–500. G500+

GAP (also see previous page) La Musardière

Simple restaurant/Cooking 2

Bravo Christophe Fouilloux! A tiny, rustic dining room, seating 20. But big-hearted offerings from a chef who clearly adores the Ecrins *montagnes* to the north (each menu has a name linked to a mountain in the *massif*). Menu C (low-end) is a memorable repast, including *St-Marcellin* (cheese) *rôti* with almonds, *gigot d'agneau son jus au porto*, *fromages de nos montagnes* and *nougat glacé au miel du Queyras*.
Menus ACD. Cards All. (Rooms: Ibis with garage – 3 min walk to SE.)
Closed 1-15 Jan. 1-15 July. Sun evg. Mon.
Post 3 pl. Révelly, 05000 Gap, Hautes-Alpes. Regions Htes-Alpes/Savoie.
Tel 92 51 56 15. Mich 146/B1. Map 6.

GERARDMER Grand Hôtel Bragard/Rest. Le Grand Cerf

Luxury hotel/Cooking 2-3
Terrace/Gardens/Swimming pool/Lift/Parking

Talented Fabienne and Claude Remy have injected a new lease of life into the old-fashioned hotel (in the second *FL*). Chef Dominique Mervelay tempts with modestly-priced menus, eaten in a deluxe environment. Relish the latter and tuck into the fare: perhaps a *marmite du pêcheur*, then an *emincé de canard aux raisins*, followed by the cheese chariot and a plate of *pâtisseries*. Work the inches off in the gym, sauna and solarium.
Menus bCDEF. Rooms (56) FG. Cards All. (Cheaper rooms: nearby Bains.)
Post pl. du Tilleul, 88400 Gérardmer, Vosges. Region Alsace.
Tel 29 63 06 31. Fax 29 63 46 81. Mich 60/B3. Map 3.

GEVREY-CHAMBERTIN Le Bonbistrot

Simple restaurant/Cooking 1-2
Terrace/Parking

Pierre Menneveau's *bistrot* is at ground level, above his rightly famed Rôtisserie, and is served by the same kitchen. Admire the l9thC pewter bar and chuckle at the toilets' washbasin. Emphatic regional tunes on the Bonbistrot piano: among them *jambon persillé*, *fricassée de coq au vin à l'ancienne* and *ami du Chambertin* cheese. Wines by the glass.
Menus ABC(à la carte). Cards Access, Visa. (Rooms: Les Grands Crus.)
Closed Feb. 1st wk Aug. Sun evg. Mon (not pub hols). (Above easy walk.)
Post 21220 Gevrey-Chambertin, Côte-d'Or. Region Burgundy.
Tel 80 34 35 14. Fax 80 34 12 30. Mich 88/B1. Map 3.

A100frs & under. B100–135. C135–165. D165–250. E250–350. F350–500. G500+

GIGONDAS   Les Florets

**Comfortable restaurant with rooms/Cooking 2
Secluded/Terrace/Gardens/Parking**

A large tree-shaded terrace is a plus: cool at midday and with lights in the
evening. Service can be off-hand. Menu C has a choice of classical, regional
and *Bourgeois plats*: *tourte de lapereau au romarin et morilles* and
roulade de pintadeau aux ravioles have been praised. *Patrons* Martine
and Pierre Bernard's family also own their own Gigondas vineyard.
Menus a(lunch)CD. Rooms (15) F. Cards All. (To the E; shown on map.)
Closed Jan. Feb. Tues evg (out of season). Wed.
Post 84190 Gigondas, Vaucluse. Region Provence.
Tel 90 65 85 01. Fax 90 65 83 80. Mich 144/C3. Map 6.

GIROUSSENS   L'Echauguette

**Comfortable restaurant with rooms/Cooking 2
Terrace**

La cuisinière, Pierrette Canonica, puts her fingers in all sorts of French
regional cooking pots: take your pick from varied delights such as *salade
Aveyronnaise, gras-double à la Lyonnaise, andouillettes* (Normandy)
and an earthy *daube de boeuf au Madiran* (Gascony). Sumptuous
home-made *pâtisseries*. Pierrette's husband, Claude, is *le patron*.
Menus ABCDE. Rooms (5) CDE. Cards All.
Closed 1st 3 wks Feb. 15-30 Sept. Sun evg and Mon (Oct to June).
Post pl. de la Mairie, 81500 Giroussens, Tarn. Region Languedoc-Rouss.
Tel 63 41 63 65. Mich 153/E2. Map 5.

GOUMOIS   Taillard

**Comfortable hotel/Cooking 2-3
Secluded/Terrace/Gardens/Swimming pool/Parking**

A blissful spot with rejuvenating views across the wooded Doubs Valley.
A long-established, now modernised family hotel, founded in 1875.
Regional and modern creations from Jean-François Taillard: *truites* in
various guises (including *au vin jaune*), *feuilleté forestier flanqué de
morilles* and super palate-tickler *sandre aux 7 épices, sauce estragon*.
Menus BCDE. Rooms (13) EF. Cards All.
Closed Nov to Feb. Wed (not Apl to Sept).
Post 25470 Goumois, Doubs. Region Jura.
Tel 81 44 20 75. Fax 81 44 26 15. Mich 77/D4. Map 3.

A100frs & under. B100–135. C135–165. D165–250. E250–350. F350–500. G500+

GOURDON
Host. de la Bouriane

Comfortable hotel/Cooking 2
Quiet/Gardens/Lift/Parking

A modern *logis* south of Gourdon's medieval centre. A host of little details make their mark: tasty appetisers and *petits fours* for example. Pretty dining room and caring *patrons*. A spiky *escalope de saumon grillée au beurre d'épices* and a luscious *coq au vin de Cahors* – with a dark pool of sauce – were the high points of an enjoyable *repas*.
Menus aBCDE. Rooms (20) EF. Cards Access, AE, Visa.
Closed Mid Jan to mid Mar. Rest: Mon (not evgs June to Oct).
Post pl. Foirail, 46300 Gourdon, Lot. Region Dordogne.
Tel 65 41 16 37. Fax 65 41 04 92. Mich 124/B4. Map 5.

GOURNAY-EN-BRAY
Aux Trois Maillets

Simple restaurant with rooms/Cooking 2-3
Terrace/Parking

The are two menus B: one *poisson*, the other *viande*. Panache describes both: *bisque de homard* and *filet de daurade* on the former; *chou farci de canard* and *pot au feu* on the latter. Philippe Colignon is a classicist and Maître Canardier: two D duck menus (above the *FWF* ceiling) offer the chance, in half-a-dozen ways, to confirm he's not a quack chef.
Menus BDE. Rooms (30) DE. Disabled. Cards All. Closed Rest only: mid Jan to mid Feb. Tues midday (mid Sept to Mar). Sat midday. Sun evg.
Post 6 r. Barbacane, 76220 Gournay-en-Bray, Seine-Maritime.
Tel 35 90 82 50. Fax 35 09 99 77. Mich 17/D3. Map 2. Region Normandy.

GRAMAT
Le Relais des Gourmands

Comfortable hotel/Cooking 2
Terrace/Gardens/Swimming pool

An enticing mix of ingredients beguile clients: colourful, bright decorations and furnishings in a modern building; a Scots' welcome from multi-lingual Susy Curtet and a confident *palette* of regional and classical specialities from husband Gérard. Memorable *assiette de deux terrines* and a blockbuster *cassoulet Périgourdin au confit d'oie*.
Menus aCD. Rooms (16) EF. Cards Access, Visa.
Closed Rest: Sun evg (winter) and Mon midday (not July/Aug).
Post av. Gare, 46500 Gramat, Lot. Region Dordogne.
Tel 65 38 83 92. Fax 65 38 70 99. Mich 125/D4. Map 5.

A100frs & under. B100–135. C135–165. D165–250. E250–350. F350–500. G500+

GRAMAT
Lion d'Or

Very comfortable hotel/Cooking 2
Terrace/Lift

A handsome stone façade with a vine-shaded terrace and a warm welcome from Suzanne and René Mommejac. René seduces with treats like *carpaccio de jambon d'Aoste au melon des côteaux du Quercy* (a tasty French and Italian marriage) and a mouthwatering *saumon rôti au lard, poireaux et tatin de champignons aux pommes*. Neo-classical and regional cooking.
Menus bCDE. Rooms (15) EF. Cards All. (Park in huge *place*.)
Closed Mid Dec to mid Jan. Rest: Mon midday (Nov to Feb).
Post pl. République, 46500 Gramat, Lot. Region Dordogne.
Tel 65 38 73 18. Fax 65 38 84 50. Mich 125/D4. Map 5.

Le GRAND-PRESSIGNY
Espérance

Comfortable restaurant with basic rooms/Cooking 2-3
Parking

Times change. Once unfussy; now the tag "grand" can be applied to whitejacketed waiters, a plague of plate covers, and to some of Bernard Torset's neo-classical and modern repertoire. Some older gems remain: *terrine de lapereau* and *brochet au beurre blanc* are a Menu B duo; and the lip-licking home-made breakfast jams of *la patronne*, Pauline Torset.
Menus BCD. Rooms (10) CD. Cards Access, DC, Visa.
Closed 5 Jan to 5 Feb. Mon (not public hols). Regions Loire/Poitou-Char.
Post 37350 Le Grand-Pressigny, Indre-et-Loire.
Tel 47 94 90 12. Mich 82/B3. Map 2.

GUINGAMP
Relais du Roy

Very comfortable restaurant with rooms/Cooking 2-3
Quiet

Victoria and Jacques Mallégol's 16th-century *hôtel particulier* (town house) has swish bedrooms. Neo-classical cooking with a Brittany flourish. Four fish creations – *petite marmite des Pêcheurs, moules de la Côte au cidre, filet de mérou bisquine* and *filet de truite de l'Argoat* – evoke to a tee the chef's well-crafted regional objectives.
Menus BCD. Rooms (7) G. Cards All. (Cheaper rooms at D'Armor.)
Closed Xmas. Sun. (Parking in *place*.)
Post pl. Centre, 22200 Guingamp, Côtes d'Armor. Region Brittany.
Tel 96 43 76 62. Fax 96 44 08 01. Mich 28/B2. Map 1.

A100frs & under. B100–135. C135–165. D165–250. E250–350. F350–500. G500+

Les HALLES   Charreton

Comfortable restaurant with rooms/Cooking 2
Parking

The *auberge*, on the D489 and at the heart of the Monts du Lyonnais, has views from the rear of both hills and woods. Pierre Charreton is both a master baker and *cuisinier*. Regional and neo-classical specialities: an enterprising *Pithiviers au Roquefort*; a sweet toothsome *cuisse de canard au Banyuls et orange*; and, no surprise, a *fromage blanc* with cream.
Menus bCD. Rooms (5) E. Cards Access, Visa.
Closed Sun evg. Wed.
Post 69610 Les Halles, Rhône. Region Lyonnais.
Tel 74 26 63 05. Mich 115/E2. Map 6.

HENDAYE   Chez Antoinette

Simple hotel/Cooking 1-2
Gardens

A mile or so from Hendaye Plage and not that far from the Spanish border. A green-shuttered (for a change) family *logis*, led by Bernard Haramboure, the *chef de cuisine*. Enjoy both *Basque* and classical fare: *merlu salsa verde, lotte au coulis de crabe, confit de cannette maison* and *noisette d'agneau à la Navarraise* are typical copious alternatives.
Menus bC. Rooms (16) DEF. Cards Access, Visa.
Closed Nov to Easter. Mon (not July/Aug). Public hols.
Post pl. Pellot, 64700 Hendaye Ville, Pyrénées-Atlantiques.
Tel 59 20 08 47. Fax 59 48 11 64. Mich 166/A1. Map 4. Region SW.

HONFLEUR   Au P'tit Mareyeur

Simple restaurant/Cooking 2

Christian Chaillou is an assured *cuisinier*. Behind the blue-fronted, ship-shape façade lies a small 18th-century dining room. There's a single-price, neo-classical menu which confirms Christian's culinary nous: a punchy *velouté de petits crabes son croûton à la crème d'ail*, an artful *escalope de saumon mi-cuit a la réglisse douce* and a saliva-stirring *tarte paysanne au miel et pommeau* are cracking creations.
Menus B. Cards Access, Visa. (Rooms: many *sans rest* hotels nearby.)
Closed 4-19 Jan. 2nd Half Nov. Thurs. Fri midday. (Parking nearby.)
Post 4 r. Haute, 14600 Honfleur, Calvados. Region Normandy.
Tel 31 98 84 23. Mich 14/C3. Map 2. (Rest. NW of La Lieutenance.)

A100frs & under. B100–135. C135–165. D165–250. E250–350. F350–500. G500+

Les HOUCHES

Auberge Beau Site/Rest. Le Pèle

Comfortable hotel/Cooking 1-2
Terrace/Gardens/Lift/Parking

Mont Blanc towers over the hotel but it is the extrovert, colourful gardens which almost steal the show. Nicole Perrin is an obliging hostess and husband Christian is a skilled chef. Primarily classical offerings such as *magret de canard au miel de montagne, féra du lac au beurre blanc, travers de porc à la Dijonnaise* and *tarte au citron.*
Menus bCD. Rooms (18) F. Cards All.
Closed 15-30 Apl. Oct to Xmas. Wed (May to 15 June & 15-30 Sept).
Post 74310 Les Houches, Haute-Savoie. Region Savoie.
Tel 50 55 51 16. Fax 50 54 53 11. Mich 119/E1. Map 6.

HOUDAN

Plat d'Etain

Comfortable restaurant with rooms/Cooking 2

Once a 16th-century *relais de poste* with a half-timbered, beamed interior and *grande cheminée.* With man-made skills from the past preserved in stone and timber no wonder, then, that the cooking is authentic classical with varying regional flourishes. Among the specialities are the famed *poule de Houdan, foie gras de canard au vieil Armagnac* and a sunny *millefeuille de boeuf à la ratatouille.*
Menus BD. Rooms (9) E. Cards Access, Visa.
Closed 1st 3 wks Aug. Mon evg. Tues. Regions Ile de France/Normandy.
Post 94 r. Paris, 78550 Houdan, Yvelines.
Tel (1) 30 59 60 28. Mich 34/C4. Map 2. (The busy N12 bypasses Houdan.)

HYERES

Jardins de Bacchus

Comfortable restaurant/Cooking 2-3
Terrace

An elegant spot with the Bacchus theme used at every turn. A top-notch *cave, bien sûr* – presented by *la patronne/sommelière*, the charming Claire Santioni. Her husband, Jean-Claude, paddles in modern Provençale pools: a right *champion marinade de canard en tapendae et huile d'olive* and a tingling-with-flavour *tian de filets de rougets et ratatouille.*
Menus BDE. Cards Acc, AE, Visa. (Rooms: Ibis & Centrotel nearby – to S.)
Closed Sat midday (summer). Sun evg (winter). Mon.
Post 32 av. Gambetta, 83400 Hyères, Var. Regions Côte d'Azur/Provence.
Tel 94 65 77 63. Mich 161/D4. Map 6.

A100frs & under. B100–135. C135–165. D165–250. E250–350. F350–500. G500+

Les ISSAMBRES   Chante-Mer

Simple restaurant/Cooking 2
Terrace

A tiny spot where 20 or so clients eat out on the covered terrace and an equal number share the air-conditioned interior. Chef Mario Battaglia is a classical fan; wife Nanette is a delightful, smiling hostess. Tuck into tempting *soupe de poissons*, drooling *petit pâté chaud, contrefilet sauce marchand de vin*, a freshly-made tart or *parfait glacé*.

Menus BCD. Cards Access, Visa. (Rooms: Plage at La Nartelle – 4 km SW.)
Closed 15 Dec-31 Jan. Sun evg (Sept-June). Mon (not evgs July/Aug).
Post 83380 Les Issambres, Var. Region Côte d'Azur.
Tel 94 96 93 23. Mich 163/E4. Map 6. (N of N98 at Hôtel Les Calanques.)

JAVRON   La Terrasse

Very comfortable restaurant/Cooking 3

One of the great highlights of our research for *FWF*. One word suffices: GO! Stylish modern *RQP* cuisine of an impeccable standard from a gifted and talented English duo: Alison Greenaway is the vivacious hostess (she puts most French *patronnes* to shame); husband Michael is a champion chef. Handsome dining room. Great cellar with over 40 halves. Come on Michelin, Michael deserves a star: don't be so wretchedly xenophobic.

Menus ACDE. Cards Access, Visa. (Rooms: Ermitage, Bagnoles-de-l'Orne.)
Closed 2-15 Jan. Sun evg. Mon. (Easy 19 km drive NW to Bagnoles.)
Post 53250 Javron-les-Chapelles, Mayenne. Region Normandy.
Tel 43 03 41 91. Mich 50/B2. Map 2.

JOIGNY   Le Rive Gauche

Comfortable hotel/Cooking 1-2
Quiet/Terrace/Gardens/Lift/Tennis/Parking/Helicopter pad

The "pad" is the sure sign that this has to be a 3-star chef's bistro; this one belongs to Michel Lorain. The riverside green-roofed hotel (zero marks for looks) is across the Yonne from his 3-star palace. Vast choice in the busy dining room. The big attraction is the buffet-style *grande table de hors d'oeuvre* – followed by main courses such as an *entrecôte marchand de vin* and sweets like *profiteroles au chocolat*.

Menus aCD. Rooms (42) EFG. Disabled. Cards All.
Post Port au Bois, 89300 Joigny, Yonne. Region Burgundy.
Tel 86 91 46 66. Fax 86 91 46 93. Mich 71/E1. Map 2.

A 100frs & under. B 100–135. C 135–165. D 165–250. E 250–350. F 350–500. G 500+

JOUCAS
Host. le Phébus

Very comfortable hotel/Cooking 2-3
Secluded/Terrace/Gardens/Swimming pool/Tennis/Parking

A super dry-stone complex in 10 acres of *garrigue*. Luxury is the word; bedrooms prices are steep (see below for nearby alternative). Enjoy the setting and chef Xavier Mathieu's classical and Provençale offerings in the two menus C: *fleurs de courgette farcies de morue fraîche* and *charlotte d'agneau de Sisteron au romarin* remain tasty memories.
Menus CDE. Rooms (17) G-G2. Disabled. Cards Access, AE, Visa.
Closed Nov to Feb. (Rooms: cheaper Résidence des Ocres, Roussillon.)
Post route Murs, 84220 Joucas, Vaucluse. Region Provence.
Tel 90 05 78 83. Fax 90 05 73 61. Mich 159/D1. Map 6.

JULIENAS
Le Coq au Vin

Simple restaurant/Cooking 2
Terrace

Multi-coloured *coqs* reign supreme at Claude Clévenot's blue-shuttered bistro – lifted, it would seem, from the pages of *Clochemerle*. The fare is a mix of modern, neo-classical and regional – with Georges Duboeuf wines almost on tap. Among many offerings we voted one cock of the walk: what else but *coq au vin de Juliénas* – the perfect mating.
Menus aCD. Cards All. (Rooms: nearby des Vignes, *sans rest.*)
Closed Tues evg and Wed (Jan/Feb).
Post pl. Marché, 69840 Juliénas, Rhône. Region Lyonnais.
Tel 74 04 41 98. Fax 74 69 68 41. Mich 102/B3. Map 6.

JUVIGNY-SOUS-ANDAINE
Au Bon Accueil

Comfortable restaurant with rooms/Cooking 2
Garage

André Cousin dips his fingers into many a French regional culinary pool at his modern *logis*: *jambon de Bayonne, terrine de canard à la Rouennaise, foie gras d'oie des Landes, escargots de Bourgogne* and *sorbet Granny Smith* are an eclectic jumble. *Bourgeoise* and classical – *ancien régime* cooking which guarantees you leave with tummies contentedly full.
Menus BCE. Rooms (8) E. Cards Access, Visa.
Closed Feb school hols. Tues evg. Wed.
Post 61140 Juvigny-sous-Andaine, Orne. Region Normandy.
Tel 33 38 10 04. Fax 33 37 44 92. Mich 50/B1. Map 2.

A100frs & under. B100–135. C135–165. D165–250. E250–350. F350–500. G500+

LACAPELLE-MARIVAL Terrasse

Simple hotel/Cooking 2
Gardens

A smart, whitewashed *logis* near the château and church. Young chef
Eric Boussac and his English-speaking wife, Clarisse, are highly thought
of by their Quercy peers and nothing is too much trouble for them. Proof
of Eric's talent shines forth in a herby *terrine de lapereau a là sauge* and
a drooling *filet de truite, beurre d'échalotes et Bergerac blanc.*
Menus ABD. Rooms (15) DE. Cards Access, Visa.
Closed Jan to mid Mar. Sun evg and Mon (Oct to Mar).
Post 46120 Lacapelle-Marival, Lot. Region Dordogne.
Tel 65 40 80 07. Mich 125/D4. Map 5.

LACAVE Pont de l'Ouysse

Very comfortable restaurant with rooms/Cooking 3
Secluded/Terrace/Gardens/Swimming pool/Parking

A roll-call of man-made and natural pleasures: a site beside the River
Ouysse, downstream from Rocamadour, just before it joins the Dordogne;
Belcastel château; cosseting comforts; and modern and regional dishes
from master chef Daniel Chambon. Especially appetising are poultry and
lamb specialities, simply roasted – made-in-heaven creations.
Menus CDEFG. Rooms (12) FG. Cards All.
Closed Jan. Feb. Mon (not evgs from May to Sept).
Post 46200 Lacave, Lot. Region Dordogne.
Tel 65 37 87 04. Fax 65 32 77 41. Mich 124/C3. Map 5.

LALINDE Château

Comfortable restaurant with rooms/Cooking 2
Terrace/Swimming pool

A down-at-heel façade for the *logis* (once a prison!) alongside the right
bank of the River Dordogne. Culinary treats generally match the fine site
and views: an *omelette aux queues de langoustines* made a pleasant
change; and both a *blanquette d'agneau aux trompettes de mortes* and
a *tarte aux pommes chaudes* were well executed, accomplished dishes.
Menus a(lunch)CD. Rooms (7) FG. Cards Access, Visa.
Closed Dec to Feb. Fri (not evgs July/Aug).
Post 1 r. Verdun, 24150 Lalinde, Dordogne. Region Dordogne.
Tel 53 61 01 82. Fax 53 24 74 60. Mich 123/D3-E3. Map 5.

A 100frs & under. B 100–135. C 135–165. D 165–250. E 250–350. F 350–500. G 500+

LAMALOU-LES-BAINS

Mas

Comfortable hotel/Cooking 1-2
Terrace/Lift/Parking

A small, shady, cool spa. The *belle époque* hotel is opposite the spa's casino. Ask English-speaking Ernest Bitsch, a friendly host, to show you the fine frescoes in the vast *salon*. Neo-classical/classical dishes: *tournedos Bordelaise à la moelle* and *omelette Norvégienne* are typical of the latter. The large terrace is a shady oasis on hot days. (For nicer bedrooms ask Ernest to put you up at a sister hotel, L'Arbousier.)
Menus ABCD. Rooms (40) BCD. Cards All.
Post 34240 Lamalou-les-Bains, Hérault. Region Languedoc-Roussillon.
Tel 67 95 62 22. Fax 67 95 67 78. Mich 155/E3. Map 5.

LANGRES

Grand Hôtel Europe

Comfortable hotel/Cooking 1-2
Parking

Highly regarded by *En Route* users (p134). A 17th-century town house at the heart of the walled town and south of the cathedral. A taste of nostalgia in the rooms, furnishings and cooking. Nothing flashy – but neither is the grub cheap and cheerful. Readers have praised the *terrine maison, bavarois de saumon fumé* and *poulet rôti à la broche*.
Menus ABD. Rooms (28) DE. Cards All.
Closed 7-21 May. 1-23 Oct. Sun evg. Mon (not evgs May to Oct).
Post 23 r. Diderot, 52200 Langres, Hte-Marne. Regions Burg/Champ-Ard.
Tel 25 87 10 88. Fax 25 87 60 65. Mich 74/C1. Map 3.

LAPOUTROIE (also see next page)

Les Alisiers

Comfortable restaurant with rooms/Cooking 2
Secluded/Terrace/Gardens/Parking

A longtime readers' favourite. Jacques and Ella Degouy's *logis* (2300 ft high) has a panoramic vista, a Chartreuse-shaded distillation of Vosges scenery. Raining? Enjoy the view from the dining room with its glass walls. Alsace and *Bourgeois plats: choucroute à l'ancienne, faux-filet au pinot noir, tarte à l'oignon* and *gâteau au chocolat sauce anglaise*.
Menus ABC. Rooms (10) DE. Cards Access, Visa.
Closed Jan. 1st wk July. Xmas. Mon evg & Tues (not rooms Mar to Nov).
Post 68650 Lapoutroie, Haut-Rhin. Region Alsace. (SW of village.)
Tel 89 47 52 82. Fax 89 47 22 38. Mich 60/C3. Map 3.

A100frs & under. B100–135. C135–165. D165–250. E250–350. F350–500. G500+

LAPOUTROIE (also see previous page) du Faudé

Comfortable hotel/Cooking 2-3
Terrace/Gardens/Swimming pool (indoor)/Parking

The much loved Baldinger family makes the *logis* zing. Thierry is the able chef; wife Chantal the English-speaking *patronne*. A cascade of menus: with stomach-fillers like *coq au Riesling* and *choucroute garnie* to personal favourites such as a silky *terrine de foie de volaille au poivre* served with *12 hors d'oeuvre et crudités* left at the table.
Menus aCD. Rooms (25) EF. Cards All.
Closed 8-23 Mar. 13 Nov to 7 Dec. (In village, which is bypassed.)
Post 68650 Lapoutroie, Haut-Rhin. Region Alsace.
Tel 89 47 50 35. Fax 89 47 24 82. Mich 60/C3. Map 3.

LAPOUTROIE Host. A La Bonne Truite

Simple hotel/Cooking 2
Parking

At Hachimette, alongside the N415 to the east. Danièle Zavialoff is an efficient hostess; husband Michel conjures up both regional and more modern creations. Choose from alternative ends of the culinary spectrum: perhaps a thumpingly good *choucroute royale au Riesling* or a smooth *terrine de sandre et du saumon au saumon fumé avec mousse au curry*.
Menus ABCDE. Rooms (10) DE. Cards Access, AE, Visa.
Closed Jan. 20-29 June. 6-22 Nov. Tues. Wed (Oct to June).
Post Hachimette, 68650 Lapoutroie, Haut-Rhin. Region Alsace.
Tel 89 47 50 07. Fax 89 47 25 35. Mich 60/C3. Map 3.

LECTOURE De Bastard

Comfortable hotel/Cooking 2-3
Quiet/Terrace/Swimming pool/Garage

A handsome 18th-century building with stylish rooms and exhilarating views. English-speaking Anne Arnaud is an informed hostess and her chef husband, Jean-Luc, thankfully offers more than just the usual Gers goose and duck permutations. Savour lighter, modern dishes such as *terrine de poissons aux champignons* and *soupe de moules aux courgettes et safran*.
Menus aCD. Rooms (29) DEF. Cards All.
Closed 23 Dec-15 Feb. Rest: Fri evg, Sat midday & Sun evg (Oct-Apl).
Post r. Lagrange, 32700 Lectoure, Gers. Region Southwest.
Tel 62 68 82 44. Fax 62 68 76 81. Mich 151/E1-F1. Map 5.

A100frs & under. B100–135. C135–165. D165–250. E250–350. F350–500. G500+

LEIGNE-LES-BOIS
Gautier

Comfortable restaurant/Cooking 2

An unpretentious little country restaurant – in a hamlet and across the road from the *église* – with smartly kitted-out, beamed dining rooms and trying hard to get small details right. Classical pleasures arrive on chef Bernard Gautier's plates: a taste of the local fields with *gâteau de lapereau en geleé*; a fresh, unfussy *cabillaud au beurre d'échalotes*; and an out-for-the-count *tournedos B. Gautier* (loosen the belts).
Menus ACD. Cards Access, Visa. (Rooms: Europe at La Roche-Posay.)
Closed Feb. Nov. Sun evg. Mon. (La Roche-Posay, a spa, 10 km to E.)
Post 86450 Leigné-les-Bois, Vienne. Regions Loire/Poitou-Charentes.
Tel 49 86 53 82. Mich 82/B4. Map 2.

LERE
Lion d'Or

Comfortable restaurant with rooms/Cooking 2-3
Terrace/Garage

A quietish site, west of the D751. Patron Jean-Paul Ridon, engineer turned chef (also past Formula 3000 driver and African reserve guide) is an ingenious cook. Elaborate creations include *petit bavarois d'araignée de mer en rémoulade* and *royale de poissons de Loire, beurre blanc, au vinaigre de canne à sucre*. Choice of over 250 wines.
Menus BCD. Rooms (8) D. Cards Access, Visa.
Closed Sun evg. Mon.
Post 18240 Léré, Cher. Regions Berry-Bourbonnais/Loire.
Tel 48 72 60 12. Fax 48 72 58 01. Mich 70/C4. Map 2.

LEVENS
Les Santons

Simple restaurant/Cooking 1-2
Terrace

Tucked away in Levens, high above the Var and Vésubie valleys. The Pellerins ask you to take your time and enjoy their hospitality. Madame is a charmer. Provençale fare and numerous fish specialities. Three-star *amuses-geules*; gutsy *timbale de moules, noisette en beurre*; a *chèvre quintet*; and sweet trolley. Note: closed evenings other than Fri & Sat.
Menus bCD. Cards Access, Visa. (Rooms: nearby La Vigneraie – to SE.)
Closed 2 Jan-8 Feb. 26 June-5 July. 2-11 Oct. Wed. Evgs (not Fri & Sat).
Post 06670 Levens, Alpes-Maritimes. Region Côte d'Azur.
Tel 93 79 72 47. Mich 165/D2. Map 6. (Near village church.)

A 100frs & under. B 100–135. C 135–165. D 165–250. E 250–350. F 350–500. G 500+

LONS-LE-SAUNIER   Comédie

Comfortable restaurant/Cooking 2-3

A tiny dining room in a pretty-as-a-picture square where every terraced house seems to be washed in a different pastel shade. Single menu A is down-to-earth largesse. Main courses have a special panache: both *joues de loup grillée au riz noir* and *cuisse de canard de Challans aux mousserons et navets confits* are exotic, virtuoso gems. A *Roquefort terrine* is a perfectly-balanced starter. Bravo Bernard Hémery.
Menus A. Cards Access, Visa. (Rooms: Nouvel, parking, 5 min walk to W.)
Closed 2nd half Apl. 1st 3 wks Aug. Sun. Mon evg.
Post 65 r. Agriculture, 39000 Lons-le-Saunier, Jura. Region Jura.
Tel 84 24 20 66. Mich 89/D4. Map 3. (Park in place Comédie opposite.)

LOUHANS   La Cotriade

Comfortable restaurant/Cooking 2

The clue for Philippe Coulon's home *pays* is in the name: Brittany *bien sûr*. He's no introvert: study the couple of dozen framed diplomas in the hall for proof of his culinary abilities. Being a Breton he's fond of fish: a Menu du Pêcheur has an *assiette de fruits de mer* and a *dos de sandre au beurre blanc*. Otherwise regional and classical numbers: *volaille de Bresse rôti, à la crème et morilles* is one highlight.
Menus ABE. Cards Access, DC, Visa. (Rooms: Host. Cheval Rouge.)
Closed 1st wk July. 15-30 Nov. Tues evg & Thurs evg (not July/Aug).
Post 4 r. Alsace, 71500 Louhans, Saône-et-Loire. Region Lyonnais.
Tel 85 75 19 91. Mich 103/D1. Map 6. (Cheval Rouge is at 5 r. Alsace.)

LUCON   La Mirabelle

Comfortable restaurant/Cooking 2-3

A UK Michelin one-star chef inspected La Mirabelle twice during a 1993 holiday. Benoît and Véronique Hermouet are a friendly and talented duo. Benoît punts both classical and Vendée streams: a *préfou* appetiser (a garlic bread *galette*); a simple and tender *filet de canard aux aromates et sa garniture* was a well-sauced classic; and *terrine froid de jarret de porc, purée légère mojettes et préfou* a mouthwatering Vendée winner.
Menus aCDE. Cards Access, Visa. (Rooms: Central at St-Michel-en-l'Herm.)
Closed Feb & Nov school hols. Tues. Sat midday. (Above 15 km to SW.)
Post 35 r. de Gaulle, 85400 Luçon, Vendée. Region Poitou-Charentes.
Tel 51 56 93 02. Fax 51 56 35 92. Mich 92/C2. Map 4.

A100frs & under. B100–135. C135–165. D165–250. E250–350. F350–500. G500+

LURBE-ST-CHRISTAU   Au Bon Coin

Comfortable hotel/Cooking 2
Terrace/Swimming pool/Parking

His regional chef peers rate Thierry Lassala and his English-speaking wife
highly. A well-named hotel – a modern blue and cream, chalet-styled
building east of the village. A thumpingly good *garbure*, melting *saumon
braisée au Jurançon* and an assiduously executed *charlotte d'agneau au
beurre de tomate* confirmed his regional and classical cooking skills.
Menus ACD. Rooms (18) E. Disabled. Cards Accss, AE, Visa.
Closed Mid Jan to mid Feb. Tues (mid Oct to Mar). Region Southwest.
Post rte des Thermes, 64660 Lurbe-St-Christau, Pyrénées-Atlantiques.
Tel 59 34 40 12. Fax 59 34 46 40. Mich 167/E3. Map 4.

LURS   Bello Visto

Simple restaurant/Cooking 1-2

Extensive views over the Durance Valley and two indoor fans are
welcome distractions on a hot summer's day (note closing details).
François Grisolle is the chef; wife Dominique *la patronne*. A *mélange* of
regional, classical and *Bourgeois* dishes: main courses are especially
flavoursome – *lapin rôti avec sa sauce poivrade* or *grillade d'agneau au
miel de thym*. Simple sweets: fruit, *pâtisserie* and *glace à la Chantilly*.
Menus aBCD. Cards Access, Visa. (Rooms: Aub. Charembeau to W, off
N100.) Closed Oct. Wed. Evgs (not high season). (*Auberge* easy drive.)
Post Lurs, 04700 Oraison, Alpes-de-Hte-Prov. Regions Htes-Alpes/Prov.
Tel 92 79 95 09. Mich 146/A4. Map 6.

MADIRAN   Le Prieuré

Simple hotel/Cooking 2
Quiet/Terrace/Gardens/Parking

Michel (the chef) and Danielle Cuénot's handsome stone hotel was once
the abbey at the famous wine village. Cleverly modernised public rooms
and bedrooms (once monks' cells!). Clever neo-classical and regional
cooking too – like light *filets de rougets aux oignons frits* and tender
agneau de lait des Pyrénées à l'ail confit. Top-notch sweets.
Menus aCDE. Rooms (10) DE. Cards All.
Closed 22-29 Jan. 13-24 Nov. Sun evg and Mon (Oct to Easter).
Post 65700 Madiran, Hautes-Pyrénées. Region Southwest.
Tel 62 31 92 50. Fax 62 31 90 66. Mich 150/B3. Map 4.

A100frs & under. B100–135. C135–165. D165–250. E250–350. F350–500. G500+

MANZAC-SUR-VERN   Lion d'Or

Comfortable restaurant with basic rooms/Cooking 2
Terrace/Gardens

Jean-Paul and Nelly Beauvais created their oasis of *RQP* charm 14 years ago. Bright and airy applies to both the dining room and cooking. Menu B may offer a first-rate *terrine de foie gras* or *salade de St-Jacques et saumon*; *méli-mélo* (an assortment) *de poissons au beurre de safran* or *magret de canard poêlée sauce au vin de noix*; and one of six desserts.
Menus ABCD. Rooms (7) D. Cards All.
Closed Feb school hols. 24 Oct to 9 Nov. Sun evg (not July/Aug). Mon.
Post 24110 Manzac-sur-Vern, Dordogne. Region Dordogne.
Tel 53 54 28 09. Mich 123/D2. Map 5.

MARANS   Porte Verte

Simple restaurant/Cooking 2
Terrace

Colourful: flowers, greenery and gourds. Once a fisherman's quayside home with a small, cool, handsome interior. Even smaller terrace. Didier Montéran keeps things classically simple: *assiette de fruits de mer* or *terrine de lapin*; *bavette sauce porto* or various fish alternatives (so fresh, still wriggling); cheese and dessert (like iced *nougat terrine*).
Menus ABC. Cards Access, Visa. (Rooms: St-Nicolas, Maillezais – to NE.)
Closed Feb school hols. Sun evg (mid Sept to mid June). Wed.
Post 20 quai Foch, 17230 Marans, Charente-Maritime. Region Poitou-Char.
Tel 46 01 09 45. Mich 93/D2. Map 4.

MARGAUX   Auberge Le Savoie

Comfortable restaurant/Cooking 2
Terrace

Yves Fougeras' two *RQP* menus boldly state his culinary philosophy: *la cuisine est un art*; *tout art est patience*. How right he is: even low-cost classical and neo-classical menus need sure, skilled hands and Yves certainly has those. Two memorable menu B (low-end) *plats*: *terrine d'aileron de raie aux câpres* and *crème de pommes au cidre doux*.
Menus A(not Sat evg)B. (Rooms: Pont Bernet, Louens – to S.)
Closed 1-22 Feb. Sun. Public hols. (Above is an easy 12 km-drive away.)
Post 33460 Margaux, Gironde. Region Southwest.
Tel 57 88 31 76. Mich 121/D2. Map 4.

A100frs & under. B100–135. C135–165. D165–250. E250–350. F350–500. G500+

MARIGNY

Comfortable restaurant/Cooking 2

The odd-ball blue-and-white façade – with three large panels depicting the varied harvests garnered from land, sea and air (and vines to boot) – leaves you in no doubt about the Manche-wide repertoire of award-winning chef, Joël Meslin. Examples include *filet de carrelet au Camembert* – a happy marriage; and an artful *noisettes de jeune cerf sur petite vinaigrette aux ciboulettes*. Banal sweets. Stylish dining room.
Menus bCDEF. Cards All. (Rooms: Ibis, St-Lô to E. Easy 12 km drive.)
Closed 1-15 Jan. 2 wks end Sept/early Oct. Sun evg. Mon.
Post pl. Wesport, 50570 Marigny, Manche. Region Normandy.
Tel 33 55 11 08. Fax 33 55 25 67. Mich 31/D2. Map 1.

MARQUISE

Very simple restaurant/Cooking 3

A down-at-heel village and a drooping Cerf – in need of a face-lift. Don't be put off: English-speaking Stéphane Pruvot is a brilliant chef. Our lunch menu B – *croustillant de crabe à la fondue de poireaux* was worthy of a 3-star God; followed by a pan-fried *rascasse* with a purée of courgettes and a potato *crêpe*; finishing with an *omelette aux pommes sauce pistache* – was the essence of modern simplicity and subtlety.
Menus A(two *plats*)BDE. Cards Access, Visa.
Closed Sun evg. Mon. (Rooms: several hotels in Boulogne and Calais.)
Post 62250 Marquise, Pas-de-Calais. Region North.
Tel 21 87 55 05. Fax 21 33 61 09. Mich 2/A2. Map 2.

MAUSSANE-LES-ALPILLES

Comfortable restaurant/Cooking 2-3
Parking

Regional tunes from the culinary piano of young, neo-classicist chef, Thierry Maffre-Bogé. Order anything which features the famed olive oil from nearby Mouriès and tuck into evocative specialities like *tomates tièdes farcies de brandade de morue au pistou* (Provence on a plate) and *terrine de gigot d'agneau à l'ail confit*. Scrumptious desserts.
Menus CDE. Cards Access, Visa. (Rooms: Touret, short walk away to W.)
Closed Jan. 16-23 Nov. Wed. Thurs midday. Region Provence.
Post av. Vallée-des-Baux, 13520 Maussane-les-Alpilles, Bouches-du-Rhône.
Tel 90 54 41 91. Mich 158/B2. Map 6. (On D17, W of village.)

A 100frs & under. B 100–135. C 135–165. D 165–250. E 250–350. F 350–500. G 500+

MAUVEZIN   La Rapière

Comfortable restaurant/Cooking 2
Terrace

Michel Fourreau, soon to be 50, started cooking at the age of 14 in the
Loire's Sologne. Marie-Thérèse, his wife, welcomes you and Michel then
challenges you to a classical and regional duel with menus notable for their
exceedingly generous choice. Signature *plats*: *terrine de faisan, saumon
sauce hollandaise* and luscious *glace aux pruneaux à l'Armagnac.*
Menus ABCDE. Cards All. (Rooms: Coin de Feu, Gimont; 14 km to S.)
Closed 14 June to 4 July. 4-19 Oct. Tues evg. Wed. (Above easy drive.)
Post 32120 Mauvezin, Gers. Region Southwest.
Tel 62 06 80 08. Mich 152/A2. Map 5.

MEGEVE   Michel Gaudin

Comfortable restaurant/Cooking 3

Alongside the N212 through Megève. Attentive English-speaking Monique
Gaudin looks after the minute dining room while husband Michel, a
modern master, does the culinary juggling backstage. Blockbusting Mont
Blanc-sized RQP. Consider the evidence in menu B: three *amuse-bouche,
soupe de poissons, canard cuit en cocotte aux olives et poivres vert,
fromage blanc, coupe de fraises à la crème Chantilly* and *petits fours.*
Menus ABCDE. Cards Access, Visa. (Rooms: L'Auguille, 3 min walk to N.)
Closed Tues (not high season). (Above quiet, *sans rest* and parking.)
Post carrefour d'Arly, 74120 Megève, Haute-Savoie. Region Savoie.
Tel 50 21 02 18. Mich 119/D1. Map 6.

MEJANNES-LES-ALES   Auberge des Voutins

Comfortable restaurant/Cooking 2-3
Terrace/Gardens/Parking

To the south-east of Alès, alongside the D981. A stone-built villa with
shady terrace and neat gardens please the eye. So, too, does the modern,
inventive cooking of René Turonnet: *filet de rascasse demi-sel* with
tomato, garlic and olive oil is just one typical taste explosion. A big plus
feature of his repertoire is the clever use he makes of regional wines.
Menus CDE. Cards All. (Rooms: Ibis, at St-Christol, to SW – easy drive.)
Closed 1st wk Mar. 1st wk Sept. Sun evg. Mon (not public hols).
Post Méjannes-lès-Alès, 30340 Salindres, Gard. Region Provence.
Tel 66 61 38 03. Mich 143/D4. Map 6.

A100frs & under. B100–135. C135–165. D165–250. E250–350. F350–500. G500+

MEURSAULT   **Relais de la Diligence**

Comfortable restaurant/Cooking 2
Parking

Beside the D23, south-east of the N74 (near *la gare*). A modern building
with four dining rooms and fine views west of *la côte*. Several menus,
efficient service and pleasing ambience. Typical *plats* include a tasty
mousse d'avocat with fresh shrimps; a well-chosen *panaché de poisson
aux deux sauces*; and a multi-choice *plateau de fromages*.
Menus ABC. Cards All. (Rooms: Les Magnolias or Les Charmes in village.)
Closed 21 Dec to 10 Feb. Tues evg. Wed. (Both above *sans rest* & quiet.)
Post r. de la gare, 21190 Meursault, Côte-d'Or. Region Burgundy.
Tel 80 21 21 32. Fax 80 21 64 69. Mich 88/A2-A3. Map 3.

MEYRUEIS   **Mont Aigoual**

Comfortable hotel/Cooking 2
Gardens/Swimming pool/Lift

The Robert family – Frédéric, Stella and Jean-Paul (the chef) – own two
Meyrueis hotels: Mont Aigoual and the nearby Europe. Both (from
father to son since 1902) have been much liked by readers for 12 years
now. I've been castigated over the *FLE* Cooking 1 rating. The new rating
does justice to the above average classical and *Bourgeoise* cuisine.
Menus ABC. Rooms (30) E. Cards Access, Visa.
Closed Nov to Mar. (Hotel's facilities available to Europe clients.)
Post r. Barrière, 48150 Meyrueis, Lozère. Region MC (Cévennes).
Tel 66 45 65 61. Fax 66 45 64 25. Mich 141/F3. Map 5.

MEZERIAT   **Les Bessières**

Comfortable restaurant with rooms/Cooking 1-2
Terrace

To the west of the sizeable *village fleuri*, near the railway station. Joël
and Raymonde Foraison are gentle, friendly folk – complementing
perfectly the unassuming restaurant, shady terrace and classical and
regional fare. Enjoy Bresse *plats* – *mousse de brochet sauce Nantua*,
filet de carpe des Dombes aux cerfeuil and *fromage blanc à la crème*.
Menus BD. Rooms (6) D. Cards Access, Visa.
Closed Mid Dec to end Jan. Mon and Tues (Sept to May).
Post 01660 Mézériat, Ain. Region Lyonnais.
Tel 74 30 24 24. Mich 102/C3. Map 6.

A100frs & under. B100–135. C135–165. D165–250. E250–350. F350–500. G500+

MIGENNES   Paris

Comfortable restaurant with rooms/Cooking 2

A vine-covered building alongside a busy main road (D943). Ghastly décor – in the style only the French know how to do so brilliantly. Attentive service, with a touch of humour, and plenty of flowers compensate – as does the classical cooking of Patrice Chauvin, the *chef/patron*. Notable touches include a deliciously flavoured *assiette de poissons* and a lip-smackingly good *île flottante crème anglaise*.

Menus aC. Rooms (9) DEF. Cards Access, Visa.
Closed 1-15 Jan. Aug. Fri evg. Sat midday. Sun evg.
Post 57 av. J.Jaurès, 89400 Migennes, Yonne. Region Burgundy.
Tel 86 80 23 22. Fax 86 80 31 04. Mich 72/A1. Map 2.

MILLAU   Château de Creissels

Comfortable hotel/Cooking 1-2
Quiet/Terrace/Gardens/Parking

A pleasing step back in time at the Austruy family hotel 2 km SW of Millau. There's an old tower and medieval church next door (at night the clock is silent). Bedrooms are well-appointed, a counterpoint to the old-world gentility of the main rooms. Classical, *Bourgeois* and regional menus (wide choice). *Roquefort* used too excessively in many dishes.

Menus ABCD. Rooms (33) DEF. Disabled. Cards All. (Alongside D992.)
Closed 28 Dec to 15 Feb. Rest: Sun evg and Mon midday (not high season).
Post rte St-Affrique, 12100 Millau, Aveyron. Region MC (Cévennes).
Tel 65 60 16 59. Fax 65 61 24 63. Mich 141/E4. Map 5.

MILLAU   La Marmite du Pêcheur

Simple restaurant/Cooking 2
Terrace

Albert Négron is no longer with us. He died last year, aged 79 and after working 65 years in various kitchens. His widow, the smiling Janine, continues Albert's classical and regional traditions – aided by 31-year-old chef, Christian Aveline. Best treats are *petite marmite du pêcheur* and, among 16 sweets, *bolet du chef Albert* – a 3-star winner.

Menus ABCD. Cards Access, AE, Visa. (Rooms: La Capelle, 200 metres N.)
Closed Wed evg (not high season). (Above hotel *sans rest* and quiet.)
Post 14 bd Capelle, 12100 Millau, Aveyron. Region MC (Cévennes).
Tel 65 61 20 44. Mich 141/E4. Map 5. (Park in large *place* opp. hotel.)

A100frs & under. B100–135. C135–165. D165–250. E250–350. F350–500. G500+

MOIDREY   Au Vent des Grèves

Comfortable restaurant/Cooking 2
Terrace/Parking

One-time director of the legendary Mère Poulard hotel/restaurant on Le
Mont-St-Michel, the talented and friendly, English-speaking Jean-Claude
Pierpaoli now entices clients to his own lair. A rich sea-water pool of
pleasures – *assiette de fruits de mer* is one example – and, just as
commendable, a juicy *gigot d'agneau de pré-salé* from the nearby marshes.
Menus ACDE. Cards Access, Visa. (Rooms: Digue, on D976, 3 km to N.)
Closed Mid Jan to mid Feb. Tues evg and Wed (not Aug).
Post 50170 Moidrey, Manche. Regions Brittany/Normandy.
Tel 33 60 01 63. Mich 30/C4. Map 1. (D976 6 km S of Le Mont-St-M.)

MOLINEUF   Poste

Comfortable restaurant/Cooking 2
Parking

An attractive village in terrific wooded country. A modern, light dining
room with striking wall frescoes. An up-and-coming young chef, Thierry
Poidras, certainly means business. Classical and neo-classical dishes: a
hunky dory duo of *dos de flétan au coulis et ravioli de homard* and
magret de canard aux langoustines et jus de truffes were perfection.
Menus aCD. Cards All. (Rooms: several hotels at Blois, 9 km to E.)
Closed Feb. Sun evg. Wed. (Ibis, Campanile & Cottage near A10 exit.)
Post 41190 Molineuf, Loir-et-Cher. Region Loire.
Tel 54 70 03 25. Fax 54 70 12 46. Mich 68/B3. Map 2.

MONESTIER-DE-CLERMONT   Au Sans Souci

Simple hotel/Cooking 2
Quiet/Terrace/Gardens/Swimming pool/Tennis/Garage/Parking

The Maurice family celebrated 60 years of ownership in 1994. The fourth
generation, Frédéric, the chef, and Michelle, *la patronne*, do a sterling
job at their mountain *logis*. Extensive choice on the classical and
Bourgeois menus: *ravioles du Royans* (W of Vercors), *omble chevalier
aux amandes*, *filet d'agneau aux cèpes* and *fromage blanc* – winners all.
Menus ABCD. Rooms (15) DE. Cards Access, Visa.
Closed 20 Dec to end Jan. Sun evg. Mon. (N of Monestier; W of N75.)
Post St-Paul-lès-Monestier, 38650 Monestier-de-Clermont, Isère.
Tel 76 34 03 60. Mich 131/E3. Map 6. Regions Hautes-Alpes/Savoie.

A100frs & under. B100–135. C135–165. D165–250. E250–350. F350–500. G500+

MONTAUBAN   Ambroisie

Comfortable restaurant/Cooking 2

The welcome new eastern N20 bypass means that Montauban is a bit
quieter these days. Sybette Fournales is the hostess at the contemporary-
styled restaurant; husband Jean-Pierre mans the *fours* in the kitchen.
Copious, multi-choice menus with classical, *Bourgeoises* and regional
specialities of the *parfait de foie de volaille, filet de truite poêlée aux
champignons, faux-filet sauce au poivre vert, îles flottantes* variety.
Menus ABCE. Cards Access, Visa. (Rooms: Climat de France, 4 km N, N20.)
Closed Sun. Public hols. (Also in town: Ingres, on Tarn's opp. bank.)
Post 41 r. Comédie, 82000 Montauban, Tarn-et-Garonne. Region Southwest.
Tel 63 66 27 40. Mich 138/B4. Map 5.

MONTAUBAN   Orsay/Rest. La Cuisine d'Alain

Comfortable restaurant with rooms/Cooking 2-3
Terrace/Lift

Opposite the station but soundproofed rooms take the sting out of
moving trains. Alain Blanc regales clients with a neo-classical display,
notable for a mix of fish dishes – *gratin de poissons aux poireaux* is one
example – and filling creations such as a *galinette de veau pâtes
fraîches.* Terrific trolley of light sweets. Nicole is *la patronne.*
Menus BCDE. Rooms (20) E. Cards All.
Closed 1st wk May. 6-22 Aug. 23 Dec-7 Jan. Sun. Mon midday. Public hols.
Post face gare, 82000 Montauban, Tarn-et-Garonne. Region Southwest.
Tel 63 66 06 66. Fax 63 66 19 39. Mich 138/B4. Map 5.

MONTBRISON   Rest. Yves Thollot/Hôtel Marytel

Comfortable restaurant & simple hotel/Cooking 2
Terrace (restaurant)/Parking

At Savigneux, beside D946 to E. Two colourful, ultra-modern buildings
side-by-side. Odd-ball bright umbrellas in dining room. Nothing odd-ball
about Yves' neo-classical repertoire: a spirited *panaché de lotte et
saumon* and an accomplished, full-of-flavour marriage of *magret de
canard aux chanterelles* are sunny memories under the indoor umbrellas.
Menus aCDE. Rooms (33) DE. Disabled. Cards Acc, AE, DC (H only), Visa.
Closed Rest only: Feb school hols. 1-15 Aug. Sun evg. Mon. Map 6.
Post 93/95 rte Lyon, 42600 Montbrison, Loire. Region MC (Auvergne).
Tel (R) 77 96 10 40. (H) 77 58 72 00. Fax (H) 77 58 42 81. Mich 115/D3.

A100frs & under. B100–135. C135–165. D165–250. E250–350. F350–500. G500+

MONTFERRAT

Ferme du Baudron

Simple restaurant/Cooking 1-2
Terrace/Gardens/Swimming pool/Tennis/Parking

Note: lunch only at the Faivre family farm. Rustic is the tag at this
Alpine-like ski-lodge, complete with vast chimney and log fire where
Daniel Faivre does most of the cooking. Readers adore the sauces and a
mushroom sextet *façon de grand-mère*. *Pâtés*, grilled *faux-filet* and *côte
de porc*, ice creams – and similar (and instant-whip chocolat mousse?).
Menus A (not Sun when à la carte C). Lunch only. (Studios for rent.)
Closed Mid Jan to end Feb. Wed. (1 km S of Montferrat.)
Post 83131 Montferrat, Var. Region Côte d'Azur.
Tel 94 70 91 03. Mich 163/D2. Map 6.

MONTMELIAN

Viboud

Simple restaurant with basic rooms/Cooking 1-2
Parking

On the hill in the old town, well away from the N6. Jacques Viboud is a
great rugger enthusiast – witness the intriguing memorabilia and the
town team's many cups displayed in the bar. Old-fashioned cooking
(little choice) with classics such as *terrine de canard au pistaches et
noisettes* and a mundane but appetising *faux-filet poêlé*.
Menus ABC. Rooms (17) BCD. Cards All.
Closed 1st 3 wks Jan. 25 Sept to 22 Oct. Sun evg. Mon.
Post 73800 Montmélian, Savoie. Region Savoie.
Tel 79 84 07 24. Mich 118/B3. Map 6.

MONTRÉAL

Chez Simone

Simple restaurant/Cooking 1-2
Terrace

Chez Simone, tucked away near the fortified *église* in the perched
bastide of Montréal, is a cool oasis of culinary Gers charm. Three plane
trees provide a shady terrace; a beamed *salle* is the indoor option.
Blockbusting Landes and Gers tummy fillers: *salmis de palombe* and
confit de canard are typical. Bravo for the toothsome *hors d'oeuvre*.
Menus aBCD. Cards All. (Rooms: Trois Lys & Logis des Cordelirs, Condom.)
Closed Sat. (Above hotels are *sans rest* and easy 15 km drive to E.)
Post pl. Eglise, 32250 Montréal, Gers. Region Southwest.
Tel 62 29 44 40. Mich 151/D1. Map 5.

A100frs & under. B100–135. C135–165. D165–250. E250–350. F350–500. G500+

MONTSALVY

Nord

Comfortable hotel/Cooking 2
Parking

Jean Cayron, a cheerful, energetic *patron*, runs the front of house; his wife, Mauricette, is *la cuisinière* at the much modernised hotel. Readers speak warmly of her artistic skills with regional, classical and *Bourgeoises* offerings such as *terrine de légumes en jardinière, quiche crèmeuse aux girolles* and *filet de St-Pierre, doré, au Noilly*.
Menus ABCD. Rooms (26) DE. Cards All.
Closed Jan to Mar.
Post 15120 Montsalvy, Cantal. Region Massif Central (Auvergne).
Tel 71 49 20 03. Fax 71 49 29 00. Mich 126/B4. Map 5.

MOUCHARD

Chalet Bel'Air/Rôtisserie

Comfortable restaurant with rooms/Cooking 1-2
Terrace (Rôtisserie)/Gardens/Parking

Chalet-style *logis* between the village and N83. Bruno and Monique Gatto do an enterprising job at their "Rôtisserie". From the open fire in the large chimney relish tasty grills with vegetables – cooked in olden-day ways: *jambon grillée, côtes d'agneau, faux-filet grillé maître d'hôtel, caille dorée en broche* and other alternatives. (Note: the *logis* and *rôtisserie* are open every day; the separate restaurant is not.)
Menus ABC (à la carte). (ADEF in rest.) Rooms (9) DEF. Cards All.
Post 39330 Mouchard, Jura. Region Jura.
Tel 84 37 80 34. Fax 84 73 81 18. Mich 89/E2. Map 3.

MOUGINS

Feu Follet

Comfortable restaurant/Cooking 2-3
Terrace

At the heart of film-set Mougins, the most expensive real estate on the coast. English-speaking Jean-Paul and Micheline Battaglia have worked wonders in creating such a success; the place is always busy. Classical cooking, no stinting on portions and quality, wide choice and opulent desserts. Take a peek at the high-tech kitchen (cost 1 million francs).
Menus CD. Cards Acc, Visa. (Rooms: du Bosquet, Pégomas to W.)
Closed Sun evg (out of season). Mon. Tues midday (mid June to mid Sept).
Post pl. Mairie, 06250 Mougins, Alpes-Maritimes. Region Côte d'Azur.
Tel 93 90 15 78. Fax 92 92 92 62. Mich 163/F2. Map 6. Note: book ahead.

A100frs & under. B100–135. C135–165. D165–250. E250–350. F350–500. G500+

MOUGINS

Very comfortable restaurant/Cooking 3
Terrace

André Surmain's wily pricing provides a top-notch bargain in some style.
Menu C can include 3 virtuoso *plats*: *gelée d'ailerons de raie aux câpres
à la crème de citron* – masterful; *morue fraîche au beurre de tomates*
(with superb Streitz young veg); and a dream *tiramisu*. Bravo André,
daughter Gigi (both speak fluent English) & chef Dominique Louis.
Menus CG. Cards Acc, AE, Visa. (Rooms: du Bosquet, Pégomas to W.)
Closed Mon (not evg July/Aug). Tues midday. (Also Le Zinc: menu A.)
Post pl. Mairie, 06250 Mougins, Alpes-Maritimes. Region Côte d'Azur.
Tel 93 90 03 47. Fax 93 75 72 83. Mich 163/F2. Map 6.

MOUTHIER-HAUTE-PIERRE

La Cascade

Comfortable hotel/Cooking 1-2
Quiet/Parking

The *logis* has scintillating views of the wooded Loue Valley far below.
Chef/patron René Savonet juggles regional and *Bourgeoises* balls on
menu B (classical, too, in DE): *croûte forestière, pâté aux foies de
volaille ou crudités*; *truite belle meunière, épaule de veau sauce
paprika ou côtes d'agneau grillée*; cheeses; dessert. One blot: awful tea.
Menus BDE. Rooms (23) E. Cards Access, Visa.
Closed Mid Nov to mid Feb.
Post 25920 Mouthier-Haute-Pierre, Doubs. Region Jura.
Tel 81 60 95 30. Fax 81 60 94 55. Mich 90/A2-B2. Map 3.

Les MOUTIERS-EN-RETZ

Bonne Auberge

Comfortable restaurant/Cooking 2

Patrice and Catherine Raimbault have bags of nous: neo-classical and
classical *plats*; a smart dining room with flowers; and a profusion of
professional touches. A clever *nouvelle formule* menu allows you to
permutate five different prices (good choice). Chef Patrice's talents shine
in numerous fish/shellfish dishes like *palourdes farcies au beurre d'ail,
marinade d'anguilles* and *coquillage à la crème de curry*.
Menus bCDE. Cards Access, AE, Visa. (Rooms: Alizes; Pornic, 8 km NW.)
Closed Feb sch. hols. Mid Nov-mid Dec. Sun evg & Mon (not July/Aug).
Post av. Mer, 44580 Les Moutiers-en-Retz, Loire-Atlantique.
Tel 40 82 72 03. Mich 78/B2. Map 1. Regions Loire/Poitou-Charentes.

A100frs & under. B100–135. C135–165. D165–250. E250–350. F350–500. G500+

MUR-DE-BARREZ   Auberge du Barrez

Comfortable hotel/Cooking 1-2
Quiet/Parking

A contemporary-styled, ultra-modern *auberge*, to the south-east of high-on-a-hill Mur-de-Barrez. Christian Gaudel's culinary brush is a lot more traditional and unfussy: few regional colours but this is more than compensated for by well-judged flavoursome dishes such as *terrine de lapin en gelée, canette braisée au vin rouge* and *terrine de fraises*.
Menus aBD. Rooms (10) DEF. Cards Access, AE, Visa.
Closed Jan to mid Feb. Rest: Sun evg (Nov to Easter). Mon.
Post 12600 Mur-de-Barrez, Aveyron. Region Massif Central (Auvergne).
Tel 65 66 00 76. Fax 65 66 07 98. Mich 126/C3. Map 5.

NAJAC   Oustal del Barry

Very comfortable restaurant with rooms/Cooking 2-3
Quiet/Terrace/Gardens/Lift

Sixth generation owners, Catherine Miquel and husband, chef Jean-Marie, weave light, colourful, modern culinary tapestries at picturesque Najac. Typical personalised creations include *filet de poisson à l'infusion d'anis et d'algues, fenouil et céleri aux moules* and *tarte aux poires et crème d'amandes, crème glacée au miel*. Slow, slow service.
Menus b(lunch)CDE. Rooms (21) EF. Cards Access, AE, Visa.
Closed Nov to Mar. Mon midday (not high season and not public hols).
Post 12270 Najac, Aveyron. Regions Dordogne/Massif Central (Cévennes).
Tel 65 29 74 32. Fax 65 29 75 32. Mich 139/E3. Map 5.

NARBONNE   L'Olibo

Comfortable restaurant/Cooking 3-4

A Michelin two-star chef at his previous Réverbère restaurant, Claude Giraud and his delectable wife, Sabine, have resurfaced in Narbonne after the financial failure of the business. At L'Olibo there's no better *RQP* goldmine in France. Examples of the modern nuggets on menu B are two gold medal winners: *bourride de morue fraîche* and j*ambonneau de poulette, farci à la girolle*. Welcome back Claude!
Menus BD. Cards Access, AE, Visa. (Rooms: La Résidence, 3 min walk NE.)
Closed 1-15 Mar. 1-21 Aug. Sun. Wed evg. (Above *sans rest* and quiet.)
Post 51 r. Parerie, 11100 Narbonne, Aude. Region Languedoc-Roussillon.
Tel 68 41 74 47. Fax 68 42 84 90. Mich 173/D2. Map 5. (Park opp. rest.)

A100frs & under. B100–135. C135–165. D165–250. E250–350. F350–500. G500+

NESTIER

Relais du Castéra

Comfortable restaurant with rooms/Cooking 2-3
Terrace/Parking

At the northern door of spectacular terrain (Col d'Aspin to the SW; St-Bertrand-de-Comminges to the SE). Man and Nature tease the eyes; here Serge Latour tempts the taste buds with regional and neo-classical creations: put my claims to the test with *croustillant de truite, cassoulet* and *feuilleté tiède aux pruneaux.* Rooms not very comfy.
Menus aCDE. Rooms (8) E. Cards All.
Closed 5-25 Jan. 9-16 June. Sun evg. Mon.
Post 65160 Nestier, Hautes-Pyrénées. Region Southwest.
Tel 62 39 77 37. Fax 62 39 77 37 (same no.). Mich 169/E2. Map 5.

NEUFCHATEL-SUR-AISNE

Le Jardin

Comfortable restaurant/Cooking 2
Gardens

The A26 (junc. 14) is 10 km away (ideal for a last lunch). Well-named; the glassed-in terrace overlooking the garden is a delight. Jean-Claude Chevallier is *le patron* and master pastry cook; son Thierry is the chef. Limited choice on menu a. Knockout regional *plats: soufflé d'anguille et filet de carpe*; and *croustillant de Picardie* (dessert).
Menus aCDE. Cards Access, Visa. (Rooms: Novotel & Ibis W of Reims.)
Closed 15-31 Jan. Sun evg. Mon. Tues evg. (Above at junc. of A26 & A4.)
Post 02190 Neufchâtel-sur-Aisne, Aisne. Regions North/Champ-Ard.
Tel 23 23 82 00. Fax 23 23 84 05. Mich 20/C3. Map 3.

NEUILLE-LE-LIERRE

Auberge de la Brenne

Comfortable restaurant/Cooking 2
Parking

François Sallé is the helpful host (ask him to fix up a nearby *chambre d'hôte*) and his wife, Ghislaine, conjures up unfussy classical/regional culinary tricks – among them *salade tourangelle, rillettes* of pork, duck and goose cooked slowly and perfectly over a log fire and *joue de boeuf mijotée* with an unctuous black sauce (*vin de Bourgueil*).
Menus aCD. Cards Acc, AE, Visa. (Rooms: Novotel & Belle Vue, Amboise.)
Closed 24 Jan to mid Mar. Tues evg. Wed. (Above easy 12 km drive to SE.)
Post 37380 Neuillé-le-Lierre, Indre-et-Loire. Region Loire.
Tel 47 52 95 05. Mich 68/A3. Map 2.

A100frs & under. B100–135. C135–165. D165–250. E250–350. F350–500. G500+

NEUILLY-LE-REAL   Logis Henri IV

Comfortable restaurant/Cooking 2
Terrace

Valdi and Patricia Persello are justly proud of their authentic 16th-century hunting lodge. They should be just as chuffed by their *RQP* menu B. Consider the evidence: a *cassolette de moules au safran*, *compotée d'endives*, tender *noisettes d'agneau de pays à la sarriette*, *fromage* and a mouthwatering *nougat glacé au miel des Cévennes*.
Menus a(lunch)BD. Cards Access, Visa. (Rooms: Ibis (N7) S of Moulins.)
Closed 15 days Feb. 28 Aug-1 Sept. Sun evg. Mon. (Above 12 km to NW.)
Post 03340 Neuilly-le-Réal, Allier. Region Berry-Bourbonnais.
Tel 70 43 87 64. Mich 100/B2. Map 5.

NIEDERSTEINBACH   Cheval Blanc

Comfortable hotel/Cooking 1-2
Quiet/Terrace/Gardens/Swimming pool/Tennis/Parking

Charles and Michel Zinck, father and son, run a successful show at their *logis* – interconnected buildings, both old and new – in the densely wooded northern Vosges. Regional and classical cooking: *presskopf de lapereau* (rabbit terrine), *truite au bleu*, *entrecôte Béarnaise*, *civet de gibier*, *tarte maison* and *vacherin glacé* is all safe-as-houses fare.
Menus aCDE. Rooms (29) E. Cards Access, Visa.
Closed Feb to mid Mar. 15-29 June. 1-15 Dec. Thurs.
Post 67510 Niedersteinbach, Bas-Rhin. Region Alsace.
Tel 88 09 55 31. Fax 88 09 50 24. Mich 43/D2. Map 3.

NOUAN-LE-FUZELIER   Le Dahu

Comfortable restaurant/Cooking 2-3
Terrace/Gardens/Parking

A beamed and cleverly glassed-in dining room in an old Solognote farm with English-style gardens and English-speaking chef, Jean-Luc Germain. Some menu C alternatives: *salade Nordique au saumon fumé* or *soupe de moules au thym*; *sandre aux poireaux* or *magret de canard à la moutarde*. Marie-Thérèse Germain is a friendly hostess.
Menus bCD. Cards Acc, AE, Visa. (Rooms: Charmilles, a short walk away.)
Closed 19 Feb to 19 Mar. Tues evg and Wed (not July/Aug).
Post 14 r. H. Chapron, 41600 Nouan-le-Fuzelier, Loir-et-Cher.
Tel 54 88 72 88. Mich 69/E3. Map 2. Region Loire.

A100frs & under. B100–135. C135–165. D165–250. E250–350. F350–500. G500+

NOYAL-SUR-VILAINE
Hostellerie les Forges

Comfortable restaurant with rooms/Cooking 2-3
Parking

André Pilard, ex-student of the Strasbourg hotel school, is the chef; his wife, Laurette, is *la patronne*. André plays a classical cooking cello, his bow tuned to the sauces strings. Among a rich repertoire of nostalgic culinary tunes the likes of *filet de boeuf sauté Périgourdine* and *gratin d'oranges au Grand Marnier* are hard to resist.
Menus BCDE. Rooms (11) DE. Cards All.
Closed 2nd half Feb. Sun evg. Public hols (evgs only).
Post 35530 Noyal-sur-Vilaine, Ille-et-Vilaine. Region Brittany.
Tel 99 00 51 08. Fax 99 00 62 02. Mich 48/C3. Map 1.

NUCES
La Diligence

Very comfortable restaurant with rooms/Cooking 2-3
Terrace/Garage/Parking

Alongside the busy N140. Don't be put off. What a surprise the stylish, cool dining room is – matched by the terrace, shaded by four large trees. Jean-Claude Lausset is the dining room boss; Joël Delmas is the chef. Neo-classical, inventive *plats* with desserts stealing the show – witness a *biscuit au chocolate noisette, glace à l'amande amère*.
Menus a(lunch)BDE. Rooms (7) E. Cards Access, Visa.
Closed Jan. 4-10 Sept. Tues evg & Wed (Sept to June but not pub. hols).
Post Nuces, 12330 Valady, Aveyron. Region Massif Central (Cévennes).
Tel 65 72 60 20. Mich 140/B2. Map 5.

NYONS (also see next page)
La Charrette Bleue

Comfortable restaurant/Cooking 2
Terrace/Parking

Four menus to choose from – *tradition*, *découverte*, *régal* and *saveur* – at this single-storey, stone-built "cart". Extremely popular with locals; join them and dig into regional, classical and *Bourgeoise* cooking. Great olives – no surprise – and two memorable highlights: *terrine de lapin aux senteurs de Provence* and *bavette poêlée à la tapenade*.
Menus aBC. Cards Access, Visa. (Rooms: Caravelle & Les Alizés, Nyons.)
Closed 11 Jan to 7 Feb. 1st wk Dec. Tues evg (not July/Aug). Wed.
Post rte de Gap, 26110 Nyons, Drôme. Region Provence. (7 km to NE.)
Tel 75 27 72 33. Fax 75 26 05 72. Mich 144/C2. Map 6.

A100frs & under. B100–135. C135–165. D165–250. E250–350. F350–500. G500+

NYONS (also see previous page) — Le Petit Caveau

Comfortable restaurant/Cooking 2-3

An aptly-named medieval site at the heart of Nyon. Christian Cormont's seven-year stint with Joël Robuchon in Paris gave him a modern cooking itch. This, married to a Provençale style, results in many flavoursome humdingers: *bouillabaisse minute de rouget et rascasse aux pistils de safran* is just one. Muriel Cormont, an expert hostess/*sommelière*, offers an enterprising three different glasses of wine at a sensible price.
Menus ACDE. Cards Access, Visa. (Rooms: Caravelle & Les Alizés, Nyons.)
Closed Dec. Sun evg and Mon (not high season).
Post 9 r. V. Hugo, 26110 Nyons, Drôme. Region Provence.
Tel 75 26 20 21. Mich 144/C2. Map 6. (Park in large *place* to the W.)

OBJAT — Pré Fleuri

Comfortable restaurant with rooms/Cooking 2-3
Terrace/Gardens

On the road to the "horse" town of Arnac-Pompadour. Jacques and Ingrid Chouzenoux have been joined by their son, Stéphane. Father and son ride regional, classical and neo-classical cooking mounts: *saumon fumé maison à la crème d'herbes* and *volaille fermière sauté aux olives et citron* are typical of the culinary hurdles jumped by the duo.
Menus aCE. Rooms (7) D. Cards Access, AE, Visa.
Closed 9-24 Jan. Mon (not in Aug).
Post rte Pompadour, 19130 Objat, Corrèze. Region Dordogne.
Tel 55 25 83 92. Mich 124/B1. Map 5.

OLORON-STE-MARIE — Alysson

Very comfortable hotel/Cooking 2
Terrace/Swimming pool/Lift/Parking

A spanking-new hotel to the west of the town. Mod-cons everywhere plus stirring views of the Pyrénées wall to the south. Plenty of choice between Philippe Maré's stop-the-tummy-rumbling regional *plats* and lighter fish alternatives: take your pick from the likes of *emincé de magret de canard au fumet de cèpes* and *tranche de thon poêlé Basquaise*.
Menus ACD. Rooms (32) EF. Disabled. Cards Access, Visa.
Closed Rest: 1st 3 wks Feb. Sat midday. Sun evg. Region Southwest.
Post bd Pyrénées, 64400 Oloron-Ste-Marie, Pyrénées-Atlantiques.
Tel 59 39 70 70. Fax 59 39 24 47. Mich 167/F2. Map 4.

A100frs & under. B100–135. C135–165. D165–250. E250–350. F350–500. G500+

OPIO   Mas des Géraniums

Very simple restaurant/Cooking 2
Terrace/Gardens/Parking

The new owners of this jewel of a *mas*, English-speaking Colette and
Michel Creusot, worked for Surmain at Mougins. Michel's classical and
Provençal repertoire has many appealing facets: menu C could include
*mousseline de rascasse à la vinaigrette de tomates, marengo de poulet
aux écrevisses, fromage blanc* and dessert (choice for each course).
Menus CD. Cards Access, Visa. (Rooms: Novotel & Ibis SE of Valbonne.)
Closed 8 Nov-8 Dec. Tue evg (out of seas). Wed. Thur *midi* (July/Aug).
Post 06650 Opio, Alpes-Maritimes. Region Côte d'Azur.
Tel 93 77 23 23. Mich 163/F2. Map 6. (Beside D7, S of D2085.)

OTTROTT-LE-HAUT   A l'Ami Fritz

Comfortable restaurant with rooms (annexe)/Cooking 2
Secluded (annexe)/Gardens (annexe)/Terrace/Parking

A 200-year-old restaurant and a spanking-new annexe 300 metres or so
away. Sophie and Patrick Fritz are a competent couple. Bravo Patrick
for your efforts to re-create old *recettes Alsaciennes*. There's nothing
prissy about *strudel de boudin noir, salade Ganzeliesel, gilerle*
(cockerel) *au Riesling* and *boeuf au rouge d'Ottrott*.
Menus BCDE. Rooms (17) DE. Cards All.
Closed 3-20 Jan. Rest: Wed.
Post 67530 Ottrott-le-Haut, Bas-Rhin. Region Alsace. Map 3.
Tel (R) 88 95 80 81. (H) 88 95 87 39. Fax 88 95 84 85. Mich 61/D1.

OTTROTT-LE-HAUT   Beau Site

Very comfortable hotel/Cooking 2-3
Terrace/Garage/Parking

Martin and Brigitte Schreiber are *les patrons*: young Pascal Steffan is *le
cuisinier*. In the beamed "Spindler" dining room (noted for its
marquetry) you can order neo-classical specialities cooked in the
modern French style. Superb cellar. For cheaper, stomach-filling Alsace
nosh head for the glass-fronted "Les 4 Saisons" bistro (menus AB).
Menus (Spindler) CEF. Rooms (7) EFG. Cards All.
Closed Rest: Sun evg. Mon.
Post 67530 Ottrott-le-Haut, Bas-Rhin. Region Alsace.
Tel 88 95 80 61. Fax 88 95 86 41. Mich 61/D1. Map 3.

A100frs & under. B100–135. C135–165. D165–250. E250–350. F350–500. G500+

OUCQUES

Commerce

Comfortable restaurant with rooms/Cooking 2

The dark-shuttered *logis* is beside the D917, to the east of the D924. The very much contemporary-styled, colourfully-upholstered dining room and bedrooms come as quite a surprise. *La patronne*, Jo Lanchais, is a delight; her husband, Jean-Pierre, drives classical and *Bourgeoises* routes: enjoy *filet de daurade et sa brunoise de légumes* and a robust *crépinette de poularde aux champignons des bois* – just the ticket.
Menus aCD. Rooms (12) DEF. Cards Access, Visa.
Closed 20 Dec-31 Jan. Sun evg (Sept-June). Mon (not evgs July/Aug).
Post 41290 Oucques, Loir-et-Cher. Region Loire.
Tel 54 23 20 41. Fax 54 23 02 88. Mich 68/B2. Map 2.

PAILHEROLS

Auberge des Montagnes

Simple hotel/Cooking 2
Quiet/Swimming pools (indoor and outdoor)/Parking

A warm-hearted family, led by André and Denise Combourieu, fusses over you at the high-altitude *auberge*. *Bourgeois*, classical and *Auvergnats* appetite-quenching meals: *pounti, truffade, tripoux* and *cornet de Murat* on one of the A menus; *terrine d'aiglefin, pavé de Salers* (beef) and a light, tempting plate of three high-quality *pâtisseries* on menu B.
Menus AB. Rooms (19) D. Cards Access, Visa.
Closed Mid Oct to 20 Dec.
Post 15800 Pailherols, Cantal. Region Massif Central (Auvergne).
Tel 71 47 57 01. Fax 71 49 63 83. Mich 126/C3. Map 5.

PASSENANS

Le Revermont

Comfortable hotel/Cooking 2
Secluded/Terr./Gardens/Swim. pool/Tennis/Lift/Garage/Parking

Michel and Marie-Claude Schmit, the owners, are an uncommunicative duo at this odd-looking, modern *logis*, run as a "business", in a lovely setting north of the village. Principally classical offerings: *mitonnée de magret de canard à la creme de lentilles* (an in-vogue dish) is a stomach filler; *petite assiette de pâtisseries* a sumptuous sweet.
Menus BCDE. Rooms (28) DEF. Cards Access, AE, Visa.
Closed Jan. Feb. Sun evg and Mon (Oct to Mar).
Post 39230 Passenans, Jura. Region Jura.
Tel 84 44 61 02. Fax 84 44 64 83. Mich 89/E3. Map 3.

A 100frs & under. B 100–135. C 135–165. D 165–250. E 250–350. F 350–500. G 500+

PERROS-GUIREC
Les Feux des Iles

Comfortable hotel/Cooking 2
Quiet/Gardens/Parking

Gardens, sea views and a modern stone building impress as much as *chef/patron* Antoine Le Roux's cooking. Menu B could include a rainbow-hued *terrine de poissons et saumon tiède au velouté vert*; a tasty and tarty *fricassée de volaille au cidre et pommes acidulées*; a *rouelle de chèvre (avec salade)*; and a lip-smacking strawberry *pâtisserie*.
Menus BDE. Rooms (15) EFG. Disabled. Cards All. Region Brittany.
Closed Feb school hols. 2-8 Oct. Sun evg and Mon (Oct to Apl).
Post 53 bd Clemenceau, 22700 Perros-Guirec, Côtes d'Armor.
Tel 96 23 22 94. Fax 96 91 07 30. Mich 28/A1. Map 1.

PEYREHORADE
Central

Comfortable hotel/Cooking 3
Lift

A fizzing *RQP* crackler. What a transformation at the hotel I've known for 20 years. Sylvie de Lalagade has worked wonders; the building is now a contemporary-styled sparkler; and her brother, Eric Galby, is a young *cuisine moderne* dazzler. Past tastebud teasers have included *sandre soufflé aux pleurottes* and *sablé aux fraises, crème vanillée*.
Menus ACD. Rooms (16) E. Cards All.
Closed 1st 3 wks Mar. 11-27 Dec. Sun evg and Mon (not July/Aug).
Post pl. A. Briand, 40300 Peyrehorade, Landes. Region Southwest.
Tel 58 73 03 22. Fax 58 73 17 15. Mich 149/D3. Map 4.

PLAISANCE
Les Magnolias

Comfortable restaurant with rooms/Cooking 2-3
Quiet/Terrace/Gardens

A bewitching spot: an old vine-covered *logis* with stones and beams and an emerald of a garden. Marie-France and Francis Roussel are charmers too. She's the English-speaking *patronne*; he's a capable *cuisinier* with a light, neo-classical touch. Hereabouts dishes like *dos de truite et son court bouillon à l'ail rose de Lautrec* are a welcome surprise.
Menus ABDE. Rooms (6) DE. Cards Access, AE, Visa.
Closed Mid Nov to end Mar.
Post 12550 Plaisance, Aveyron. Region Languedoc-Roussillon.
Tel 65 99 77 34. Fax 65 99 70 57. Mich 154/C1. Map 5.

A100frs & under. B100–135. C135–165. D165–250. E250–350. F350–500. G500+

PLAISANCE
La Ripa Alta

Comfortable restaurant with rooms/Cooking 3 (see text)

Generous-hearted, English-speaking Maurice Coscuella, cooking for almost 35 years, has had his fair share of problems over the decades I've known him and his gentle wife, Irène. Maurice is one of a rare breed – a truly innovative chef capable of pulling modern, regional and neo-classical tricks from his culinary *valise. Quod sapit nutrit* he claims: spot-on with delights like a *soupe de châtaigne aux grattons de foie gras.*
Menus ACD (menu A – rating 2). Rooms (12) DE. Cards All.
Closed Jan. Mon midday (not mid May to mid Sept).
Post 32160 Plaisance, Gers. Region Southwest.
Tel 62 69 30 43. Fax 62 69 36 99. Mich 150/C3. Map 4.

PLAN-DU-VAR
Cassini

Comfortable restaurant with rooms/Cooking 2
Terrace

Beside the N202. A rural-style dining room and a warm welcome from the Cassini-Martin foursome – all talented restaurateurs. Philippe Martin is a clever classicist with many light-fingered touches. Two main courses epitomise those skills: a super *truite saumonée à la crème de persil* and a gutsy *pavé de boeuf aux morilles.* Delicious desserts.
Menus BCD. Rooms (22) CDE. Cards Access, AE, Visa. Region Côte d'Azur.
Closed 8-21 Jan. 12-25 June. Sun evg & Mon (not July/Aug).
Post rte Nationale, Plan-du-Var, 06670 Levens, Alpes-Maritimes.
Tel 93 08 91 03. Fax 93 08 45 48. Mich 165/D2-D3. Map 6.

PLOUMANAC'H
Rochers

Very comfortable restaurant with rooms/Cooking 2-3

Bracing views of a landlocked bay from Renée Justin's acclaimed restaurant will leave laser-etched memories. Whether the classical *plats* will impress as much is open to doubt. Menu C offers no choice: to start, a well-executed *terrine de lapereau aux fruits sec, chutney de légumes*; followed by a fresh-as-daisies *filet de carrelet au coulis de langoustines*; finishing with a *parfait glacé St-James, crème vanille.*
Menus CDF. Rooms (15) E. Cards Access, Visa.
Closed Oct to Easter. Rest: Wed (out of season).
Post Ploumanac'h, 22700 Perros-Guirec, Côtes d'Armor. Region Brittany.
Tel 96 91 44 49. Fax 96 91 43 64. Mich 28/A1. Map 1.

A100frs & under. B100–135. C135–165. D165–250. E250–350. F350–500. G500+

POLIGNY   Paris

Simple hotel/Cooking 1-2
Swimming pool (indoor)/Garage

André Biétry's ugly *logis* is in the centre of Poligny. A choice for each
course is a big plus – as is the indoor pool. Choose from alternatives
such as *terrine* or *soupe de poissons*; *truite meunière, civet de lièvre* –
the latter both rich and filling – or *lapereau aux herbes garni*; Jura
cheeses and a vast selection of desserts, including *vacherin glacé*.
Menus ACD. Rooms (25) CDE. Cards Access, Visa.
Closed Nov to Jan. Rest: Mon and Tues midday (not July/Aug).
Post 7 r. Travot, 39800 Poligny, Jura. Region Jura.
Tel 84 37 13 87. Mich 89/E3. Map 3.

PONT-A-MOUSSON   Auberge des Thomas

Simple restaurant/Cooking 2
Terrace

Flowers caress the eyes both inside and in the gardens at Michel and
Solange Thomas' *auberge* – at Blénod, two km south of the town in the
unattractive Moselle Valley. Thierry Pernot is the neo-classical chef: he
makes good use of the local wine in a tasty *sandre à la lie de pinot noir
de Toul*. Brilliant desserts – like *charlotte à la poire*.
Menus BCD. Cards All. (Rooms: Bagatelle, *sans rest*, in Pont-à-Mousson.)
Closed Feb school hols. 1st 3 wks Aug. Sun evg. Mon. Wed evg.
Post 100 av. V. Claude, 54700 Blénod-lès-Pont-à-Mousson, Meurthe-et-M.
Tel 83 81 07 72. Mich 41/D3. Map 3. Regions Alsace/Champagne-Ard.

PONTAUMUR   Poste

Simple hotel/Cooking 1-2
Garage

Pierrette Quinty is a welcoming hostess; and her husband, Jean-Paul, is
both an enthusiastic rugger fan and lover of *Auvergnats*, classical and
Bourgeois specialities: *tête de veau gribiche, jambon d'Auvergne* and
rable de lièvre aux figues are among the many Quinty pleasures. A top-
notch sweet is a lip-licking *nougat glacé au miel et aux noix*.
Menus aCD. Rooms (15) DE. Cards Access, Visa.
Closed Mid Dec to end Jan. Sun evg and Mon (not July/Aug).
Post 63380 Pontaumur, Puy-de-Dôme. Region Massif Central (Auvergne).
Tel 73 79 90 15. Fax 73 79 73 17. Mich 112/C1. Map 5.

A100frs & under. B100–135. C135–165. D165–250. E250–350. F350–500. G500+

PONT-DE-VAUX   Commerce

Comfortable restaurant with rooms/Cooking 2-3
Garage

Monique Patrone is an attractive, attentive *patronne*. Competition is murderous in the small town, its houses looking quite colourful these days. What about this for a colourful menu B? Silky *gâteau de foies de volaille*; *escalope de saumon sauce curry et fruits* – a stormy marriage; and a *tarte aux pommes chaude, caramel et glace canelle*.

Menus a(lunch)BCD. Rooms (10) DE. Cards All.
Closed 19 Nov to 21 Dec. Tues and Wed (not July/Aug and public hols).
Post 01190 Pont-de-Vaux, Ain. Region Lyonnais.
Tel 85 30 30 56. Mich 102/C2. Map 6.

PONT-DE-VAUX   Le Raisin

Comfortable restaurant with rooms/Cooking 3
Garage

A coffee-shaded façade in a street of houses with many-hued exteriors. The menus, too, have many shades of taste and choice. Consider the cheapest: from 4 starters a *terrine de chef* and *assiette de crudités*; from a main-course trio, a robust *paillard de boeuf grillée*; *crêpes Parmentier*; and, from four sweets, *fromage blanc à la crème*.

Menus bCDE. Rooms (8) DE. Cards All.
Closed Jan. Sun evg and Mon (not public hols).
Post 01190 Pont-de-Vaux, Ain. Region Lyonnais.
Tel 85 30 30 97. Fax 85 30 67 89. Mich 102/C2. Map 6.

PORT-VENDRES   Côte Vermeille

Comfortable restaurant/Cooking 2

The brothers Bessière – Philippe, younger by two years, is the chef; Guilhem runs the front of house – are fish addicts; there's no use coming here if you're a carnivore. The trawler alternatives are a knockout: like *soupe de poissons, anchois de Collioure marinés, fantasie de poissons et crustacés marinés, merlan de palangre et pétoncles* and *filets de rougets de roche en salmis*. (You'll be hard pressed to find such a roll-call of super fish dishes anywhere.) Forget the chips!

Menus a(lunch)CD. Cards Access, Visa. (Rooms: St-Elme, *sans rest*.)
Post quai du Fanal, 66660 Port-Vendres, Pyrénées-Orientales.
Tel 68 82 05 71. Mich 177/F3. Map 5. Region Languedoc-Roussillon.

A100frs & under. B100–135. C135–165. D165–250. E250–350. F350–500. G500+

POUILLY-SOUS-CHARLIEU de la Loire

Very comfortable restaurant/Cooking 2
Terrace/Gardens/Parking

Brigitte and Alain Rousseau (he trained at Troisgros in Roanne) have a handsome dining room and lime-shaded terrace – 100 m from the Loire. Alain rings all the culinary-style bells: *rillette aux deux saumons*; a blockbuster pan-fried *pièce Charolaise au beurre vigneron* or a lighter *filet de cabillaud à la Basquaise*; and a dessert duo – all on menu C.
Menus aCDE. Cards All. (Rooms: Relais de l'Abbaye, Charlieu.) Closed 2-7 Jan. Feb sch. hols. 1-10 Sept. Sun evg. Mon. Wed evg (not high seas).
Post 42720 Pouilly-sous-Charlieu, Loire. Region Lyonnais.
Tel 77 60 81 36. Mich 101/E3. Map 5. (Hotel is easy 5 min-drive to E.)

La PRENESSAYE Motel d'Armor/Rest. Le Boléro

Comfortable hotel/Cooking 2
Gardens/Parking

Beside the N164, 8 km east of Loudéac. Wooded grounds, a warm welcome from Madeleine Fraboulet and modern cooking from her husband Daniel. Clever menu choice. First-class fish dishes served on huge plates: *le délice Nordique* (*galette de blé noir, poisson fumé*) and *le superbe filet de lieu côtier à l'estragon* are among the memorable highlights.
Menus aBCD. Rooms (10) E. Cards Access, Visa.
Closed Feb school hols. Rest: Sun evg. Mon midday.
Post La Prénessaye, 22210 Plémet, Côtes d'Armor. Region Brittany.
Tel 96 25 90 87. Fax 96 25 76 72. Mich 47/D1. Map 1.

PUSIGNAN La Closerie

Very comfortable restaurant/Cooking 2-3
Terrace/Gardens/Parking

Gilles Troump's Louis XV-styled restaurant is more easily found if Pusignan is approached from the A432 Satolas road. Classical is the best tag for the cooking, service and fittings. An original *carpaccio de canard* – which didn't quite work – and impressive *blanquette de veau* (no relation to the basic mundane version) were enjoyable. Pretty gardens.
Menus BCDE, Cards All. (Rooms: Sofitel & Climat de France, – 7 km to S.)
Closed 7-21 Aug. Sun evg. Mon. (Both above at Lyon-Satolas airport.)
Post 4 pl. Gaîté, 69330 Pusignan, Rhône. Region Lyonnais.
Tel 78 04 40 50. Mich 116/B2. Map 6. (Pusignan is 23 km E of Lyon.)

A100frs & under. B100–135. C135–165. D165–250. E250–350. F350–500. G500+

RAGUENES-PLAGE   Chez Pierre

Comfortable hotel/Cooking 1-2
Quiet/Terrace/Gardens/Parking

Chez Pierre has had many a face-lift over the decades – including a new modern annexe. Gentle, English-speaking *patronne*, Dany Guillou, and her chef husband, Xavier, work hard to please their largely *pension* clients. Copious classical and *Bourgeoises plats*: *colin au champagne* and *gigot d'agneau* as examples. *Vacherin* a mini Mt-Blanc concoction.
Menus bCD. Rooms (35) DEF. Disabled. Cards Access, Visa.
Closed Oct to Mar. Rest: Wed (June to mid Sept).
Post Raguenès-Plage, 29139 Névez, Finistère. Region Brittany.
Tel 98 06 81 06. Mich 45/E3. Map 1.

REALMONT   Noël

Very comfortable restaurant with rooms/Cooking 2
Terrace

Young chef Jean-Paul Granier hangs classical and regional *plats* on the Noël tree; and his wife Michèle takes your requests. The green-shuttered house and shady terrace remain the same from times past – as does the cooking. Menu B could be a *salade de foie de dinde au vinaigre de Xérès*; *noix de boeuf au poivre*; cheeses; and *croustillant aux pommes*.
Menus BDE. Rooms (9) DE. Cards All.
Closed Feb school hols. Sun evg and Mon (not July/Aug).
Post r. H. de Ville, 81120 Réalmont, Tarn. Region Languedoc-Roussillon.
Tel 63 55 52 80. Mich 154/A2. Map 5.

ROCAMADOUR   Beau Site et Notre Dame/Rest. Jehan de Valon

Very comfortable hotel/Cooking 2-3
Terrace/Lift/Parking

A well-named site, halfway up the cliff-hanger medieval *cité*. Modern and old apply to the two buildings (straddling the pedestrian-crowded road) and to Christophe Besse's cooking. On one hand a melting *millefeuille de truite rose à la crème de ciboulette*; on the other a belt-stretching *cuisse de canard confite à l'ancienne*. Wide choice on menus.
Menus ACD. Rooms (44) EF. Cards All.
Closed Mid Nov to Mar.
Post 46500 Rocamadour, Lot. Region Dordogne.
Tel 65 33 63 08. Fax 65 33 65 23. Mich 124/C4. Map 5.

A100frs & under. B100–135. C135–165. D165–250. E250–350. F350–500. G500+

ROCHEFORT
Tourne-Broche

Comfortable restaurant/Cooking 1-2

Dina Klein and her husband, chef Jean, contrive to pull off a series of culinary rope tricks with no less than four qualifying menus. The two C menus are largesse: *nos propositions du marché* offers a wide choice for each course; a *dégustation* has eight courses. Fish, shellfish, *grillades au feu de bois*, classical and regional alternatives provide the most varied of options. Simpler grills on the two cheapest menus.
Menus BCD. Cards Access, AE, Visa. (Rooms: Ibis to N – with parking.)
Closed 20-28 Feb. 24 June to 7 July. Last wk Oct. Sat midday.
Post 56 av. Ch. de Gaulle, 17300 Rochefort, Char.-Mar. Region Poit-Char.
Tel 46 99 20 19. Fax 46 99 72 06. Mich 106/B1-Cl. Map 4.

La ROCHELLE
L'Entracte

Comfortable restaurant/Cooking 2-3

Easy to get to from the western side; park near the famous Tour de la Lanterne. L'Entracte is Michelin 2-star chef Richard Coutanceau's bistro (about 300 metres from his restaurant). A "theatre-programme" menu: four acts (starters, fish, *viandes*, desserts) and you choose from three. Wide choice of modern, classical and regional *plats* like *mouclade*, *morue fraîche, faux-filet grillée sauce Bordelaise* and *jonchée*.
Menus C Cards Access, Visa. (Rooms: Les Brises & Majestic – both to W.)
Closed Sun. (Les Brises has super site/parking; Majestic much cheaper.)
Post 22 r. St-Jean du Pérot, 17000 La Rochelle, Charente-Maritime.
Tel 46 50 62 60. Fax 41 41 99 45. Mich 92/C3. Map 4.

RODEZ
St-Amans

Comfortable restaurant/Cooking 2

Jack Amat is fast approaching his 50th birthday. Thirty years ago he won the coveted best apprentice chef in France award; he also had a long seven-year stint at Taillevent in Paris. That honed and buffed polish in Paris shows in his classical and neo-classical repertoire: menu B could be *oeuf poché aux asperges, saumon poêlé aux algues*, a *granité, filet de porc au citron vert, fromage* and a cracking sweet.
Menus BE. Cards Access, Visa, (Rooms: Tour Maje – adjacent to parking.)
Closed Mid Feb to mid Mar. (Above 200 metres-walk to NW.)
Post 12 r. Madeleine, 12000 Rodez, Aveyron. Region MC (Cévennes).
Tel 65 68 03 18. Mich 140/B2-C2. Map 5.

A100frs & under. B100–135. C135–165. D165–250. E250–350. F350–500. G500+

La ROQUE-GAGEAC

Belle Etoile

Comfortable hotel/Cooking 1-2
Terrace/Garage

Guy and chef Régis Ongaro's *logis* has a fabulous Dordogne-side site. The first-floor terrace is a cool haven for summer lunches. Plenty of choice but no little extras. A typical menu could be a drooling *ballotine de canard au foie gras et sa salade*, a *magret de canard sauce citron*, *cabécou de Rocamadour* and a "so-so" *crème brûlée à la cassonade*. Menus BCDE. Rooms (17) DEF. Cards Access, Visa.
Closed Mid Oct to Easter.
Post 24250 La Roque-Gageac, Dordogne. Region Dordogne.
Tel 53 29 51 44. Fax 53 29 45 63. Mich 124/A3. Map 5.

ROSCOFF

Le Temps de Vivre

Very comfortable restaurant/Cooking 3

If you are using Roscoff to cross the Channel then find an excuse to nose out Jean-Yves Crenn, one of Brittany's best chefs. A modern master creating gilt-edged *plats* and capitalising cleverly on Finistère's rich and varied larder. Simple, complex and robust sit cheek by jowl: *choux farcis d'araignée aux oignons roses de Roscoff* and a *museau de cochon farci* are both star-winning stunners – and ample evidence of what I mean. Menus bCDE. Cards Access, Visa. (Rooms: adjacent Ibis.)
Closed Feb and Nov school hols. Sun evg. Mon.
Post pl. Eglise, 29680 Roscoff, Finistère. Region Brittany.
Tel 98 61 27 28. Mich 27/D1. Map 1.

ROUDOUALLEC

Bienvenue

Comfortable restaurant/Cooking 2-3
Parking

A run-of-the-mill exterior but don't be fooled: the airy, cool dining room is a refreshing tonic (the turquoise wall covering is English). Refined and intense neo-classical cuisine from Jean-Claude Spégagne. Two cracking specialities have links with Scotland: Scottish salmon in a sorrel sauce and giant *langoustines grillées flambées au whisky*. Menus aCDE. Cards Access, AE, Visa. (Rooms: Relais de Cornouaille – at)
Closed 1-15 Feb. Tues evg & Wed (out of season). (Châteauneuf-du-Faou.)
Post 56110 Roudouallec, Morbihan. Region Brittany.
Tel 97 34 50 01. Mich 45/E1. Map 1. (Easy drive NW to Chat.-du-Faou.)

A100frs & under. B100–135. C135–165. D165–250. E250–350. F350–500. G500+

ROUFFACH   A la Ville de Lyon/Rest. Philippe Bohrer

Simple hotel and very comfortable restaurant/Cooking 3
Lift/Parking

Two adjacent buildings (the hotel exterior needs a face-lift). Attentive waitress service. Neo-classical fare from chef Philippe Bohrer: a wholesome *hure de queue de boeuf en gelée*, flavoursome *blanc de volaille aux senteurs des Mascareignes* and a saliva-stirring *terrine de quetsches et sa glace cannelle*. Also cheaper Chez Julien *winstub* (wine bar).
Menus BDEF (winstub AB). Rooms (43) EF. Cards All.
Closed 1st 3 wks Mar. Rest: Mon. (On town's northern exit.)
Post r. Poincaré, 68250 Rouffach, Haut-Rhin. Region Alsace. Map 3.
Tel (R) 89 49 62 49. (H) 89 49 65 51. Fax 89 49 76 67. Mich 61/D4.

Les ROUSSES   France

Very comfortable hotel/Cooking 3
Terrace/Parking

For many decades Roger Petit has been charming both French and Swiss clients (the border is just minutes away) at his mountain chalet-hotel 1100 metres above sea-level. Step back many decades, to the days of the legendary Fernand Point, for painstakingly-created classical offerings. One more endearing dividend: plenty of half-bottles of wine.
Menus CDF. Rooms (33) F. Cards All.
Closed 20 Nov to 14 Dec. 5-30 June.
Post 39220 Les Rousses, Jura. Region Jura.
Tel 84 60 01 45. Fax 84 60 04 63. Mich 104/B1. Map 6.

ROUTOT   L'Ecurie

Comfortable restaurant/Cooking 2-3

Danièlle and Jacques Thierry are a delightful, ambitious duo. Great dining room (not the *écurie* – stable – which is used for large parties) and equally stylish menus, a roll-call of sumptuous classical dishes. Try these for size: *les rouelles de lapereau tièdes, vinaigrette au jus de truffe*; *trois terrines maison*; *canard de Duclair façon Ecurie*; Normandy cheeses; and *charlotte au chocolat crème au café*.
Menus aCD. Cards Acc, Visa. (Rooms: Normotel-La Marine, Caudebec.)
Closed Feb school hols. 1st wk Aug. Sun evg. Mon. Wed evg (Oct-June).
Post 27350 Routot, Eure. Region Normandy. (Caudebec 20 km to N.)
Tel 32 57 30 30. Mich 15/E4. Map 2. (Park in huge *place*.)

A100frs & under. B100–135. C135–165. D165–250. E250–350. F350–500. G500+

ROYE
Central/Rest. Florentin

Comfortable restaurant with rooms/Cooking 2

A modern, smart-looking spot in the centre of the town (near the huge place H. de Ville). The dining room, with garish neo-classical pillars and murals, is much too crowded for comfort. Chef Denis Devaux does a competent classical/regional job: enjoy, from a wide choice for each course on menu C (low-end), *tourteau froid mayonnaise*; gutsy *coq au vin*; cheese; and a filling, intense *gâteau au chocolat*.

Menus aCD. Rooms (8) DE. Cards All.
Closed 23 Dec to 4 Jan. 6-13 Mar. 19-27 Aug. Sun evg. Mon.
Post 36 r. Amiens, 80700 Roye, Somme. Region North.
Tel 22 87 11 05. Fax 22 87 42 74. Mich 18/B2. Map 2.

RUMILLY
L'Améthyste

Comfortable restaurant/Cooking 2-3

Easily found if you enter the town from the north; the restaurant is on the right, before the river bridge. Chef Julien Valéro, a modern *cuisinier*, was once a student of glamour-puss Marc Veyrat (near Annecy). Julien's invention shows – though not that well in a *noisettes de thon au curry*. More resounding successes are *cuisse de lapereau au jus de thyme* and a clever *duo chaud-froid* strawberry dessert.

Menus BDEF. Cards Access, Visa. (Rooms: Relais du Clergeon at Moye.)
Closed 23 July to 11 Aug. (Moye is 4 km to NW – quiet village and site.)
Post 27 r. Pont-Neuf, 74150 Rumilly, Haute-Savoie. Region Savoie.
Tel 50 01 02 52. Mich 118/A1. Map 6.

ST-AFFRIQUE
Moderne

Comfortable hotel/Cooking 2

A considerable favourite with readers over the years. Built in 1970, the *logis* lives up to its modern-day name as the place has been extensively refurbished and painted up a treat; the interior is a permanent art exhibition. Jean-François Decuq does the brush work front of house; brother Yves mixes the colours in the kitchen. Classical and regional canvases with *Roquefort* (down the road) popping up all over the show.

Menus ACDE. Rooms (28) EF. Cards Access, AE. Visa.
Closed 18 Dec to 15 Jan. 9-15 Oct (not hotel).
Post 54 av. A.-Pezet, 12400 St-Affrique, Aveyron. Region MC (Cévennes).
Tel 65 49 20 44. Fax 65 49 36 55. Mich 155/D1. Map 5.

A 100frs & under. B 100–135. C 135–165. D 165–250. E 250–350. F 350–500. G 500+

ST-AMAND-MONTROND
Boeuf Couronné

Simple restaurant/Cooking 2
Parking

Three dining rooms in this small restaurant at a busy junction NW of the town. A Grand Canyon wide choice of dishes is an impressive feature. Menu B has 6 starters, 4 main course dishes and 11 desserts. Typical bounty could include *saumon fumé* (home-made and delicious), gutsy *confit de canard maison aux cèpes* and a simple *crème caramel*.
Menus aBCD. Cards Access, Visa. (Rooms: Le Noirlac, 2 km to NW.)
Closed 3-17 Jan. 28 June to 12 July. Tues evg. Wed. (Above on N144.)
Post 86 r. Juranville, 18200 St-Amand-Montrond, Cher.
Tel 48 96 42 72. Mich 84/C4. Map 2. Region Berry-Bourbonnais.

ST-ANTHEME
Pont de Raffiny

Simple hotel/Cooking 2
Parking

Alain Beaudoux has to try so much harder at this remote *logis* 5½ km south of St-Anthème. Modernised bedrooms and an unusual dining room with fountain and small pool; ask, too, to see the *salon*. Classical fare: *civet de sanglier sauce Grand Marnier*, *pavé de boeuf au poivre* and *rable de lièvre aux pâtes fraîches* will stop tummies rumbling for days.
Menus aBC. Rooms (12) D. Cards Access, Visa.
Closed Jan to mid Feb. Sun evg and Mon (mid Sept to June).
Post Raffiny, 63660 St-Anthème, Puy-de-Dôme. Region MC (Auvergne).
Tel 73 95 49 10. Fax 73 95 80 21. Mich 114/C3. Map 5.

ST-AVOLD
Europe

Comfortable hotel/Cooking 2
Lift/Garage/Parking

I first visited Eugène and Charlotte Zirn's modern hotel when I was researching my *En Route* guide (p41). Eugène drives both traditional and modern cooking *autoroutes*: *jarret de porc sur choucroute nouvelle*, *moules marinières*, *escalope de saumon à la crème de ciboulette* are typical *plats*. (S from A4; left after Novotel; right at T.)
Menus BCDE. Rooms (34) EF. Cards All.
Closed Rest: 1-15 Aug. Sat midday. Sun.
Post 7 r. Altmayer, 57500 St-Avold, Moselle. Region Alsace.
Tel 87 92 00 33. Fax 87 92 01 23. Mich 41/F1. Map 3.

A100frs & under. B100–135. C135–165. D165–250. E250–350. F350–500. G500+

ST-CAST-LE-GUILDO

Le Biniou

Comfortable restaurant/Cooking 2
Parking

Panoramic views of the sea from the smart modern Breton "bagpipe". Yvette and Jean-Claude Menard are the pipers at "Le Biniou". The Armor's piscatorial harvests – treasures all – dominate the menus: oysters, mussels, *soupe de poissons aux étrilles, filet de lieu, terrine de poissons, maquereaux, saumon*. Who needs to eat meat here?
Menus aBDE. Cards Access, Visa. (Rooms: Dunes & Bon Abri.)
Closed Mid Nov to mid Mar. Tues (mid Sept to mid June).
Post Plage de Pen-Guen, 22380 St-Cast-le-Guildo, Côtes d'Armor.
Tel 96 41 94 53. Mich 29/E2. Map 1. Region Brittany.

ST-CERE

France

Comfortable hotel/Cooking 2
Terrace/Gardens/Swimming pool/Parking

A modern *logis*, away from St-Céré's busy centre, with spacious lounges, dining room and shady terrace/garden. English-speaking Isabelle Lherm is an attractive young hostess; husband Patrick an assured, able chef. Classical and regional offerings: invigorating *soupe paysanne en croûte, saumon fumé Parmentier* and a diet-killing *pièce de boeuf grillée*.
Menus bCDE. Rooms (22) EF. Cards Access, Visa.
Closed Mid Nov to Feb. Tues midday. Sat midday.
Post av. F. de Maynard, 46400 St-Céré, Lot. Region Dordogne.
Tel 65 38 02 16. Fax 65 38 02 98. Mich 125/D3. Map 5.

ST-CHELY-D'AUBRAC

Voyageurs-Vayrou

Simple hotel/Cooking 1-2

Christiane Vayrou and her son-in-law, Patrick Amilhat (his wife, Brigitte, is the sister of Régine Caralp at Le Méjane, Espalion), are the cooks at the long-established family hotel. Classical and regional *cuisine soignée* (see the dining room photographs): *tripoux, terrine de canard, assiette de charcuterie, cou farci et magret fumé* and *aligot du chef* – all dishes which are the very essence of Aubrac.
Menus ABC. Rooms (14) E. Cards Access, Visa.
Closed Oct to Mar. Sat (not July/Aug).
Post 12470 St-Chély-d'Aubrac, Aveyron. Region Massif Central (Auvergne).
Tel 65 44 27 05. Mich 141/D1. Map 5.

A 100frs & under. B 100–135. C 135–165. D 165–250. E 250–350. F 350–500. G 500+

ST-CIRQ-LAPOPIE   Auberge du Sombral "Aux Bonnes Choses"

Comfortable restaurant with rooms/Cooking 1-2
Quiet/Terrace

The medieval village, high above the Lot, is a photographer's dream; so, too, is Gilles Hardeveld's *auberge* and the evocative place de la Mairie. Unabashed regional nosh: *salade de cabécous rôtis, cuisse de canarde confite, poulet aux champignons, truite au vieux Cahors* and *gigot d'agneau* are typical. Tricky parking.
Menus ACD. Rooms (8) EF. Cards Access, Visa.
Closed 11 Nov to end Mar. Tues evg. Wed.
Post 46330 St-Cirq-Lapopie, Lot. Region Dordogne.
Tel 65 31 26 08. Fax 65 30 26 37. Mich 138/C2. Map 5.

ST-DIZIER   La Gentilhommière

Comfortable restaurant/Cooking 1-2

New owners, Florémond, the chef, and Corinne Descharmes, have worked in numerous swish French and Swiss hotels since they won their hotel school diplomas a decade ago. Flowers and shutters dominate the façade (are the two figures still there?). Elegant interior. Neo-classical treats from the chef: *rouelles de dos de lapin à la sauge et ses graines de moutarde* is a typical assured creation. (Rooms: simple Picardy or Ibis.)
Menus ABC. Cards Access, Visa. (Ibis N of town; Picardy 600 m walk.)
Closed Sat midday. Sun evg. Mon evg. Region Champagne-Ardenne.
Post 29 r. J. Jaurès, 52100 St-Dizier, Haute-Marne.
Tel 25 56 32 97. Mich 57/F1. Map 3. (Alongside D384 Troyes road.)

ST-FELIX-LAURAGAIS   Auberge du Poids Public

Comfortable hotel/Cooking 2-3
Terrace/Gardens/Garage/Parking

Panoramic views from the large beamed dining room appeal – perhaps as much as the cooking of acclaimed chef, Claude Taffarello. Both modern and regional dishes. Menu B could be a block of *rillettes de canard, confiture d'oignons*; *thon poêlé, beurre de tomate*; *noisettes* (rissoles) *de pied de porc au jus*; and *pain perdu à l'ancienne* (French toast).
Menus BCDE. Rooms (13) E. Cards Access, AE, Visa.
Closed Jan. Sun evg (Oct to Apl). Region Languedoc-Roussillon.
Post 31540 St-Félix-Lauragais, Haute-Garonne.
Tel 61 83 00 20. Fax 61 83 86 21. Mich 153/E4. Map 5.

A100frs & under. B100–135. C135–165. D165–250. E250–350. F350–500. G500+

ST-FLOUR   Grand Hôtel Voyageurs

Comfortable hotel/Cooking 2-3
Lift/Garage

In the *haute ville* with the most delectable of secret sun-trap terraces
(alas, not used for meals). Diego Quinonero mixes creative neo-classical
with regional. The latter, in menu B, included a *cochonnaille des Monts
d'Auvergne* (*charcuterie*), a pungent *volaille fermière Brayaude aux
morilles, lentilles, fromages* and yummy *milliard aux griottes*.
Menus aBCD. Rooms (33) CDE. Cards Access, DC, Visa.
Closed Nov to Mar.
Post 25 r. College, 15100 St-Flour, Cantal. Region MC (Auvergne).
Tel 71 60 34 44. Fax 71 60 00 21. Mich 127/D2. Map 5.

ST-FLOUR   Les Messageries/Rest. Nautilus

Comfortable hotel/Cooking 2
Terrace/Swimming pool/Garage/Parking

North of the busy N9, in the low town and near the station. Chef Bruno
Giral (son of the high town Europe's owners) and his wife, Catherine, do
a sound job. Mix of regional, neo-classical and modern creations: on one
hand a light *sandre grillé aux mousserons* and at a more basic, gutsy
level both *tripoux* and *noisette de porc au curry*.
Menus ABCDE. Rooms (16) DEF. Cards Access, Visa.
Closed Mid Jan to mid Feb. Fri and Sat midday (Nov to Mar).
Post 23 av. Ch. de Gaulle, 15100 St-Flour, Cantal. Region MC (Auvergne).
Tel 71 60 11 36. Fax 71 60 46 79. Mich 127/D2. Map 5.

ST-GENIEZ-D'OLT   France

Comfortable hotel/Cooking 1-2
Lift/Swimming pool & Tennis (see text)

St-Geniez, beside the River Lot (Olt is local *patois*), is a busy place.
Clients of Madeleine and Michel Crouzet can use the facilities (see
above) at their Club Marmotel, one km away. France's cooking?
Regional and classical. Especially noteworthy is the Menu Aveyronnais
(A): *charcuterie, terrine de tripoux, aligot* and *cabécou grillé*.
Menus ACD. Rooms (48) E. Cards Access, Visa.
Closed Mid Nov to mid Mar.
Post 12130 St-Geniez-d'Olt, Aveyron. Regions MC (Auvergne/Cévennes).
Tel 65 70 42 20. Fax 65 47 41 38. Mich 141/D2. Map 5.

A 100frs & under. B 100–135. C 135–165. D 165–250. E 250–350. F 350–500. G 500+

ST-HILAIRE-LE-CHATEAU   du Thaurion

Very comfortable restaurant with rooms/Cooking 3
Terrace/Gardens/Parking

Either qualifying menu (a or C) is *RQP* at its best: the first offers a choice at each of three courses; the second, with no choice, provides the chance for you to try five regional *plats*. Regional, neo-classical and modern fare: whatever your choice, I cannot recommend chef Gérard Fanton and his English-speaking wife, Marie-Christine, enough.
Menus aCDEF. Rooms (10) DEFG. Cards All.
Closed Jan to end Feb. 21 to 27 Dec. Wed. Thurs midday.
Post 23250 St-Hilaire-le-Château, Creuse. Region Poitou-Charentes.
Tel 55 64 50 12. Fax 55 64 90 92. Mich 111/D1. Map 5.

ST-JEAN-DU-BRUEL   Midi-Papillon

Simple hotel/Cooking 2
Quiet/Gardens/Swimming pool/Parking

At the heart of one of Nature's most beguiling corners this spruced-up *logis* appeals to all: a riverside setting; involved fourth-generation owners, Maryse and Jean-Michel Papillon; and the latter's cooking, of all styles, makes clever use of his own home-grown vegetables, home-reared poultry and home-made *charcuterie, foies gras et confits*.
Menus aBD. Rooms (19) ACD. Cards Access, Visa.
Closed 11 Nov to 24 Mar.
Post 12230 St-Jean-du-Bruel, Aveyron. Region Massif Central (Cévennes).
Tel 65 62 26 04. Fax 65 62 12 97. Mich 141/F4. Map 5.

ST-JOSSE-SUR-MER   Le Relais de St-Josse

Simple restaurant/Cooking 2

A four-star *village fleuri* where a young couple are working wonders. Fabienne Delmer is a quiet, English-speaking *patronne*; husband Etienne a classical cavalier chef. Stylish, assured specialities (three choices for each course). Examples in C: *marbre de queue de boeuf, pot-au-feu de lotte, plâteau de fromages* and *tarte Tatin servi tiède*. Only debit: barn-like dining room. (Rooms: many hotels at Le Touquet.)
Menus ACDE. Cards Access, Visa. (Ibis, on beach, recommended.)
Closed Mid Jan to early Feb. Sun evg. Mon. (Le Touquet 9 km to NW.)
Post 62170 St-Josse-sur-Mer, Pas-de-Calais. Region North.
Tel 21 94 61 75. Mich 2/A4. Map 2.

A100frs & under. B100–135. C135–165. D165–250. E250–350. F350–500. G500+

ST-JULIEN-CHAPTEUIL   Vidal

Very comfortable restaurant/Cooking 2-3

I can vouch for chef Jean-Pierre Vidal's references (he was trained by
Forges at Riorges, Troisgros at Roanne and Rostang at Antibes – all in my
earlier guides). Neo-classical virtuosity – exemplified by an accomplished
aromatic *cannette rôtie aux épices et pommes gaufrettes*. Chantal Vidal
is a bespectacled, smiling *patronne/sommèliere*. (Rooms: Moulin de
Barette, Pont de Sumène – N88, 13 km to WNW: also see below.)
Menus bCDEF. Cards Access, AE, Visa. (Rooms: also Barriol in village.)
Closed 19 Jan to end Feb. Mon evg. Tues (out of season).
Post 43260 St-Julien-Chapteuil, Haute-Loire. Region MC (Ardèche).
Tel 71 08 70 50. Fax 71 08 40 14. Mich 129/D2. Map 5.

ST-LAURENT-DE-LA-SALANQUE   Auberge du Pin

Simple hotel/Cooking 2
Terrace/Gardens/Parking

Philippe Got, after stints elsewhere in France, California and other
overseas outposts, took over from his parents a few years ago. Readers
enjoy his *Catalane* and neo-classical cooking. Menu C is typical: *filets
de rougets au coulis d'olives*; *magret de canard au Banyuls*; *chèvre
frais aux figues*; and the ubiquitous *crème Catalane*.
Menus BCD. Rooms (19) DE. Cards Access, Visa.
Closed Jan. Feb. Sun evg and Mon (out of season). Region Lang-Rouss.
Post rte Perpignan, 66250 St-Laurent-de-la-Salanque, Pyr.-Or.
Tel 68 28 01 62. Fax 68 28 39 14. Mich 173/D4. Map 5.

ST-LAURENT-DE-LA-SALANQUE   Commerce

Comfortable restaurant with rooms/Cooking 2
Garage

Raymonde Siré is the hostess; husband Jean-Louis is the chef. Enjoy
classical cuisine, with the odd dip in the *Catalane* pool, in a light,
yellow-washed dining room. Noteworthy specialities on menu C include
an exemplary *bouillabaisse de lotte à la Catalane*, a sea-scented *méli-
mélo* (mixture) *de palourdes et moules bouchots* and *crème Catalane* .
Menus aCD. Rooms (14) DE. Cards Access, Visa. Region Lang-Rouss.
Closed School hols in Feb and Nov. Sun evg and Mon (not July/Aug).
Post 2 bd Révolution, 66250 St-Laurent-de-la-Salanque, Pyr.-Or.
Tel 68 28 02 21. Mich 173/D4. Map 5.

A100frs & under. B100–135. C135–165. D165–250. E250–350. F350–500. G500+

ST-MALO   Le Chalut

Comfortable restaurant/Cooking 2

At last! Michelin have woken up to the talents of chef Jean-Philippe
Foucat (true, too, of at least a dozen old *FL* favourites); he wins an entry
and an accolade. My *FLE* words still apply: go once and you'll return
often. What better compliment can I pay this congenial fish restaurant?
Fresh fish is laid out on an open-air counter; shellfish are in a dining
room tank. Classical fare. Not for carnivores.
Menus aCD. Cards Access, AE, Visa. (Rooms: several nearby hotels.)
Closed 15-31 Oct. Sun evg (out of season). Mon. Region Brittany.
Post 8 r. Corne de Cerf, 35400 St-Malo, Ille-et-Vilaine.
Tel 99 56 71 58. Mich 30/A4. Map 1. (In NE corner of walled town.)

ST-MARCELLIN   Savoyet-Serve

Simple hotel (comfortable annexe)/Cooking 1-2
Lift/Parking

The multi-floored annexe is soulless modern – but with all mod-cons. St-
Marcellin is famed for its cow's milk cheese; Jean-Pierre Serve's
restaurant is acclaimed locally for his classical and regional *RQP* menus:
ravioles de Royans (down the road) – don't miss 'em; *poulet sauté aux
écrevisses*; and *chevreuil Grand Veneur* are typical *plats*.
Menus aBCD. Rooms (60) BCDEF. Cards Access, Visa.
Closed Sun evg. Regions Hautes-Alpes/Savoie.
Post 16 bd Gambetta, 38160 St-Marcellein, Isère.
Tel 76 38 04 17. Fax 76 64 02 99. Mich 130/C2. Map 6.

ST-MARTIN-D'ARMAGNAC   Auberge du Bergerayre

Comfortable restaurant with rooms/Cooking 2-3
Secluded/Terrace/Gardens/Swimming pool/Parking

Pierrette Sarran is *la cuisinière* at this delectable old farm – west of the
village and surrounded by vineyards and fields – seemingly infused with
the spirit of Armagnac. Rustic dining rooms. Madame's classical and
regional repertoire epitomises Gers: witness *salade paysanne aux
gesiers confits* and *pintadeau rôti, jus court à l'ail* as evidence.
Menus aBD. Rooms (14) EF. Disabled. Cards Access, Visa.
Closed Mid Jan to mid Feb. Rest: Wed.
Post 32110 St-Martin-d'Armagnac, Gers. Region Southwest.
Tel 62 09 08 72. Fax 62 09 09 74. Mich 150/B2. Map 4.

A100frs & under. B100–135. C135–165. D165–250. E250–350. F350–500. G500+

ST-MARTIN-DE-LONDRES   Les Muscardins

Very comfortable restaurant/Cooking 3

Multi-prize-winning *cuisinier* Georges Rousset, a longtime *FL* favourite, leaves much of the modern and neo-classical cooking these days to his talented 30-year-old son, Thierry. The contents of menu b vary each day – depending what's at the market. Menu C can include a lipsmackingly good *cabillaud demi-sel en croûte légère* and a brilliantly conceived *agneau en trilogie (noisettes, poitrine farci et navarin)*.
Menus b(lunch)CDEF. Cards All. (Rooms: Juvena – 18 km SE, D986.)
Closed Feb. Mon (not public hols). Tues (not evgs in summer).
Post 19 rte Cévennes, 34380 St-Martin-de-Londres, Hérault.
Tel 67 55 75 90. Fax 67 55 70 28. Mich 156/B2. Map 5. Region Lang-Rouss.

ST-MARTIN-EN-BRESSE   Au Puits Enchanté

Simple hotel/Cooking 2
Parking

Well-named and a worthwhile detour from the A6. Chef Jacky Chateau and his wife, Nadine, are *RQP* winners. Elegant but simple applies to both furnishings and cooking: start with a sumptuous *terrine de pintade aux foies de canards en gelée blonde*; then a lighter *rosettes de saumon à la fondue les jeunes poireaux*, cheese and sweet (typical menu B).
Menus aBCD. Rooms (14) CDE. Cards Access, Visa. Closed 16-31 Jan.
Feb sch. hols. 1-7 Sept. Sun evg (not July/Aug). Mon (out of season). Tues.
Post 71620 St-Martin-en-Bresse, Saône-et-Loire. Regions Burg/Lyonnais.
Tel 85 47 71 96. Fax 85 47 74 58. Mich 88/B3. Map 3.

ST-MEDARD   Le Gindreau

Very comfortable restaurant/Cooking 3-4
Terrace

An old school house with green views over the Vert Valley and a cool chestnut-shaded terrace. Some school house – these days very chic. Elegant Martine and Alexis Pélissou, the chef, beguile with a flavour-personified RQP menu: wide choice including *magret de canard macéré façon carpaccio*, local lamb and drooling *gateau aux trois chocolats*.
Menus CDE. Cards Acc, AE, Visa. (Rooms: Campanile & France, Cahors.)
Closed 13 Nov to 7 Dec. Sun evg (out of season). Mon (not public hols).
Post 46150 St-Médard, Lot. Region Dordogne.
Tel 65 36 22 27. Fax 65 36 24 54. Mich 138/B1. Map 5.

A100frs & under. B100–135. C135–165. D165–250. E250–350. F350–500. G500+

ST-MELIOR-DES-ONDES   Le Coquillage

Comfortable restaurant/Cooking 2-3
Secluded/Gardens/Parking

I'm no fan of the latest French chef comet, two-star Olivier Roellinger –
Gault Millau's 1994 Chef of the Year. He, too, has opened a bistro –
housed in the Hôtel de Bricourt-Richeux, a deluxe Relais & Châteaux
annexe for his famed Cancale restaurant. "Sea" and "spices" are the
words which flood the aromatic *RQP* repertoire. Superb views.
Menus BC. Cards All. (Rooms: Nuit & Jour, Cancale; Terminus, Rotheneuf.)
Closed Mid Nov to mid Dec. Mon. Tues midday (not July/Aug).
Post le Point-du-Jour, 35350 St-Méloir-des-Ondes, Ille-et-Vilaine.
Tel 99 89 64 76. Fax 99 89 88 47. Mich 30/A4. Map 1. Region Brittany.

ST-MELOIR-DES-ONDES   Hôtel Tirel-Guérin

Very comfortable hotel/Cooking 3
Gardens/Swimming pool (indoor)/Tennis/Parking

A family closed shop: Roger Tirel (son of the owners) married Annie
Guérin; her brother, Jean-Luc, hitched-up with Roger's sister, Marie-
Christiane. Great favourite with readers. Modern and classical *plats*.
Fresh-as-daisies fish and shellfish: oysters, mussels, scallops, *colin*,
saumon, lieu et al. Fine sauces. *RQP* grub with cosseting comforts.
Menus BDE. Rooms (60) EF. Disabled. Cards All. (S of St-Méloir.)
Closed Mid Dec to mid Jan. Rest: Sun evg (Oct to Easter).
Post la gare, La Gouesnière, 35350 St-Méloir-des-Ondes, Ille-et-Vilaine.
Tel 99 89 10 46. Fax 99 89 12 62. Mich 30/A4. Map 1. Region Brittany.

ST-NEXANS   La Vieille Grange

Comfortable restaurant/Cooking 1-2
Terrace/Gardens/Parking

An old barn, 6 km SE of Bergerac. A mixture of rustic and Louis XIII –
and Italian and Périgourdine cuisine from Catherine Cassaresi, born
locally and married to an Italian. There's nothing bland about her varied
specialities – among them *mignon de veau au gorgonzola, tortellini aux
quatre fromages, caneton rôti au miel au citron* and *tiramisu*.
Menus BCD. Cards All. (Rooms: Climat de France & Campanile, Bergerac.)
Closed Tues evg and Wed (not July/Aug). (Above SW of Bergerac – D936.)
Post La Petite Forêt, 24520 St-Nexans, Dordogne. Region Dordogne.
Tel 53 24 32 21. Mich 123/D4. Map 5.

A 100frs & under. B 100–135. C 135–165. D 165–250. E 250–350. F 350–500. G 500+

ST-PAUL-DE-VENCE   La Brouette

Simple restaurant/Cooking 1-2
Terrace/Parking

The English-speaking Danish family Bornemann – Olé, Birgitte and son
Michel – mix Scandinavian and French at their extrovert base. Menu C is
"salty and smoky" goodies galore – with a *terrine de foie* (Viking recipe),
filet mignon, flétan fumé (*ou saumon mariné*), *harengs marinées ou
saumon fumé* (both *Danois*), *truite fumé* and dessert. *Olé!*
Menus ACD. Cards Acc, Visa. (D36 Cagnes-Vence road, E of St-Paul.)
Closed Feb. Mon (out of season). (Rooms: Le Hameau, D7 W of St-Paul.)
Post 830 rte de Cagnes, 06570 St-Paul, Alpes-Mar. Region Côte d'Azur.
Tel 93 58 67 16. Mich 165/D3. Map 6.

ST-PEE-SUR-NIVELLE   Fronton

Comfortable restaurant with rooms/Cooking 2-3
Terrace

Jean-Baptiste and Maritxu (Maritchu) Daguerre are passionate about their
métier. It shows in their unpretentious, flower-dominated Basque home.
Menu B is primarily neo-classical: dishes like *filet de truite saumonée au
beurre blanc, civet de canard aux petits oignons* and *île flottante.* A
super menu of reworked old Basque recipes is, alas, in price range D.
Menus BD. Rooms (7) E. Cards All. (At Ibarron – 2 km to W.)
Closed Mid Feb to mid Mar. Tues evg and Wed evg (not high season).
Post 64310 St-Pée-sur-Nivelle, Pyrénées-Atlantiques. Region Southwest.
Tel 59 54 10 12. Mich 148/B4. Map 4.

ST-PERE-SOUS-VEZELAY   Le Pré des Marguerites

Comfortable restaurant/Cooking 2-3
Terrace/Gardens/Parking

Another three-star chef's bistro (Marc Meneau). How's this for a low-end
menu C with a choice for each course: a bravura *galantine de canard* or
unfussy *saucisson chaud pommes*; a feisty, ear-to-the-ground *oreilles de
porc aux lentilles*; and a discreetly flavoured *sable aux pommes crème
anglaise* or a robust *tarte aux raisins de vendange.* Fine service.
Menus aCD. Cards All. (Rooms: La Renommée, *sans rest,* at St-Père.)
Closed Mon (not public holidays).
Post Gde-Rue, 89450 St-Père-sous-Vézelay, Yonne, Region Burgundy.
Tel 86 33 33 33. Fax 86 33 34 73. Mich 72/B4. Map 3.

A100frs & under. B100–135. C135–165. D165–250. E250–350. F350–500. G500+

ST-PIERRE-DES-NIDS

Dauphin

Comfortable restaurant with rooms/Cooking 2
Parking

Don't be put off by the exterior. Hidden behind the dull façade is the remarkable Jean Etienne, an English-speaking *patron/chef* (once with the *French Line*) and dynamic promoter of his *pays*. *French Line* classical cooking: *escalope de saumon d'Ecosse sur lit vert* and a local *cuisse de canard confite à la Pôôtéenne* (the local *pays*) are show stoppers.
Menus ACDE. Rooms (9) CDE. Cards Access, Visa.
Closed Feb school hols. 2nd half Aug. Wed.
Post rte Alençon, 53370 St-Pierre-des-Nids, Mayenne. Region Normandy.
Tel 43 03 52 12. Fax 43 03 55 49. Mich 50/C2. Map 2.

ST-PIERRE-LANGERS

Le Jardin de l'Abbaye

Very comfortable restaurant/Cooking 2
Parking

Two rustic dining rooms, both with chimneys, at the happy home of Alain and Catherine Duval. The couple love their *métier*; she's a friendly hostess; he walks the classical cloisters. Relish the Menu Abbaye (three choices for each of three courses; top-end B): *nage de daurade au basilic* and *faux-filet au poivre de Guinéc* are top of the pops treats.
Menus ABE. Cards Access, Visa. (Rooms: Michelet, Granville, 11 km NW.)
Closed 3 wks Feb. 23 Sept to 9 Oct. Sun evg (not July/Aug). Mon.
Post Croix Barrée, 50530 St-Pierre-Langers, Manche. Region Normandy.
Tel 33 48 49 08. Fax 33 48 18 50. Mich 30/C3. Map 1.

ST-POURCAIN-SUR-SIOULE

Chêne Vert

Comfortable hotel/Cooking 2-3
Terrace/Garage

A welcome gale of fresh air, in the shape of new owners Jean-Guy and Martine Siret, has blown away the old cobwebs. The tag spick and span describes the beefed up hotel fabric and J-G's neo-classical dishes. Get stuck into *saumon cru mariné au gros sel*, *terrine de faisan en gelée*, *omble chevalier poêlé*, *civet de chevreuil* and a selection of *sorbets*.
Menus aBCD. Rooms (32) EF. Cards All.
Closed Last 3 wks Jan. Sun evg (Oct to Apl). Rest: Mon.
Post bd Ledru-Rollin, 03500 St-Pourçain-sur-Sioule, Allier.
Tel 70 45 40 65. Fax 70 45 68 50. Mich 100/A3. Map 5. Region Berry-B.

A 100frs & under. B 100–135. C 135–165. D 165–250. E 250–350. F 350–500. G 500+

ST-RAPHAEL   Pastorel

Comfortable restaurant/Cooking 2-3
Terrace

At the heart of old St-Raphaël, north of the railway line. There's nowt
flippant about the restaurant or the cooking; chef Charles Floccia has
both Provençal and classical nous. An almost faultless meal of a tasty
amuse-bouche, nine oysters with rye bread, an as-it-should-be *blanquette
d'agneau à l'ancienne*, *salade de Roquefort aux noix* and a sweet.
Menus CD. Cards All. (Rooms: Epulias, next door; L'Oasis, Fréjus-Plage.)
Closed Midday in Aug. Sun evg & Mon (not Aug). (L'Oasis: quiet/parking.)
Post 54 r. Liberté, 83700 St-Raphaël, Var. Region Côte d'Azur.
Tel 94 95 02 36. Fax 94 95 64 07. Mich 163/E3. Map 6.

ST-REMY-DE-PROVENCE   La Maison Jaune

Comfortable restaurant/Cooking 2-3
Terrace

A three-storey town house in the centre of St-Rémy. Chef François
Pérraud (previously at La Regalido in Fontvieille – *FLE* p325) and his
English-speaking wife, Catherine, opened their new home at the end of
1993. Stylish and clever taste combinations like *minestrone*, *toasts aux
olives noires* and *blanc de volaille à l'aïoli et au safran*.
Menus b(lunch)CDE. Cards Access, Visa. (Rooms: Soleil – 3 min-walk S.)
Closed Mid Feb to mid Mar. Sun evg. Mon. (Above quiet/parking/pool.)
Post 15 r. Carnot, 13210 St-Rémy-de-Provence, Bouches-du-Rhône.
Tel 90 92 56 14. Mich 158/B2. Map 6. Region Provence.

ST-THEGONNEC   Auberge St-Thégonnec

Comfortable hotel/Cooking 2
Terrace/Gardens/Parking

A modern, stone-built *logis* across the road from one of the famed
enclos paroissiaux. English-speaking Alain Le Coz (he gives a lot of
help to Leicester Catering College students) favours flavour in his
cuisine: witness a *salade de magret tièdes à l'huile de noix* and a *poêlée
de rougets barbets aux pleurottes*. Finish with local Plougastel *fraises*.
Menus aBCD. Rooms (19) EFG. Disabled. Cards All.
Closed Mid Dec to end Jan. Sun evg & Mon (mid Sept to mid June).
Post 29410 St-Thégonnec, Finistère. Region Brittany.
Tel 98 79 61 18. Fax 98 62 71 10. Mich 27/D2. Map 1.

A100frs & under. B100–135. C135–165. D165–250. E250–350. F350–500. G500+

ST-VAAST-LA-HOUGUE   France et Fuchsias

Comfortable hotel/Cooking 1-2
Terrace/Gardens

Famed for exceptional gardens. The owners, the Brix family, make good use of produce grown on their farm. Plenty of fish courses, too: *crabe mayonnaise* and *filet de cabillaud* are champion; so, too, are *tarte framboise* and *nougat glace*. Cooking rating scuppered by kindergarten standard *amuse-guèle* (offal), vegetable soup and chicken-liver terrine.
Menus aBCD. Rooms (32) CDEF. Cards All.
Closed 9 Jan to 19 Feb. Mon (mid Sept to Apl). Tues midday (Nov to Apl).
Post 50550 St-Vaast-la-Hougue, Manche. Region Normandy.
Tel 33 54 42 26. Fax 33 43 46 79. Mich 12/C3. Map 1.

ST-VALLIER   Terminus/Rest. Albert Lecomte

Very comfortable restaurant with rooms/Cooking 2-3
Garage

Don't be put off by the exterior and the site – by *la gare* and beside the N7. Double-glazed bedrooms, a modern dining room and a first-class classical chef more than compensate. Albert hails from St-Jean-en-Royans (Vercors) – the area's famed *ravioles* appear in a salade with *magret fumé* and with a *filet de sandre*.
Menus CDEF. Rooms (10) EF. Cards All.
Closed Feb school hols. 14-25 Aug. Sun evg. Mon.
Post 116 av. J. Jaurès, 26240 St-Vallier, Drôme. Region MC (Ardèche).
Tel 75 23 01 12. Fax 75 23 38 82. Mich 130/A1. Map 6.

STE-MENEHOULD   Cheval Rouge

Simple hotel/Cooking 1-2

Catherine and François Fourreau are the hosts at the vine-covered *logis*; Jean-Robert Lafois is the busy chef. He juggles classical, *Bourgeois* and varying regional culinary trotters. Relish *choucroute d'empereur* or an *onglet de veau à la Niçoise*; or tuck into local treats like the famed *pied de cochon à la Ste-Menehould* and *délice d'Argonne*. Some rooms noisy: Le Jabloire (*sans rest*) at Florent-en-Argonne much quieter.
Menus aCD. (Brasserie A.) Rooms (18) DE. Cards All. (Above 8 km to NE.)
Closed Sun evg (not hotel). Mon (Sept to Apl).
Post 1 r. Chanzy, 51800 Ste-Menehould, Marne. Region Champagne-Ard.
Tel 26 60 81 04. Fax 26 60 93 11. Mich 39/E2. Map 3.

A100frs & under. B100–135. C135–165. D165–250. E250–350. F350–500. G500+

STES-MARIES-DE-LA-MER

Pont de Gau

Comfortable restaurant with rooms/Cooking 2-3
Terrace/Parking

Jean and Monique Audry's *logis,* at the heart of the Camargue, is next door to the renowned Parc Ornithologique. Vivid regional and classical *plats* from chef Jean – including a gutsy Menu Camarguais. Tuck into the likes of *bouille de congre à la rouille,* a beefy *marinade de toros à la provençale* or *faux-filet grillé sauce forestière au poivre.*
Menus ABD. Rooms (9) D. Cards Access, AE, Visa. (5 km N – D570.)
Closed 3 Jan to 19 Feb. Wed (mid Oct to Easter – but not school hols).
Post 13460 Stes-Maries-de-la-Mer, Bouches-du-Rhône. Region Provence.
Tel 90 97 81 53. Fax 90 97 98 54. Mich 157/E3-E4. Map 6.

SALIGNAC-EYVIGUES

La Meynardie

Comfortable restaurant/Cooking 2-3
Terrace/Gardens/Parking

A dead-end road (follow signs N) leads you to an exquisite setting (woods and pastures) and an old farm with stone walls and deep casement windows. Little touches abound. Hearty regional – *assiette gourmand du Périgord (foie, magret, gésiers, d'oie, crudités)* – and lighter dishes like a spirited *saumon à la feuille de chou, sauce gingembre.*
Menus ACDE. Cards Access, Visa. (Rooms: La Terrasse in village.)
Closed Mid Nov to mid Dec. Mon midday (July to Sept). Wed (Oct to June).
Post 24590 Salignac-Eyvigues, Dordogne. Region Dordogne.
Tel 53 28 85 98. Fax 53 28 82 79. Mich 124/B3. Map 5.

SARPOIL

La Bergerie

Comfortable restaurant/Cooking 3
Parking

Menu B at Laurent and Isabelle Jury's remote *bergerie* is superb *RQP.* Clever use of regional produce in Laurent's creative culinary rainbow: terrine of lentils, trout and smoked salmon; *pansettes* (faggots) of lamb stuffed with wild thyme & herbs; 12 Auvergne cheeses; and *oeufs à la neige.* (Rooms: use the exquisite Château de Pasredon, 2 km to the NW.)
Menus BCDE. Cards All. (Above *chambres d'hôtes*; low-end F inc' bkft; at)
Closed Jan. Sun evg. Mon. (63500 St-Rémy-de-Chargnat; tel 73 71 00 67.)
Post Sarpoil, 63490 St-Jean-en-Val, Puy-de-Dôme. Region MC (Auvergne).
Tel 73 71 02 54. Mich 113/E3. Map 5. (La Bergerie 10 km SE of Issoire.)

A100frs & under. B100–135. C135–165. D165–250. E250–350. F350–500. G500+

SARZEAU   Espadon

Comfortable restaurant/Cooking 2-3
Parking

A modern façade gives no inkling of the art museum interior with stone, beams and panelling; almost every square inch of wall is covered with pictures. Bravura classical cooking: *soupe de poisson, blanc de poulet bourguignonne* and *île flottante* on a give-away menu A which will please anyone keen to keep wallets full. Excellent fish *plats* & sweets.
Menus ACDE. Cards All. (Rooms: Mur du Roy – Penvins.)
Closed Sun evg & Mon (Oct to May). (Penvins 1 km N.)
Post La Grée-Penvins, 56370 Sarzeau, Morbihan. Region Brittany.
Tel 97 67 34 26. Fax 97 67 38 43. Mich 62/C3. Map 1. (SE of Sarzeau.)

SARZEAU   Le Tournepierre

Simple restaurant/Cooking 2

A tiny, beamed dining room in a small stone cottage opposite the village church of St-Colombier (NE of Sarzeau). Rich, gutsy classical offerings: *fricassée de ris d'agneau et ses copeaux de foie gras de canard* (a bit too high-octane opulent for me), *noisettes d'agneau poêlés aux cocos blancs et son beurre de noix, chèvre chaud* and a dessert of *pommes rôti au miel* is a typical appetite-satisfying menu C.
Menus a(lunch)CDE. Cards Access, AE, Visa. (Rooms: see previous entry.)
Closed 15-31 Jan. 15-30 Nov. Sun evg & Mon (not July/Aug).
Post St-Colombier, 56370 Sarzeau, Morbihan. Region Brittany.
Tel 97 26 42 19. Mich 62/C2-C3. Map 1.

SAULZET-LE-CHAUD   Auberge de Montrognon

Comfortable restaurant/Cooking 2
Parking

By the end of 1994 Gilles and Florence Bettiol should have moved into their spanking new restaurant. Spanking good menus too – changed every three days. Dig into Gilles' varied kaleidoscope of specialities: among them *meunière de saumon au coulis de crustacés, vinaigrette de volaille aux myrtilles* and *rable de lapereau aux champignons des bois*.
Menus bCDE. Cards Acc, Visa. (Rooms: La Châtaigneraie, Ceyrat; 2 km N.)
Closed Tues evg. Wed. Region Massif Central (Auvergne).
Post Saulzet-le-Chaud, 63540 Romagnat, Puy-de-Dôme.
Tel 73 61 30 51. Fax 73 61 34 09. Mich 113/D2. Map 5.

A100frs & under. B100–135. C135–165. D165–250. E250–350. F350–500. G500+

SAUXILLANGES   Chalut

Very simple restaurant with basic rooms/Cooking 2
Garage

Have you a sweet tooth? Then head here for a 5-pudding dessert menu
(C). Most of us will be content with François Chalut's neo-classical and
regional concoctions: a *salade de lapereau tiède et sa ballotine*, *filet de
canard aux poires épicées*, Auvergne cheeses and *crème brulée aux
mûres* all appear on an aptly-named, multi-choice Menu Plaisir (C).
Menus aBCE. Rooms (6) CD. Cards Access, Visa.
Closed 1-25 Feb. 4-24 Sept. Sun evg & Mon (not July/Aug).
Post 63490 Sauxillanges, Puy-de-Dôme. Region Massif Central (Auvergne).
Tel 73 96 80 71. Fax 73 96 87 25. Mich 113/E3. Map 5.

SEMBLANCAY   Mère Hamard

Simple hotel/Cooking 2
Gardens/Parking

An elegant dining room and friendly owners – English-speaking Patrick
and Monique Pégué. The gardens and rear aspect are more eye-pleasing
than the modest façade. Nothing modest about the grub: a satisfying menu
B of *terrine de canard au foie gras*, rich *rognons de veau au Bourgueil et
à l'échalote, salade au Ste-Maure chaude* and a chocolate sweet.
Menus aBD. Rooms (9) D Cards Access, Visa.
Closed Sch. hols Feb/Nov. Sun evg & Mon (not hotel mid Apl-mid Oct).
Post pl. Eglise, 37360 Semblançay, Indre-et-Loir. Region Loire.
Tel 47 56 62 04. Fax 47 56 53 61. Mich 67/E3. Map 2.

SETE   Les Terrasses du Lido

Comfortable hotel/Cooking 2
Terrace/Swimming pool/Lift/Garage/Parking

West of Sète, on La Corniche (on D2 – not the N112), and with views of
the distant Med and famed Bassin de Thau. Cool elegance prevails: in
the dining room and on the flower-bedecked terrace beside the first-floor
pool. Colette Guironnet is *la cuisinière*. A welcome emphasis on fish
dishes (mainly classical) and *coquillages* from the nearby *bassin*.
Menus BDE. Rooms (8) EF. Disabled. Cards All.
Closed Feb. Rest: Sun evg & Mon (not July/Aug).
Post rond-point Europe, 34200 Sète, Hérault. Region Languedoc-Rouss.
Tel 67 51 39 60. Fax 67 53 26 96. Mich 156/B4. Map 5.

A100frs & under. B100–135. C135–165. D165–250. E250–350. F350–500. G500+

SOUSCEYRAC   Au Déjeuner de Sousceyrac

Comfortable restaurant with basic rooms/Cooking 2-3

Fluent English-speaking Laurence Piganiol and her brilliant young chef husband, Richard, do a great job in an unprepossessing village. A panelled dining room is a handsome backdrop. Starters – *terrine de boeuf froide en gelée* and a *brandade de morue et crispie de poitrine fumée* – were star quality; alas, meat dishes were undercooked to the point of being almost inedible; and desserts were flamboyantly top notch.
Menus bCD. Rooms (10) CD. Cards Access, Visa.
Closed Jan (rooms only). Feb. Sun evg and Mon (not July/Aug).
Post 46190 Sousceyrac, Lot. Region Dordogne.
Tel 65 33 00 56. Fax 65 33 04 37. Mich 125/E3. Map 5.

SOUVIGNY-EN-SOLOGNE   Perdrix Rouge

Comfortable restaurant/Cooking 2
Gardens

A super village with pretty "green" and unusual church with *caquetoir*. The English-speaking *patronne*, Dominique Beurienne, and the small, beamed dining room are also eye-pleasers. Husband, Jean-Noël, treads all cooking paths – witness *filet de sandre au beurre blanc, éminçé de boeuf au poivre vert* and *tarte tiède aux pommes façon Sologne*.
Menus aCDE. Cards Acc, Visa. (Rooms: Charmilles, Nouan-le-Fuzelier, SW.)
Closed 2-11 Jan. 24 Fe-15 Mar. 28 Au-5 Sep. Mon (not *midi* Ap-Oct). Tues.
Post 41600 Souvigny-en-Sologne, Loir-et-Cher. Region Loire.
Tel 54 88 41 05. Fax 54 88 05 56. Mich 69/F3. Map 2.

STAINVILLE   La Petite Auberge

Comfortable restaurant/Cooking 3

Why is it that guides like Gault Millau turn their backs on outposts of old-fashioned excellence like La Petite Auberge? Owner Mme Abalti first won a Michelin star in the 70s. Today, chef Philippe Perée conjures up the same classical culinary tricks. Refined *ancien régime* cooking with *filet de boeuf (avec pleurotes ou morilles), filet de poisson poché au champagne* and an unbeatable old-timer – *gâteau au chocolat*.
Menus CDE. Cards All. (Rooms: Ibis, N of St-Dizier; 18 km W on N4.)
Closed 21 July to 12 Aug. Fri evg. Sat. Sun evg.
Post 55500 Stainville, Meuse. Region Champagne-Ardenne.
Tel 29 78 60 10. Mich 39/F4. Map 3.

A100frs & under. B100–135. C135–165. D165–250. E250–350. F350–500. G500+

TAMNIES   Laborderie

Comfortable hotel/Cooking 2
Secluded/Terrace/Gardens/Swimming pool/Parking

A much modernised and extended *logis* "business" on a hilltop site with
fine views over the Beune Valley. A *Périgourdin* menu C includes feisty,
filling dishes such as *foie gras d'oie mi-cuit, cuisse de canarde confite
avec cèpes et pommes forestière, cabécou chaud* with an aromatic
walnut-oil salad and an inevitable *soufflé glace aux noix*.
Menus BCDE. Rooms (36) EF. Cards Access, Visa.
Closed Nov to Mar.
Post 24620 Tamniès, Dordogne. Region Dordogne.
Tel 53 29 68 59. Fax 53 29 65 31. Mich 124/A3. Map 5.

TARNAC   Voyageurs

Simple hotel/Cooking 2
Quiet

Readers have consistently praised this modest *logis*, tucked away in
adorable Corrèze. The same adjective could be tied to both Ghislaine
and Jean Deschamps – and to his classical and *Bourgeoise* cuisine.
Sauces with all beef dishes are considered "wonderful" and *escargots*
"the best ever". Autumn bonuses of *cèpes, pleurottes* and *girolles*.
Menus aBC. Rooms (17) CD. Cards Access, Visa.
Closed Mid Dec to mid Mar. Sun evg & Mon (Oct to May; not public hols).
Post 19170 Tarnac, Corrèze. Region Poitou-Charentes.
Tel 55 95 53 12. Fax 55 95 40 07. Mich 111/E2. Map 5.

TENCE   Grand Hôtel Placide

Comfortable hotel/Cooking 3
Gardens/Parking

A string of compliments from readers for the young, 4th-generation *chef/
patron*, Pierre-Marie Placide (trained by Chabran at Pont-de-l'Isère) and
his bubbling, English-speaking wife, Véronique. Modern and regional
masterpieces: dither over choices like lightly-smoked *cochon aux
lentilles de Puy* and *terrine chaude de cèpes, sauce au brebis frais*.
Menus bCDEF. Rooms (17) EF. Cards Access, AE, Visa.
Closed Mid Nov to mid Feb. Sun evg and Mon (not high season).
Post av. Gare, 43190 Tence, Haute-Loire. Region MC (Ardèche).
Tel 71 59 82 76. Fax 71 65 44 46. Mich 129/E2. Map 6.

A100frs & under. B100–135. C135–165. D165–250. E250–350. F350–500. G500+

THANNENKIRCH
Auberge la Meunière

Simple hotel/Cooking 2
Terrace/Parking

Timber predominates in this bright *logis* – both inside and out – and in the extensive Vosges forest views. Other pluses: a jacuzzi, sauna and billiards. Francesca Dumoulin is the hostess; husband, Jean-Luc, mans the stoves. Particularly tasty starters and sweets; among them *canapés de Munster chaud au cumin* and *parfait aux griottes de Thannenkirch.*
Menus aBCD. Rooms (15) EF. Cards Access, AE, Visa.
Closed Mid Nov to end Mar.
Post 68590 Thannenkirch, Haut-Rhin. Region Alsace.
Tel 89 73 10 47. Fax 89 73 12 31. Mich 61/D2. Map 3.

THIEZAC
Casteltinet

Comfortable hotel/Cooking 2
Terrace/Lift/Parking

Built a decade ago with extensive views and now less noise from the main road (new bypass to E). Nelly Macua is a helpful hostess; husband Faust is a creative chef. One dish alone – a bursting with flavour *escalopes de sandre, fondue de poireaux et fricassée de trompettes aux lardons* – made the trip worthwhile. Another bonus: great Auvergne cheeses.
Menus aBCD. Rooms (23) DE. Cards Access, Visa.
Closed Mid Oct to Xmas. Easter to mid May.
Post 15450 Thiézac, Cantal. Region Massif Central (Auvergne).
Tel 71 47 00 60. Mich 126/C2. Map 5.

THOMERY
Le Vieux Logis

Very comfortable restaurant with rooms/Cooking 2-3
Terrace/Swimming pool/Parking

Punt upstream on the Seine and Loing and you are in Impressionist *pays*. Monique-Antonia Plouvier's *hostellerie* is equally eye-pleasing. Jean-Luc Daligault continues the theme with vibrant modern cooking canvases: menu C could include *saumon croustillé en peau, polenta et jus de viande* and a luscious *crème brûlée à la cassonade et vanille Bourbon.* Another plus: a dozen sensibly-priced, first-class half-bottles of wine.
Menus CD. Rooms (14) F. Cards Access, AE, Visa. Region Ile de France.
Post 5 r. Sadi-Carnot, 77810 Thomery, Seine-et-Marne.
Tel (1) 60 96 44 77. Fax (1) 60 96 42 71. Mich 54/C2. Map 2.

A100frs & under. B100–135. C135–165. D165–250. E250–350. F350–500. G500+

THONES   Nouvel Hôtel du Commerce

Comfortable hotel/Cooking 2
Lift/Garage

Don't be put off by either the name or the façade. The 3rd-generation
owners of the 80-year-old *logis* are a cracking duo. Attractive Christiane
Bastard-Rosset is the welcoming hostess; husband Robert is an assertive
chef. Classical & *Savoyards* menus: the former could include a *mousse
de brochet soufflé*; the latter, a filling *farcement*.
Menus aBCDE. Rooms (25) DEF. Cards Access, Visa.
Closed Nov. Rest: Sun evg and Mon (not high season).
Post r. Clefs, 74230 Thônes, Haute-Savoie. Region Savoie.
Tel 50 02 13 66. Fax 50 32 16 24. Mich 118/Cl. Map 6.

TORCY   Vieux Saule

Very comfortable restaurant/Cooking 2-3
Terrace/Parking

South of Le Creusot. Marie-Madeleine Hervé is a helpful *patronne*; and
her husband Christian is a down-to-earth *cuisinier*. His Menu du Terroir
(C) is a four-course, appetite-quenching blockbuster with two especially
hearty *plats* – a *chausson d'escargots au beurre d'orties* and *estouffade
de joues de boeuf à la charolaise*. Excellent desserts.
Menus b(lunch)CDE. Cards Access, Visa. (Rooms: Novotel, Montchanin.)
Closed Sun evg. Mon. (Above easy 4 km drive to SE; use N80.)
Post 71210 Torcy, Saône-et-Loire. Region Burgundy.
Tel 85 55 09 53. Mich 87/F4. Map 3.

TORNAC   Demeures du Ranquet

Very comfortable hotel/Cooking 2-3
Quiet/Terrace/Gardens/Swimming pool/Parking

A heavenly wooded site south of Tornac. Anne Majourel is a self-taught
cuisinière and her Menu du Terroir (C) is the sole *FWF* qualifier: relish a
*tarte fine chaude à la brandade de morue; cuisse de canard confite
aux lentilles; salade au pélardon frit*; and a sweet. Lunch is perfect:
afterwards relax by the pool. Cheaper rooms? See two lines below.
Menus CDE. Rooms (10) G. D'bled. Cards Acc, Visa. (Porte des Cévennes.)
Closed Jan to Mar. Tues evg & Wed (mid Sept-mid June). (NW of Anduze.)
Post Tornac, 30140 Anduze, Gard. Regions Languedoc-Roussillon/Provence.
Tel 66 77 51 63. Fax 66 77 55 62. Mich 143/D4. Map 5.

A100frs & under. B100–135. C135–165. D165–250. E250–350. F350–500. G500+

TOURNUS   Terminus

Comfortable restaurant with rooms/Cooking 2
Terrace/Parking

Alongside both the N6 and station. A bright exterior, lined with boxes of
geraniums; the interior hides the exciting surprise of a 1900 Gasparini
mechanical organ – in the dining room! Michel Rigaud pulls out all the
stops in his classical/regional tunes. How about a prize-winning *gâteau
de foie blond* and an evocative *quenelle de brochet soufflé*?
Menus aBCDE. Rooms (13) DE. Cards Access, Visa.
Closed 3-25 Jan. 21-29 Nov. Tues evg and Wed (not July/Aug).
Post 21 av. Gambetta, 71700 Tournus, Saône-et-Loire. Region Lyonnais.
Tel 85 51 05 54. Fax 85 32 55 15. Mich 102/C1. Map 6.

TOURNUS   Terrasses

Comfortable restaurant with rooms/Cooking 2
Garage/Parking

Competition is fierce in this "intriguing" town (see *Mapaholics' France*;
map sheet 102). Like the entry above, the vine-covered, busy-lizzied
logis is also alongside the N6. Michel Carrette is a friendly host and
competent chef. Menu B (low-end) is bravura classical: we recall, with
relish, a pungent *cuisse de lapin en civet au Mâcon rouge*.
Menus aBCD. Rooms (18) E. Cards Access, Visa.
Closed 2-31 Jan. 19-25 June. Sun evg. Mon.
Post 18 av. 23-Janvier, 71700 Tournus, Saône-et-Loire. Region Lyonnais.
Tel 85 51 01 74. Fax 85 51 09 99. Mich 102/C1. Map 6.

TOURRETTES-SUR-LOUP   Petit Manoir

Comfortable restaurant/Cooking 2

A perched *cité*. The manoir is *petit*, accessible only on foot (for the sure-
footed only), 150 metres from the D2210. Françoise and Dominique
Taburet make you welcome at their old stone house. Chef Dominique is
a classical master: savour carefully sauced and prepared *croustade
d'escargots, beurre Provençal*; filling *aiguillettes de boeuf braisée aux
carottes*, cheese and a choice of desserts. English spoken.
Menus a(lunch)CD. Cards Access, AE, Visa. (Rooms: Floréal or Miramar.)
Closed 2nd half Feb. 15-30 Nov. Sun evg. Wed. (Above at Vence to E.)
Post 21 Gde Rue, 06140 Tourrettes-s-Loup, Alpes-Mar.
Tel 93 24 19 19. Mich 163/F2. Map 6. Region Côte d'Azur.

A100frs & under. B100–135. C135–165. D165–250. E250–350. F350–500. G500+

La TRINITE-SUR-MER   L'Azimut

Very comfortable restaurant/Cooking 2-3
Terrace

Blue and white umbrellas and awnings brighten up the stone-built house
overlooking the port. Marie-Hélène & Hervé Le Calvez have an
impressive culinary c.v. (in France & Switzerland). Menu du Terroir (B),
Menu Marin (C) and grills from the open fire. *Saumon, bar et haddock
fumés*, sardines stuffed with an artichoke cream, *saumon sauvage laqué
en peau au miel* and a lime charlotte is a typical menu C.
Menus ABCD. Cards Access, Visa. (Rooms: La Licorne, *sans rest*, Carnac.)
Post 56470 La Trinité-s-Mer, Morbihan. Region Brittany. (Above 5 km W.)
Tel 97 55 71 88. Fax 97 55 80 15. Mich 62/B2. Map 1.

Les TROIS-EPIS   Croix d'Or

Simple hotel/Cooking 1-2
Terrace/Parking

Views are the highlight at this small hotel, 2000 ft above sea-level and
only 14 km from Colmar. Catherine Bruley and Marianne Gebel stick
with a regional, classical and *Bourgeoise* repertoire – a formula which
includes *canard de Barbarie à l'orange*, *choucroute garnie* and the
buffet-style *hors d'oeuvre*, tagged *la table Hans im Schnokeloch*.
Menus aBCD. Rooms (12) DE. Cards Access, Visa.
Closed Mid Nov to mid Dec. Tues.
Post 68410 Les Trois-Epis, Haut-Rhin. Region Alsace.
Tel 89 49 83 55. Fax 89 49 87 14. Mich 61/D3. Map 3.

TURENNE   Maison des Chanoines

Simple restaurant with comfortable rooms/Cooking 2
Quiet/Terrace

A tiny, 16th-century stone-built house at the heart of the *bourg* – with a
shady terrace across the alley. Plenty of choice. A typical regional meal
could incorporate an inventive *terrine chaude aux noix, Roquefort et
poires*; a filling *médaillon de veau du Limousin sauce Quercynoise*;
and a refreshing *glace aux noix maison*. All appetising grub.
Menus b(lunch)CD. Rooms (3) EF. Cards Access, Visa.
Closed 11 Nov to end Feb. Tues evg and Wed (not July/Aug).
Post 19500 Turenne, Corrèze. Region Dordogne.
Tel 55 85 93 43. Mich 124/C2. Map 5.

A100frs & under. B100–135. C135–165. D165–250. E250–350. F350–500. G500+

TY SANQUER   Auberge Ty Coz

Comfortable restaurant/Cooking 1-2
Parking

Beside the D770 – 7 km N of Quimper and E of the N165 *voie express* –
the sombre, dark granite exterior is brightened-up no end by a splash of
flowers. Jean-Pierre Marrec's classical and *Bourgeois* wide-choice menus
brighten-up spirits and fill empty stomachs: oysters, mussels, smoked
salmon, *gigot, faux-filet, confit de canard* and similar.
Menus aCD. Cards Access, Visa. (Rooms: Ibis, NE corner of Quimper.)
Closed 25 Apl to 14 May. 5-24 Sept. Sun evg. Mon. (Above easy drive.)
Post Ty Sanquer, 29000 Quimper, Finistère. Region Brittany.
Tel 98 94 50 02. Mich 45/D2. Map 1.

VALBONNE   Auberge Fleurie

Comfortable restaurant/Cooking 2-3
Terrace/Parking

A top *RQP* favourite. Jean-Pierre Battaglia's *métier* is polished classical.
Good choice for each course on all menus. Even menu B has gems like
pâté de canard et ses aubergines confites, filet de rascasse au vin rouge
and *pavé de chocolat crème anglaise*. How rewarding it has been to see
Jean-Pierre succeed so well during the 18 years we've known him.
Menus BCD. Cards Access, Visa. (Rooms: Novotel/Ibis 6 km to SE.)
Closed Mid Dec to end Jan. Wed. (Both above at Sophia-Antipolis.)
Post 06560 Valbonne, Alpes-Maritimes. Region Côte d'Azur.
Tel 93 12 02 80. Fax 93 12 22 27. Mich 163/F2. Map 6. (On D3, to S.)

VALLOIRE   La Sétaz/Rest. Le Gastilleur

Comfortable hotel/Cooking 2
Gardens/Swimming pool/Parking

The large modern *logis* has two attractive amenities (see above). But, for
me, the first-floor dining room and the chef, whom I was fortunate
enough to meet, are better bonuses. Jacques Villard is a clever classicist:
a superlative *suprême de poulet avec morilles et champignons des bois*
and a lip-smacking dessert trolley remain vivid memories.
Menus bCD. Rooms (22) EF. Cards Access, AE, Visa.
Closed 25 Apl to 2 June. 25 Sept to 15 Dec.
Post 73450 Valloire, Savoie. Regions Hautes-Alpes/Savoie.
Tel 79 59 01 03. Fax 79 59 00 63. Mich 132/C1. Map 6.

A100frs & under. B100–135. C135–165. D165–250. E250–350. F350–500. G500+

VALS-LES-BAINS
Chez Mireille

Simple restaurant/Cooking 1-2

The sainted duo, Albert and Renée Mazet, now run their Hôtel Europe *sans rest* (an ideal base – a short walk away). This alternative, in the same *rue*, does very nicely thank you. A warm welcome from Colette Martin and classical temptations from husband Daniel. How about this permutation? A salad of fresh and smoked salmon; *petits rôtis de pintade à la crème de laurier*; cheese; and a *parfait aux marrons*. Or, *escargots au St-Péray* to start; then *filet de sole à la crème de homard*?
Menus ABCD. Cards Access, Visa. (Rooms: see text above.)
Post 3 r. J. Jaurès. 07600 Vals-les-Bains, Ardèche. Region MC (Ardèche).
Tel 75 37 49 06. Mich 129/E4. Map 6.

VALS-LES-BAINS
Vivarais

Comfortable hotel/Cooking 2-3
Terrace/Swimming pool/Lift/Parking

A fifth-generation chef, Christiane Guiliani-Brioude, is making a name for herself at the multi-floored, 30s-style spa hotel. Neo-classical delights mixed with reworked, old regional recipes: a typical meal could be a mysterious *salade picodonne*; *parmentier d'agneau en crépinettes* with a wild mushroom sauce; and a seductive sweet (choose from 14).
Menus CDE. Rooms (47) EFG. Cards All.
Closed Rest: Feb.
Post av. C. Expilly, 07600 Vals-les-Bains, Ardèche. Region MC (Ardèche).
Tel 75 94 65 85. Fax 75 37 65 47. Mich 129/E4. Map 6.

VANNES
La Morgate

Simple restaurant/Cooking 2

Vannes is a busy town and came close to not being included. This small beamed restaurant, between the cathedral and *gare*, is well worth the detour. Exceptionally helpful *patrons*, Vincenza and Daniel Le Blay. Chef Daniel stirs classical pots: tuck into the likes of 10 oysters, an invigorating *dos de bar rôti en peau*, *fleur de sel de Guérande*, cheese and a mouthwatering *fondant au chocolat amer, compote d'oranges*.
Menus ABCD. Cards Access, Visa. (Rooms: Anne de Bretagne, near *gare*.)
Closed Mar. Sun evg (out of seas). Mon. (Above 5 min walk N; garage.)
Post 21 r. La Fontaine, 56000 Vannes, Morbihan. Region Brittany.
Tel 97 42 42 39. Mich 62/C2. Map 1.

A100frs & under. B100–135. C135–165. D165–250. E250–350. F350–500. G 500+

VAUX La Petite Auberge

Comfortable restaurant/Cooking 2
Terrace/Parking

The duo Mansour took over the tiller here, a Yonne-side *auberge*, a few years back when the Barnabets paddled downstream to their new restaurant in Auxerre. Classical cuisine with safe, assured specialities such as *compote de lapereau en gelée, pièce de boeuf à la moutarde* and *île flottante, creme anglaise à la vanille.*
Menus CD. Cards Access, Visa. (Rooms: Ibis, A6 Auxerre-Sud exit.)
Closed Sun evg. Mon (not public hols). (Also several hotels in Auxerre.)
Post Vaux, 89290 Auxerre, Yonne. Region Burgundy. (6 km SE of Auxerre.)
Tel 86 53 80 08. Fax 86 53 65 62. Mich 72/A2. Map 2.

VELARS-SUR-OUCHE Auberge Gourmande

Very comfortable restaurant/Cooking 2
Terrace/Parking

The stone-built, flower-bedecked restaurant – rustic, yet refined – is west of Dijon and south of the A38 exit. Chef André Barbier and his wife, Louise, play a Burgundy fiddle: *escargots, oeufs pochés en meurette, coq au vin* and *jambon persillé dijonnais* are all on the menus. You'll not complain about lack of choice here – that's for sure.
Menus aCD. Cards Access, Visa. (Rooms: La Bonbonnière, Talant, 6 km E.)
Closed 15-31 Jan. Sun evg. Mon. (Above *sans rest* & quiet, W of Dijon.)
Post 21370 Velars-sur-Ouche, Côte-d'Or. Region Burgundy.
Tel 80 33 62 51. Fax 80 33 65 83. Mich 74/A4. Map 3.

VERCHAIX Rouge Gorge

Very simple restaurant/Cooking 1-2

Simplicity personified in a fabulous valley (be sure to head east to the dead-end *cirque* before or after your meal). *"Derrière la poste"* and between the village and D907. Françoise Thirvaudey tends the tiny *salle*; Roland, her chef husband, paints a classical *palette*: a *feuilleté de Chavignol sur salade verte, darne de saumon sauce tartare, plateau de fromages* and a *tarte* is a typical tempting menu C.
Menus ACD. Cards Access, Visa. (Rooms: simple Chalet Fleuri nearby.)
Closed 15-30 June. 15 Nov-6 Dec. Sun evg. Mon. (More hotels at Samoëns.)
Post 74440 Verchaix, Haute-Savoie. Region Savoie.
Tel 50 90 16 77. Mich 105/E3. Map 6.

A100frs & under. B100–135. C135–165. D165–250. E250–350. F350–500. G500+

VILLEFORT
Balme

Simple hotel/Cooking 2-3
Terrace/Garage

A small, handsome corner of old-world France. Michel Gomy, an English-speaking Parisian (and tennis nut), and his wife, Micheline, work hard to promote their adopted *pays* (Lozère) in the Far East every year. Touches of the Orient surface in Michel's work – together with modern creations and *Cévenols* treats. Mont Lozère-sized choice in menu C.
Menus BCD. Rooms (20) CDE. Cards All.
Closed 4-9 Oct. Mid Nov to mid Feb. Sun evg and Mon (out of season).
Post 48800 Villefort, Lozère. Region Massif Central (Cévennes).
Tel 66 46 80 14. Fax 66 46 85 26. Mich 142/C2. Map 5.

VILLENEUVE-DE-MARSAN
Europe

Comfortable hotel/Cooking 2-3
Terrace/Gardens/Swimming pool/Parking

I'm giving another chance to Robert and Maïté Garrapit (dropped from *FLE* because of Madame's wayward *addition* arithmetic). Robert has had health problems and now leaves the cooking to young Franck Augé, a *cuisine moderne* chef. Among typical menu B treats are *gelée de tête de veau*, *croustillant de filet de saumon*, *lapin farci au basilic et son jus réduit* and a masterly *gratin de fruits frais à la crème d'amandes*.
Menus BDE. Rooms (13) CDE. Cards All.
Post 40190 Villeneuve-de-Marsan, Landes. Region Southwest.
Tel 58 45 20 08. Fax 58 45 34 14. Mich 150/A1. Map 4.

VILLERS-BOCAGE
Trois Rois

Very comfortable restaurant with rooms/Cooking 2
Gardens/Parking

The modern *logis*, alongside the N175, will, one of these days, have a welcome bypass (has any ever taken so long to complete?). Chef Henri Martinotti is a classical champ: he's renowned for his *tripes à la mode de Caen*; he boxes clever with numerous fish dishes; an appetite-busting *tournedos sauté*; and an artful, heady *nougat glace au Cointreau*.
Menus BDE. Rooms (14) DEF. Cards All.
Closed Jan. Last wk June. Sun evg and Mon (not public hols).
Post 14310 Villers-Bocage, Calvados. Region Normandy.
Tel 31 77 00 32. Fax 31 77 93 25. Mich 31/F2. Map 1.

A100frs & under. B100–135. C135–165. D165–250. E250–350. F350–500. G500+

VITRAC   Auberge de la Tomette

Simple hotel/Cooking 1-2
Quiet/Terrace/Gardens/Swimming pool

A warm welcome from kindly Odette Chausi at her stone-built *logis* in chestnut-tree terrain. There's nothing prissy about husband Daniel's regional fare. From a trio of choices for each course on the regional menu B dig into *plats* such as *jambon de pays*, *bouriol à la crème fraîche*, *poulet farci aux pruneaux*, Auvergne cheeses and *tarte*.
Menus ABC. Rooms (20) E. Cards Access, AE, Visa.
Closed Jan to Mar.
Post 15220 Vitrac, Cantal. Region Massif Central (Auvergne).
Tel 71 64 70 94. Fax 71 64 77 11. Mich 126/A4. Map 5.

VITRAC   La Ferme

Simple restaurant/Cooking 1-2
Parking

An isolated site, 200 metres from the River Dordogne – at Caudon, east of Vitrac. *Périgourdine* fare at Dominique and Arlette Lacour-Escalier's long-established business. Gutsy grub: *soupe de campagne au pain de seigle*; *rillettes Sarladaises*; *faux-filet grillé* and *côtes d'agneau* are some of the non-cissy stomach fillers. Air-conditioned *salle*.
Menus ABC. Cards Access, Visa. (Rooms: Mas de Castel, 3 km S of Sarlat.)
Closed Oct. Xmas to end Jan. Sun evg (not high season). Mon.
Post Caudon-de-Vitrac, 24200 Sarlat-la-Canéda, Dordogne.
Tel 53 28 33 35. Mich 124/A3-B3. Map 5. Region Dordogne.

VITRAC   La Sanglière

Comfortable restaurant/Cooking 2
Gardens/Swimming pool/Parking

A pleasant drive west and north from Vitrac leads you to an isolated and elevated modern restaurant "home" in extensive gardens. Unrelenting regional dishes dominate the menus: *salade de magret ou gésier, cuisse de canard garnie* and a heavyweight *civet de gésier* are typical. A lightweight option is *flétan à l'oseille*. Top-notch desserts.
Menus ACDE. Cards Access, Visa. ((Rooms: see previous entry.)
Closed Jan. Feb. Sun evg and Mon (not July/Aug).
Post 24200 Vitrac, Dordogne. Region Dordogne.
Tel 53 28 33 51. Fax 53 28 52 31. Mich 124/A3-B3. Map 5.

A100frs & under. B100–135. C135–165. D165–250. E250–350. F350–500. G500+

VITRE   Hôtel Petit Billot/Rest. Petit Billot

Simple hotel and restaurant/Cooking 1-2

I first visited the simple, beamed restaurant when researching *En Route*, my *autoroute* guide (p109). Marie-Thérèse Lancelot welcomes you; husband Bernard works both *Bourgeoises* and classical chopping blocks (*billot* – block): *fromage de tête, rillettes de pays, terrine de maison et son chutney, escalope de veau Viennoise, crème caramel* and *île flottante* are typical. The hotel is run as a separate business by M. Fournel. Menus AB. Rooms (22) CDE. Cards Access, Visa. Map 1.
Closed Mid Dec to mid Jan. Fri evg (not high season). Sat. Hotel: Sun.
Post 5 pl. Mar. Leclerc, 35500 Vitré, Ille-et-Vilaine. Region Normandy.
Tel (R) 99 74 68 88. (H) 99 75 02 10. Fax 99 74 72 96. Mich 49/D3.

VIVONNE   La Treille

Very simple restaurant with very basic rooms/Cooking 2

A couple I love dearly will please all readers – especially those with few francs to spare. Geneviève Monteil is a bubbly angel; husband, chef Jacquelin, is an ardent supporter of both regional and classical *plats*. Refer to the regional lists for notes on *mouclade, farci Poitevin, bouilliture d'anguilles*, etc. (Better rooms: Mondial, quiet, *sans rest*, at Croutelle, N10, 14 km to N; and Ibis-Sud, near A10 exit 20.)
Menus ACD. Rooms (4) ABC. Cards Access, AE, Visa.
Closed Feb school hols. Wed (not midday in high season).
Post av. Bordeaux, 86370 Vivonne, Vienne. Region Poitou-Charentes.
Tel 49 43 41 13. Mich 95/D2. Map 5.

VONNAS   La Résidence des Saules/Rest. L'Ancienne Auberge

Comfortable hotel & simple restaurant/Cooking 2-3
Quiet (hotel)/Terrace

3-star chef George Blanc's bistro. Watch supplements on menu C (with 8 dessert options). Two finger-licking hits: a *pâté chaud feuilleté sauce porto* and *crème de champignons aux petites quenelles de volaille*. One disaster: overcooked, mushy *filet de lieu jaune à l'échalote*. Great service. Vonnas? No – "Blancville" ("*le business*" at every turn).
Menus a(lunch)CD. Rooms (6) G. Cards All. (Cheaper rooms: Beaujolais.)
Closed 2 Jan-9 Feb. Sun evg & Mon (not pub hols). (Mâcon, E bank Saône.)
Post pl. Marché, 01540 Vonnas, Ain. Region Lyonnais.
Tel 74 50 11 13. Fax 74 50 08 80. Mich 102/C3. Map 6.

A100frs & under. B100–135. C135–165. D165–250. E250–350. F350–500. G500+

WANGENBOURG   Parc

Comfortable hotel/Cooking 2
Quiet/Gardens/Swimming pool (indoor)/Tennis/Lift/Parking

A super site in wooded, hilly terrain nicknamed the Swiss Vosges. Owned by the same family for 150 years; the 6th generation, Elisabeth and Daniel Gihr, are spirited owners. A gym and sauna – and walks galore – to sweat off the inches after tucking into the likes of *truite au Riesling* and *civet de chevreuil* (infused with *essence de genièvre*).
Menus BCDE. Rooms (34) DEF. Cards Access, Visa.
Closed 2 Jan to 20 Mar. 2 Nov to 21 Dec.
Post 67710 Wangenbourg, Bas-Rhin. Region Alsace.
Tel 88 87 31 72. Fax 88 87 38 00. Mich 42/C4. Map 3.

WIMEREUX   Atlantic Hôtel

Very comfortable restaurant with rooms/Cooking 2-3
Lift/Parking

New owners, Aron and Marie-France Misan (he worked in London for many years), and young chef, Alain Morville, have blown bracing air through the first-floor restaurant. Classical offerings with emphasis on fish creations: *terrine de turbotin à la mousse de crabe* and *feuilleté de fruits de mer sauce corail* are typical. (Also cheaper *brasserie*.)
Menus bCD. Rooms (11) F. Cards Access, Visa.
Closed Dec to Feb. Sun evg and Mon (not July/Aug).
Post digue de mer, 62930 Wimereux, Pas-de-Calais. Region North.
Tel 21 32 41 01. Fax 21 87 46 17. Mich 2/A2. Map 2.

WIMEREUX   Epicure

Comfortable restaurant/Cooking 3

A small, whitewashed restaurant on the corner of the D940 and rue de la Gare. Claudette Carrée is *la patronne*; husband Philippe is the *cuisine moderne* magician. How welcome a mixture of eclectic flavours are: *cabillaud au cerfeuil et poivre de Sichuan* (a Chinese-cracker trick); *navarin de langoustines aux lentilles* (contemporary sleight of hand); and *tarte croustillant de banane et noix de coco* (Indies deception).
Menus CD. Cards Access, Visa. (Rooms: Ibis-Plage, Boulogne, 6 km D940.)
Closed 9-29 Oct. Sun evg. Wed. (Above easy drive to S.)
Post 1 r. Gare, 62930 Wimereux, Pas-de-Calais. Region North.
Tel 21 83 21 83. Mich 2/A2. Map 2.

A100frs & under. B100–135. C135–165. D165–250. E250–350. F350–500. G500+

Glossary of Menu Terms

A point medium rare

Abatis (Abattis) poultry giblets

Abats offal

Ablette freshwater fish

Abricot apricot

Acajou cashew nut

Acarne sea-bream

Achatine snail (from Far East)

Ache celery

Acidulé(e) acid

Affiné(e) improve; ripen, mature (common term with cheeses)

Africaine (à l') African style: with aubergines, tomatoes, *cèpes*

Agneau lamb

Agneau de pré-salé lamb fed on salt marshes

Agnelet young lamb

Agnès Sorel thin strips of mushroom, chicken and tongue

Agrumes citrus fruits

Aïado lamb with herbs and garlic

Aiglefin haddock

Aigre-doux sweet-sour

Aigrelette sharp sauce

Aiguillette thin slice

Ail garlic

Aile (Aileron) wing (winglet)

Aillade garlic sauce

Aïoli mayonnaise, garlic, olive oil

Airelles cranberries

Albert white cream sauce, mustard, vinegar

Albuféra *béchamel* sauce, sweet peppers

Alénois watercress-flavoured

Algues seaweed

Aligot purée of potatoes, cream, garlic, butter and fresh Tomme de Cantal (or Laguiole) cheese

Allemande a *velouté* sauce with egg yolks

Allemande (à l') German style: with sauerkraut and sausages

Allumette puff pastry strip

Alose shad (river fish)

Alouette lark

Alouette de mer sandpiper

Aloyau sirloin of beef

Alsacienne (à l') Alsace style: with sauerkraut, sausage and sometimes *foie gras*

Amande almond

Amande de mer small clam-like shellfish with nutty flavour

Amandine almond-flavoured

Amer bitter

Américaine (à l') Armoricaine (à l') sauce with dry white wine, cognac, tomatoes, shallots

Amourettes ox or calf marrow

Amuse-bouche appetiser

Amuse-geule appetiser

Amusette appetiser

Ananas pineapple

Anchoïade anchovy crust

Anchois anchovy

Ancienne (à l') in the old style

Andalouse (à l') Andalusian style: tomatoes, sweet red peppers, rice

Andouille smoked tripe sausage

Andouillette small chitterling (tripe) sausage

Aneth dill

Ange angel

Ange à cheval oyster, wrapped in bacon and grilled

Angevine (à l') Anjou style: with dry white wine, cream, mushrooms, onions

Anglaise (à l') plain boiled

Anguille eel

Anis aniseed

Anis étoile star anise (a star-shaped fruit)

Ansé basted with liquid

Arachide peanut

Araignée de mer spider crab

Arc en ciel rainbow trout

Ardennaise (à l') Ardenne style: with juniper berries

Arête fish bone

Argenteuil asparagus flavoured (usually soup)

Arlésienne stuffed tomatoes *à la provençale,* eggplant, rice

Armoricaine see *Américaine*

Aromates aromatic; either spicy or fragrant

Arômes à la gêne Lyonnais cow's or goat's cheese soaked in *marc*

Artichaut artichoke

Asperges asparagus

Assaisonné flavoured or seasoned with; to dress a salad

Assiette (de) plate (of)

Aubergine aubergine, eggplant

Aulx (plural of *ail*) garlic

Aumônière pancake drawn up into shape of beggar's purse

Aurore (à l') pink sauce, tomato flavoured

Auvergnate (à l') Auvergne style: with cabbage, sausage and bacon

Aveline hazelnut

Avocat avocado pear

Avoine oat(s)

Azyme unleavened (bread)

Baba au rhum sponge dessert with rum syrup

Baguette long bread loaf

Baie berry

Baigné bathed or lying in

Ballotine boned and stuffed poultry or meat in a roll

Banane banana

Bar sea-bass

Barbarie Barbary duck

Barbeau barbel

Barbeau de mer red mullet

Barbue brill

Barigoule (à la) brown sauce with artichokes and mushrooms

Baron de lapereau baron of young rabbit

Barquette boat-shaped pastry

Basilic basil

Basquaise (à la) Basque style:

Bayonne ham, rice and peppers

Bâtarde butter sauce, egg yolks

Bâtarde pain crusty white loaf

Batavia salad lettuce

Bâton stick-shaped bread loaf

Baudroie monkfish, anglerfish

Bavaroise bavarois mould, usually of custard, flavoured with fruit or chocolate. Can describe other dishes, particularly shellfish

Bavette skirt of beef

Baveuse runny

Béarnaise thick sauce with egg yolks, shallots, butter, white wine and tarragon vinegar

Béatilles (Malin de) sweetbreads, livers, kidneys, cockscombs

Beaugency *Béarnaise* sauce with artichokes, tomatoes, marrow

Bécasse woodcock

Bécassine snipe

Béchamel creamy white sauce

Beignet fritter

Beignet de fleur de courgette courgette flower in batter

Belle Hélène poached pear with ice cream and chocolate sauce

Belon oyster (see *Huîtres*)

Berawecka Christmas fruit bread stuffed with dried fruit, spices and laced with *kirsch*

Bercy sauce with white wine and shallots

Bergamot variety of pear or orange

Bergamote orange-flavoured sweet

Berlingot mint-flavoured sweet

Berrichone *Bordelaise* sauce

Bêtisse hard mint

Betterave beetroot

Beuchelle à la Tourangelle kidneys, sweetbreads, morels, cream and truffles

Beurre (Echiré) butter. (Finest butter from Poitou-Charentes)

Beurre blanc sauce with butter, shallots, wine vinegar and sometimes dry white wine

Beurre noir sauce with browned butter, vinegar, parsley

Biche female deer

Bière à la pression beer on tap

Bière en bouteille bottled beer

Bifteck steak

Bigarade (à la) orange sauce

Bigarreau type of cherry

Bigorneau winkle

Billy By mussel soup

Biscuit à la cuiller sponge finger

Bisque shellfish soup

Blanc (de volaille) white breast (of chicken): can describe white fish fillet or white vegetables

Blanchaille whitebait

Blanquette white stew

Blé corn or wheat

Blé noir buckwheat

Blettes Swiss chard

Blinis small, thick pancakes

Boeuf à la mode beef braised in red wine

Boeuf Stroganoff beef, sour cream, onions, mushrooms

Boletus type of edible fungi

Bombe ice cream

Bon-chrétien variety of pear

Bonne femme (à la) white wine sauce, shallots, mushrooms

Bonne femme (à la) potato, leek and carrot soup

Bordelais(e) (à la) Bordeaux style: brown sauce with shallots, red wine, beef bone marrow

Bouchée mouthful size (either a tart or *vol-au-vent*)

Boudin sausage-shaped mixture

Boudin blanc white coloured; pork and sometimes chicken

Boudin noir black pudding

Bouillabaisse Mediterranean fish stew and soup

Bouilliture eel stew (see *matelote d'anguilles*)

Bouillon broth, light consommé

Boulangère sauce of onions and potatoes

Boulette small ball of fish or meat

Bouquet prawn

Bouquet garni bunch of herbs used for flavouring

Bourdaloue hot poached fruit

Bourdelot whole apple pastry

Bourgeoise (à la) sauce of carrots, onions and diced bacon

Bourguignonne (à la) Burgundy style: red wine, onions, bacon and mushrooms

Bouribot duck stewed in red wine

Bourrache borage, a herb used in drinks and salads

Bourride creamy fish soup with *aïoli*

Bourriole sweet or savoury pancake

Boutargue grey mullet roe paste

Braisé braised

Brandade de morue salt cod

Brassado (Brassadeau) doughnut

Bréjaude cabbage and bacon soup

Brème bream

Brési thin slices dried beef

Bretonne sauce with celery, leeks, beans and mushrooms

Brioche sweet yeast bread

Broche (à la) spit roasted

Brochet pike

Brochette (de) meat or fish on a skewer

Brouet broth

Brouillade stewed in oil

Brouillés scrambled

Broutard young goat

Brugnon nectarine

Brûlé(e) toasted

Brunoise diced vegetables

Bruxelloise sauce with asparagus, butter and eggs

Bucarde cockle

Buccin whelk

Bugne sweet pastry fritter
Cabillaud cod
Cabri kid (young goat)
Cacahouète roasted peanut
Cacao cocoa
Caen (à la mode de) cooked in Calvados and white wine
Café coffee
Cagouille snail
Caille quail
Caillé milk curds
Caillette pork and vegetable faggot
Cajasse sweet pastry (sometimes made with black cherries)
Cajou cashew nut
Calissons almond and crystallised fruit sweetmeats
Calmar (Calamar) inkfish, squid
Campagne country style
Canapé a base, usually bread
Canard duck
Canard à la presse (Rouennaise) duck breast cooked in blood of carcass, red wine and brandy
Canard au sang see above
Canard sauvage wild duck
Caneton (canette) duckling
Cannelle cinnamon
Capilotade small bits or pieces
Capoum scorpion fish
Caprice whim (a dessert)
Capucine nasturtium
Carbonnade braised beef in beer, onions and bacon
Cardinal *béchamel* sauce, lobster, cream, red peppers
Cardon cardoon, a large celery-like vegetable
Cari curry powder
Caroline chicken consommé
Carpe carp
Carré d'agneau lamb chops from best end of neck
Carré de porc pork cutlets from best end of neck
Carré de veau veal chops from best end of neck
Carrelet flounder, plaice
Carvi caraway seed
Casse-croûte snack
Cassis blackcurrant
Cassolette small pan
Cassonade soft brown sugar
Cassoulet casserole of beans, sausage and/or pork, goose, duck
Caviar d'aubergine aubergine (eggplant) purée
Cebiche raw fish marinated in lime or lemon juice
Cedrat confit a crystallised citrus fruit
Céleri celery
Céleri-rave celeriac
Cendres (sous les) cooked (buried) in hot ashes
Cèpe fine, delicate mushroom
Cerfeuil chervil
Cerise (noire) cherry (black)
Cerneau walnut
Cervelas pork garlic sausage
Cervelle brains
Cévenole (à la) garnished with mushrooms or chestnuts
Champignons (des bois) mushrooms (from the woods)
Chanterelle apricot-coloured mushroom
Chantilly whipped cream, sugar
Chapon capon
Chapon de mer *rascasse* or scorpion fish
Charbon de bois (au) grilled on charcoal
Charcuterie cold meat cuts
Charcutière sauce with onions, white wine, gherkins
Charlotte sponge fingers, cream, etc.
Charolais (Charollais) beef
Chartreuse a mould shape
Chasse hunting (season)

Chasseur sauce with white wine, mushrooms, shallots
Châtaigne sweet chestnut
Chateaubriand thick fillet steak
Châtelaine garnish with artichoke hearts, tomatoes, potatoes
Chaud(e) hot
Chaudrée fish stew
Chausson pastry turnover
Chemise (en) pastry covering
Cheveux d'ange vermicelli
Chevreau kid (young goat)
Chevreuil roe-deer
Chevrier green haricot bean
Chichi doughnut-like fritter
Chicon chicory
Chicorée curly endive
Chiffonnade thinly-cut
Chinoise (à la) Chinese style: with bean sprouts and soy sauce
Chipirones see *calmars*
Choisy braised lettuce, sautéed potatoes
Choix (au) a choice of
Choron *Béarnaise* sauce with the addition of tomatoes
Chou (vert) cabbage
Choucroute (souring of vegetables) usually white cabbage (sauerkraut), peppercorns, boiled ham, potatoes and Strasbourg sausages
Chou-fleur cauliflower
Chou-frisé kale
Chou-pommé white-heart cabbage
Chou-rave kohlrabi
Chou-rouge red cabbage
Choux (au fromage) puffs (made of cheese)
Choux de Bruxelles Brussels sprouts
Choux (pâte à) pastry
Ciboule spring onion
Ciboulette chive
Cidre cider
Citron (vert) lemon (lime)

Citronelle lemon grass
Citrouille pumpkin
Civet stew
Civet de lièvre jugged hare
Clafoutis cherries in pancake batter
Claires oysters (see *Huîtres*)
Clamart with petits pois
Clou de girofle clove (spice)
Clouté (de) studded with
Clovisse small clam
Cocherelle type of mushroom
Cochon pig
Cochonailles pork products
Coco coconut; also small white bean
Cocotte (en) cooking pot
Coeur (de) heart (of)
Coeur de palmier palm heart
Coffret (en) in a small box
Coing quince
Colbert (à la) fish, dipped in milk, egg and breadcrumbs
Colin hake
Colvert wild duck
Compote stewed fruit
Concassé(e) coarsely chopped
Concombre cucumber
Condé creamed rice and fruit
Confiserie confectionery
Confit(e) preserved or candied
Confiture jam
Confiture d'oranges marmalade
Congre conger eel
Consommé clear soup
Contrefilet sirloin, usually tied for roasting
Copeaux literally shavings
Coq (au vin) chicken in red wine sauce (or name of wine)
Coque cockle
Coque (à la) soft-boiled or served in shell
Coquelet young cockerel
Coquillages shellfish
Coquille St-Jacques scallop

Corail (de) coral (of)
Coriandre coriander
Cornichon gherkin
Côte d'agneau lamb chop
Côte de boeuf side of beef
Côte de veau veal chop
Côtelette chop
Cotriade Brittany fish soup
Cou (d'oie) neck (of goose)
Coulemelle mushroom
Coulibiac hot salmon *tourte*
Coulis (de) thick sauce (of)
Coupe ice cream dessert
Courge pumpkin
Courgette baby marrow
Couronne circle or ring
Court-bouillon aromatic
   poaching liquid
Couscous crushed semolina
Crabe crab
Crambe sea kale
Cramique raisin or currant loaf
Crapaudine (à la) grilled game
   bird with backbone removed
Crapinaude bacon pancake
Craquelot herring
Crécy with carrots and rice
Crème cream
Crème (à la) served with cream or
   cooked in cream sauce
Crème à l'anglaise light custard
   sauce
Crème brûlée same, less sugar and
   cream, with praline (see *brûlée*)
Crème pâtissière custard filling
Crème plombières custard filling:
   egg whites, fresh fruit flavouring
Crémets fresh cream cheese,
   eaten with sugar and cream
Crêpe thin pancake
Crêpe dentelle thin pancake
Crêpe Parmentier potato pancake
Crêpe Suzette sweet pancake
   with orange liqueur sauce
Crépinette (de) wrapping (of)
Cresson watercress

Cressonière purée of potatoes and
   watercress
Crête cockscomb
Creuse long, thick-shelled oyster
Crevette grise shrimp
Crevette rose prawn
Cromesquis croquette
Croque Monsieur toasted cheese
   or ham sandwich
Croquette see *boulette*
Crosne Chinese/Japanese
   artichoke
Croustade small pastry mould
   with various fillings
Croûte (en) pastry crust (in a)
Croûtons bread (toast or fried)
Cru raw
Crudité raw vegetable
Crustacés shellfish
Cuillère soft (cut with spoon)
Cuisse (de) leg (of)
Cuissot (de) haunch (of)
Cuit cooked
Cul haunch or rear
Culotte rump (usually steak)
Cultivateur soup or chopped
   vegetables
Dariole basket-shaped pastry
Darne slice or steak
Dartois savoury or sweet filled
   puff-pastry rectangles
Datte date
Daube stew (various types)
Daurade sea-bream
Décaféiné decaffeinated coffee
Dégustation tasting
Délice delight
Demi-glace basic brown sauce
Demi-sel lightly salted
Diable seasoned with mustard
Diane (à la) peppered cream
   sauce
Dieppoise (à la) Dieppe style:
   white wine, cream, mussels,
   shrimps
Dijonnaise (à la) with mustard

sauce

Dijonnaise (à la belle) sauce made from blackcurrants

Dinde young hen turkey

Dindon turkey

Dindonneau young turkey

Diot pork and vegetable sausage

Dodine (de canard) cold stuffed duck

Dorade sea-bream

Doré cooked until golden

Doria with cucumbers

Douceurs desserts

Douillon pear wrapped in pastry

Doux (douce) sweet

Dragée sugared almond

Du Barry cauliflower soup

Duxelles chopped mushrooms, shallots and cream

Echalote shallot

Echine loin (of pork)

Echiquier in checkered fashion

Eclade (de moules) (mussels) cooked over pine needles

Ecrasé crushed (as with fruit)

Ecrevisses freshwater crayfish

Ecuelle bowl or basin

Effiloché(e) frayed, thinly sliced

Emincé thinly sliced

Encornet cuttlefish, squid

Encre squid ink, used in sauces

Endive chicory

Entrecôte entrecôte, rib steak

Entremets sweets

Epaule shoulder

Eperlan smelt (small fish)

Epice spice

Epinard spinach

Epis de maïs sweetcorn

Escabèche fish (or poultry) marinated in *court-bouillon*; served cold

Escalope thinly cut (meat or fish)

Escargot snail

Espadon swordfish

Estouffade stew with onions, herbs, mushrooms, red or white wine (perhaps garlic)

Estragon tarragon flavoured

Esturgeon sturgeon

Etrille crab

Etuvé(e) cooked in little water or in ingredient's own juices

Exocet flying fish

Façon cooked in a described way

Faisan(e) pheasant

Fane green top of root vegetable

Far Brittany prune flan

Farci(e) stuffed

Farine flour

Faux-filet sirloin steak

Favorite a garnish of *foie gras* and truffles

Favouille spider crab

Fécule starch

Fenouil fennel

Fenouil marin samphire

Féra lake fish, like salmon.

Ferme (fermier) farm (farmer)

Fermière mixture of onions, carrots, turnips, celery, etc.

Feuille de vigne vine leaf

Feuilleté light flaky pastry

Fève broad bean

Ficelle (à la) tied in a string

Ficelles thin loaves of bread

Figue fig

Filet fillet

Financière (à la) Madeira sauce with truffles

Fine de claire oyster (see *Huîtres*)

Fines herbes mixture of parsley, chives, tarragon, etc.

Flageolet kidney bean

Flamande (à la) Flemish style: bacon, carrots, cabbage, potatoes and turnips

Flambé flamed

Flamiche puff pastry tart

Flan tart

Flétan halibut

Fleur (de courgette) flower

(courgette flower, usually stuffed)

Fleurons puff pastry crescents

Flie small clam

Florentine with spinach

Flûte long thin loaf of bread

Foie liver

Foie de veau calves liver

Foie gras goose liver

Foies blonds de volaille chicken liver mousse

Foin (dans le) cooked in hay

Fond (base) basic stock

Fondant see *boulette*: a bon-bon

Fond d'artichaut artichoke heart

Fondu(e) (de fromage) melted (cheese with wine)

Forestière bacon and mushrooms

Fouace dough cakes

Four (au) baked in oven

Fourré stuffed

Frais (Fraîche) fresh or cool

Fraise strawberry

Fraise des bois wild strawberry

Framboise raspberry

Française (à la) mashed potato filled with mixed vegetables

Frangipane almond custard filling

Frappé frozen or ice cold

Friandises sweets (*petits fours*)

Fricadelle minced meat ball

Fricandeau slice topside veal

Fricassée braised in sauce of butter, egg yolks and cream

Frisé(e) curly

Frit fried

Frite chip

Fritot fritter

Frittons see *grattons*

Friture small fried fish

Frivolle fritter

Froid cold

Fromage cheese

Fromage de tête brawn

Fruit de la passion passion fruit

Fruits confits crystallised fruit

Fruits de mer seafood

Fumé smoked

Fumet fish stock

Galantine cooked meat, fish or vegetables in jelly, served cold

Galette pastry, pancake or cake

Galimafrée (de) stew (of)

Gamba large prawn

Ganache chocolate and *crème fraîche* mixture used to fill cakes

Garbure (Garbue) vegetable soup

Gardiane beef stew with red wine, black olives, onions and garlic

Gardon small roach

Gargouillau pear tart or cake

Garni(e) with vegetables

Garniture garnish

Gasconnade leg of lamb roasted with anchovies and garlic

Gâteau cake

Gâtinaise (à la) with honey

Gaufre waffle

Gayette faggot

Gelée aspic jelly

Géline chicken

Gendarme smoked or salted herring: flat, dry sausage

Genièvre juniper

Génoise rich sponge cake

Gentiane liqueur made from gentian flowers

Germiny sorrel and cream soup

Germon long-fin tuna

Gésier gizzard

Gibelotte see *fricassée*

Gibier game

Gigot (de) leg of lamb. Can describe other meat and fish

Gigot brayaude leg of lamb in white wine with red beans and cabbage

Gigue (de) shank (of)

Gingembre ginger

Girofle clove

Girolle apricot-coloured fungus

Givré frosted

Glacé iced. Crystallised. Glazed

Glace ice cream

Gnocchi dumplings of semolina, potato or *choux* paste

Godard see *financière (à la)*

Gougère round-shaped, egg and cheese *choux* pastry

Goujon gudgeon

Goujonnettes (de) small fried pieces (of)

Gourmandises sweetmeats; can describe *fruits de mer*

Gousse (de) pod or husk (of)

Graine (de capucine) seed (nasturtium)

Graisse fat

Graisserons duck or goose fat scratchings

Grand Veneur sauce with vegetables, wine vinegar, redcurrant jelly and cream

Granité water ice

Gratin browned

Gratin Dauphinois potato dish with cream, cheese and garlic

Gratin Savoyard potato dish with cheese and butter

Gratiné(e) sauced dish browned with butter, cheese, breadcrumbs, etc.

Gratinée Lyonnaise clear soup with port, beaten egg and cheese (grilled brown)

Grattons pork fat scratchings

Gravette oyster (see *Huîtres*)

Grecque (à la) cooked vegetables served cold

Grelette cold sauce, based on whipped cream, for fish

Grenade pomegranate

Grenadin thick veal escalope

Grenouille (cuisses de grenouilles) frog (frogs' legs)

Gribiche mayonnaise sauce with gherkins, capers, hardboiled egg yolks and herbs

Grillade grilled meat

Grillé(e) grilled

Grilot small bulb onion

Griotte (Griottine) bitter red cherry

Griset mushroom

Grisotte parasol mushroom

Grive thrush

Grondin gurnard, red gurnet

Gros sel coarse rock or sea salt

Groseille à maquereau gooseberry

Groseille noire blackcurrant

Groseille rouge redcurrant

Gruyère hard, mild cheese

Gyromitre fungus

Habit vert dressed in green

Hachis minced or chopped-up

Hareng herring
    à l'huile cured in oil
    fumé kippered
    salé bloater
    saur smoked

Haricot bean

Haricot blanc dried white bean

Haricot rouge red kidney bean

Haricot vert green/French bean

Hochepot thick stew

Hollandaise sauce with butter, egg yolk and lemon juice

Homard lobster

Hongroise (à la) Hungarian style: sauce with tomato and paprika

Hors d'oeuvre appetisers

Huile oil

Huîtres oysters
    Les claires: the oyster-fattening beds in Marennes terrain (part of the Charente Estuary, between Royan and Rochefort, in Poitou-Charentes).
    Flat-shelled oysters:
    Belons (from the River Belon in Brittany);
    Gravettes (from Arcachon in the Southwest);
    both the above are cultivated in

their home oyster beds.
Marennes are those transferred from Brittany and Arcachon to *les claires*, where they finish their growth.

Dished oysters (sometimes called *portugaises*):
these breed mainly in the Gironde and Charente estuaries; they mature at Marennes.

Fines de claires and *spéciales* are the largest; *huîtres de parc* are standard sized.

All this lavish care covers a time span of two to four years.

Hure (de) head (of). Brawn. Jellied
Ile flottante unmoulded soufflé of beaten egg white and sugar
Imam bayeldi aubergine with rice, onions and sautéed tomatoes
Impératrice (à la) desserts with candied fruits soaked in kirsch
Indienne (à l') Indian style: with curry powder
Infusion herb tea
Italienne (à l') Italian style: artichokes, mushrooms, pasta
Jalousie latticed fruit or jam tart
Jambon ham
Jambonneau knuckle of pork
Jambonnette (de) boned and stuffed (knuckle of ham or poultry)
Jardinière diced fresh vegetables
Jarret de veau stew of shin of veal
Jarreton cooked pork knuckle
Jerez sherry
Jésus de Morteau smoked Jura pork sausage
Joinville *velouté* sauce with cream, crayfish tails and truffles
Joue (de) cheek (of)
Judru cured pork sausage
Julienne thinly-cut vegetables: also ling (cod family, see *lingue*)

Jus juice
Kaki persimmon fruit
Lait milk
Laitance soft roe
Laitue lettuce
Lamproie eel-like fish
Langouste spiny lobster or crawfish
Langoustine Dublin Bay prawn
Langue tongue
Languedocienne (à la) mushrooms, tomatoes, parsley garnish
Lapereau young rabbit
Lapin rabbit
Lapin de garenne wild rabbit
Lard bacon
Lard de poitrine fat belly of pork
Lardons strips of bacon
Laurier bay-laurel, sweet bay leaf
Lavaret lake fish, like salmon trout
Lèche thin slice
Léger (Légère) light
Légume vegetable
Lieu cod-like fish
Lièvre hare
Limaçon snail
Limande lemon sole
Limon lime
Lingue ling (cod family)
Lit bed
Livèche lovage (like celery)
Longe loin
Lotte de mer monkfish, anglerfish
Lotte de rivière (de lac) burbot, a river (or lake) fish, like eel; liver a great delicacy
Lou magret see *magret*
Loup de mer sea-bass
Louvine (loubine) grey mullet, like a sea-bass (Basque name)
Lyonnaise (à la) Lyonnais style: sauce with wine, onions, vinegar
Macédoine diced fruit or veg
Mâche lamb's lettuce; small, dark, green leaf
Macis mace (spice)

Madeleine tiny sponge cake

Madère sauce *demi-glace* and Madeira wine

Madrilène Madrid style: with chopped tomatoes

Magret (de canard) breast (of duck); now used for other poultry

Maigre fish, like sea-bass

Maigre non-fatty, lean

Maillot carrots, turnips, onions, peas and beans

Maïs maize flour

Maison (de) of the restaurant

Maître d'hôtel sauce with butter, parsley and lemon

Maltaise an orange flavoured *hollandaise* sauce

Manchons see *goujonnettes*

Mandarine tangerine

Mangetout edible peas and pods

Mangue mango

Manière (de) style (of)

Maquereau mackerel

Maraîchère (à la) market-gardener style: *velouté* sauce with vegetables

Marais marsh or market-garden

Marbré(e) marbled

Marc pure spirit

Marcassin young wild boar

Marché market

Marchand de vin sauce with red wine, chopped shallots

Marée fresh seafood

Marengo tomatoes, mushrooms, olive oil, white wine, garlic, herbs

Marennes (blanche) flat-shelled oyster (see *Huîtres*)

Marennes (verte) green shell

Mareyeur fishmonger

Marinade, Mariné(e) pickled

Marinière see *moules*

Marjolaine marjoram

Marjolaine almond and hazelnut

sponge cake with chocolate cream and praline

Marmite stewpot

Marquise (de) water ice (of)

Marrons chestnuts

Marrons glacés crystallised sweet chestnuts

Massepains marzipan cakes

Matelote (d'anguilles) freshwater red wine fish stew (of eels)

Matignon mixed vegetables, cooked in butter

Mauviette lark

Médaillion (de) round piece (of)

Mélange mixture or blend

Melba (à la) poached peach, with vanilla ice cream, raspberry sauce

Mélisse lemon-balm (herb)

Ménagère (à la) housewife style: onions, potatoes, peas, turnips and carrots

Mendiant (fruits de) mixture of figs, almonds and raisins

Menthe mint

Mer sea

Merguez spicy grilled sausage

Merlan whiting (in Provence the word is used for hake)

Merle blackbird

Merlu hake

Merluche dried cod

Mérou grouper (sea fish)

Merveilles hot, sugared fritters

Mesclum mixture of salad leaves

Meunière (à la) sauce with butter, parsley, lemon (sometimes oil)

Meurette red wine sauce

Miel honey

Mignardises *petits fours*

Mignon (de) small round piece

Mignonette coarsley ground white pepper

Mijoté(e) cooked slowly in water

Milanaise (à la) Milan style: dipped in breadcrumbs, egg, cheese

Millassou sweet maize flour flan

Mille-feuille puff pastry with numerous thin layers

Mimosa chopped hardboiled egg

Mique stew of dumplings

Mirabeau anchovies, olives

Mirabelles golden plums

Mirepoix cubes carrot, onion, ham

Miroir smooth

Miroton (de) slices (of)

Mitonée (de) soup (of)

Mode (à la) in the manner of

Moelle beef marrow

Mojettes pulse beans in butter

Moka coffee

Montagne (de) from mountains

Montmorency with cherries

Morilles edible, dark brown, honeycombed fungi

Mornay cheese sauce

Morue cod

Morvandelle (jambon à la) ham with a piquant cream sauce, wine and wine vinegar (from Burgundy)

Morvandelle rapée baked eggs, cream and cheese, mixed with grated potato (from Burgundy's Morvan)

Mostèle (Gâteau de) cod mousse

Mouclade mussel stew

Moule mussel

Moules marinière mussels cooked in white wine and shallots

Mourone Basque red bell pepper

Mourtayrol stew with beef, chicken, ham, vegetables and bread (from the Auvergne)

Mousse cold, light, finely-minced ingredients with cream and egg whites

Mousseline *hollandaise* sauce with whipped cream

Mousseron edible fungus

Moutarde mustard

Mouton mutton

Mulet grey mullet

Mûre mulberry

Mûre sauvage (de ronce) blackberry

Muscade nutmeg

Museau de porc (de boeuf) sliced muzzle of pork (beef) with shallots and parsley in *vinaigrette*

Myrtille bilberry (blueberry)

Mystère a meringue desert with ice cream and chocolate; also cone-shaped ice cream

Nage (à la) *court-bouillon*: aromatic poaching liquid

Nantua sauce for fish with crayfish, white wine, tomatoes

Nappé sauce covered

Nature plain

Navarin stew, usually lamb

Navets turnips

Nègre dark (e.g. chocolate)

Newburg sauce with lobster, brandy, cream and Madeira

Nid nest

Nivernaise (à la) Nevers style: carrots and onions

Noilly sauce based on vermouth

Noisette hazelnut

Noisette sauce of lightly browned butter

Noisette (de) round piece (of)

Noix nuts

Noix (de veau) topside of leg (veal)

Normande (à la) Normandy style: fish sauce with mussels, shrimps, mushrooms, eggs and cream

Nouille noodle

Nouveau (nouvelle) new or young

Noyau sweet liqueur from crushed stones (usually cherries)

Oeufs à la coque soft-boiled eggs

Oeufs à la neige see *île flottante*

Oeufs à la poêlé fried eggs

Oeufs brouillés scrambled eggs

Oeufs durs hard-boiled eggs
Oeufs moulés poached eggs
Oie goose
Oignon onion
Oison rôti roast gosling
Omble chevalier freshwater char;
looks like large salmon trout
Ombre grayling
Ombrine fish, like sea-bass
Omelette brayaude omelette with
bacon, cream, potatoes and
cheese
Onglet flank of beef
Oreille (de porc) ear (pig's)
Oreillette sweet fritter, flavoured
with orange flower water
Orge (perlé) barley (pearl)
Origan oregano (herb)
Orléannaise (à l') Orléans style:
chicory and potatoes
Orly dipped in butter, fried and
served with tomato sauce
Ortie nettle
Ortolan wheatear (thrush family)
Os bone
Oseille sorrel
Osso bucco à la Niçoise veal
braised with orange zest,
tomatoes, onions and garlic
Ouillat Pyrénées soup; onions,
tomatoes, goose fat, garlic
Oursins sea-urchins
Pageot sea-bream
Paillarde (de veau) grilled veal
escalope
Paille fried potato stick
Pailletté (de) spangled (with)
Paillettes pastry straws
Pain bread
  bis brown bread
  de campagne round white loaf
  d'épice spiced honey cake
  de mie square white loaf
  de seigle rye bread
  doré bread soaked in milk and
eggs and fried

  entier/complet wholemeal
  grillé toast
Paleron shoulder
Palmier palm-shaped sweet puff
pastry
Palmier (coeur de) palm (heart)
Palombe wood pigeon
Palomête fish, like sea-bass
Palourde clam
Pamplemousse grapefruit
Pan bagna long split bread roll,
brushed with olive oil and filled
with olives, peppers, anchovies,
onions, lettuce
Panaché mixed
Panade flour or bread paste
Panais parsnip
Pané(e) breadcrumbed
Panier basket
Panisse fried chickpea or maize
fritter
Pannequets like *crêpes*, smaller
and thicker
Pantin pork filled small pastry
Paon peacock
Papeton fried or puréed
aubergines, arranged in ring
mould
Papillon small oyster (butterfly)
from the Atlantic coast
Papillote (en) cooked in oiled
paper (or foil)
Paquets (en) parcels
Parfait (de) a mousse (of)
Paris-Brest cake of *choux* pastry,
filled with butter cream, almonds
Parisienne (à la) leeks, potatoes
Parmentier potatoes
Pascade sweet or savoury pancake
Pascaline (de) see *quenelle* (of)
Passe Crassane variety of pear
Passe-pierres seaweed
Pastèque watermelon
Pastis (sauce au) aniseed based
Pâté minced meats (of various
types) baked. Usually served

cold

Pâte pastry, dough or batter

Pâte à choux cream puff pastry

Pâte brisée short crust pastry

Pâte d'amande almond paste

Pâté en croûte baked in pastry crust

Pâtes (fraîches) fresh pasta

Pâtés (petits) à la Provençale anchovy and ham turnovers

Pâtisserie pastry

Pâtisson custard marrow

Patte claw, foot, leg

Pauchouse see *pochouse*

Paupiettes thin slices of meat of fish, used to wrap fillings

Pavé (de) thick slice (of)

Pavot (graines de) poppy seeds

Paysan(ne) (à la) country style

Peau (de) skin (of)

Pêche peach

Pêcheur fisherman

Pèlerine scallop

Perce-pierre samphire (edible sea fennel)

Perche perch

Perdreau young partridge

Perdrix partridge

Périgourdine (à la) goose liver and sauce *Périgueux*

Périgueux sauce with truffles and Madeira

Persil parsley

Persillade mixture of chopped parsley and garlic

Petit-beurre biscuit made with butter

Petit gris small snail

Petite marmite strong consommé with toast and cheese

Petits fours miniature cakes, biscuits, sweets

Petits pois tiny peas

Pétoncle small scallop

Pets de nonne small soufflé fritters

Picanchâgne (piquenchâgne) a

pear tart with walnut topping

Picholine large green table olives

Pied de cheval large oyster

Pied de mouton blanc creamcoloured mushroom

Pied de porc pig's trotter

Pigeonneau young pigeon

Pignon pine nut

Pilau rice dish

Pilon drumstick

Piment (doux) pepper (sweet)

Pimpernelle burnet (salad green)

Pintade (pintadeau) guinea-fowl (young guinea-fowl)

Piperade omelette or scrambled eggs with tomatoes, peppers, onions and, sometimes, ham

Piquante (sauce) sharp-tasting sauce with shallots, capers, wine

Piqué larded

Pissenlit dandelion leaf

Pistache green pistachio nut

Pistil de safran saffron (*pistil* from autumn-flowering crocus)

Pistou vegetable soup bound with *pommade*

Plateau (de) plate (of)

Pleurote mushroom

Plie franche plaice

Plombières sweet with vanilla ice cream, *kirsch,* candied fruit and *crème chantilly*

Pluche sprig

Pluvier plover

Poché(e) Pochade poached

Pochouse freshwater fish stew with white wine

Poêlé fried

Pogne sweet brioche flavoured with orange flower water

Poire pear

Poireau leek

Pois peas

Poisson fish

Poitrine breast

Poitrine fumée smoked bacon

143

Poitrine salée unsmoked bacon

Poivrade a peppery sauce with wine vinegar, cooked vegetables

Poivre noir black pepper

Poivre rose red pepper

Poivre vert green pepper

Poivron (doux) pepper (sweet)

Pojarsky minced meat or fish, cutlet shaped and fried

Polenta boiled maize flour

Polonaise Polish style: with buttered breadcrumbs, parsley, hard-boiled eggs

Pommade thick, smooth paste

Pomme apple

Pommes de terre potatoes
　à l'anglaise boiled
　allumettes thin and fried
　boulangère sliced with onions
　brayaude baked
　château roast
　dauphine croquettes
　duchesse mashed with egg yolk
　en l'air hollow potato puffs
　frites fried chips
　gratinées browned with cheese
　Lyonnaise sautéed with onions
　vapeur boiled

Pomponette savoury pastry

Porc (carré de) loin of pork

Porc (côte de) pork chop

Porcelet suckling pig

Porchetta whole roasted young pig, stuffed with offal, herbs, garlic

Porto (au) port

Portugaise (à la) Portuguese style: fried onions and tomatoes

Portugaises oysters with long, deep shells (see *Huîtres*)

Potage thick soup

Pot-au-crème dessert, usually chocolate or coffee

Pot-au-feu clear meat broth served with the meat

Potée heavy soup of cabbage, beans, etc.

Potimarron pumpkin

Potjevleisch northern terrine of mixed meats (rabbit, pork, veal)

Pouchouse see *pochouse*

Poularde large hen

Poulet chicken

Poulet à la broche spit-roasted chicken

Poulet Basquaise chicken with tomatoes and peppers

Poulet de Bresse corn-fed, white flesh chicken

Poulet de grain grain-fed chicken

Poulette young chicken

Poulpe octopus

Pounti small, egg-based, savoury soufflé with bacon or prunes

Pourpier purslane (salad green, also flavours dishes); a weed

Pousse-pierre edible seaweed

Poussin small baby chicken

Poutargue grey mullet roe paste

Praire small clam

Praline caramelised almonds

Praslin caramelised

Pré-salé (agneau de) lamb raised on salt marshes

Primeur young vegetable

Princesse *velouté* sauce, asparagus tips and truffles

Printanièr(e) (à la) garnish of diced vegetables

Produit (de) product (of)

Profiterole *choux* pastry, custard filled puff

Provençale (à la) Provençal style: tomatoes, garlic, olive oil, etc.

Prune plum

Pruneau prune

Purée mashed

Quasi (de veau) thick part of loin of veal (chump)

Quatre-épices four blended ground spices (ginger, cloves, nutmeg and white pepper)

Quatre-quarts cake made with equal weights of eggs, butter, sugar and flour (four-quarters)

Quenelle light dumpling of fish or poultry

Quetsche small, purple plum

Queue tail

Queue de boeuf oxtail

Quiche (Lorraine) open flan of cheese, ham or bacon

Râble de lièvre (lapin) saddle of hare (rabbit)

Raclette scrapings from specially made and heated cheese

Radis radish

Ragoût stew, usually meat, but can describe other ingredients

Raie (bouclée) skate (type of)

Raifort horseradish

Raisin grape

Raïto sauce served over grilled fish (red wine, onions, tomatoes, herbs, olives, capers and garlic)

Ramequin see *cocotte (en)*

Ramier wood pigeon

Rapé(e) grated or shredded

Rascasse scorpion fish

Ratafia brandy and unfermented Champagne. Almond biscuit

Ratatouille aubergines, onions, courgettes, garlic, red peppers and tomatoes in olive oil

Ratte de Grenoble white potato

Raves (root) turnips, radishes,etc.

Ravigote sauce with onions, herbs, mushrooms, wine vinegar

Ravioles ravioli

Ravioles à la Niçoise pasta filled with meat or Swiss chard and baked with cheese

Ravioles du Royans small ravioli pasta with goat cheese filling (from the terrain under the western edges of the Vercors)

Régence sauce with wine, truffles, mushrooms

Réglisse liquorice

Reine chicken and cream

Reine-Claude greengage

Reinette type of apple

Réjane garnish of potatoes, bone-marrow, spinach and artichokes

Rémoulade sauce of mayonnaise, mustard, capers, herbs, anchovy

Rillettes (d'oie) potted pork (goose)

Rillons small cubes of fat pork

Ris d'agneau lamb sweetbreads

Ris de veau veal sweetbreads

Rissettes small sweetbreads

Rivière river

Riz rice

Riz à l'impératrice cold rice pudding

Riz complet brown rice

Riz sauvage wild rice

Robe de chambre jacket potato

Robert sauce *demi-glace*, white wine, onions, vinegar, mustard

Rocambole wild garlic

Rognon kidney

Rognonnade veal and kidneys

Romanoff fruit marinated in liqueur; mostly strawberries

Romarin rosemary

Roquette salad green

Rosé meat cooked to pink stage

Rosette large pork sausage

Rossini see *tournedos*

Rôti roast

Rouelle (de) round piece or slice

Rouget red mullet

Rouget barbet red mullet

Rouget grondin red gurnard (larger than red mullet)

Rouille orange-coloured sauce with peppers, garlic and saffron

Roulade (de) roll (of)

Roulé(e) rolled (usually *crêpe*)

Rousette rock salmon; dog fish

Roux flour, butter base for sauces

Royan fresh sardine

Rutabaga swede
Sabayon sauce of egg yolks, wine
Sablé shortbread
Sabodet Lyonnais sausage of pig's head, pork, beef; served hot
Safran saffron (see *pistil de*)
Sagou sago
Saignant(e) underdone, rare
Saindoux lard
St-Germain with peas
St-Hubert sauce *poivrade*, bacon and cooked chestnuts
St-Jacques (coquille) scallop
St-Pierre John Dory
Saisons (suivant) depending on the season of the year
Salade Niçoise tomatoes, beans, potatoes, black olives, anchovy, lettuce, olive oil, perhaps tuna
Salade panachée mixed salad
Salade verte green salad
Salé salted
Salicornes marsh samphire (edible sea-fennel)
Salmigondis meat stew
Salmis red wine sauce
Salpicon meat or fish and diced vegetables in a sauce
Salsifis salsify (vegetable)
Sanciau thick sweet or savoury pancake
Sandre freshwater fish, like perch
Sang blood
Sanglier wild boar
Sanguine blood orange
Sanguines mountain mushrooms
Santé potato and sorrel soup
Sarcelle teal
Sarrasin buckwheat
Sarriette savory, bitter herb
Saucisse freshly-made sausage
Saucisson large, dry sausage
Saucisson cervelas saveloy
Sauge sage
Saumon salmon
Saumon blanc hake

Saumon fumé smoked salmon
Sauté browned in butter, oil or fat
Sauvage wild
Savarin see *baba au rhum*
Savoyarde with Gruyère cheese
Scarole *endive* (chicory)
Scipion cuttlefish
Seiche squid or cuttlefish
Sel salt
Selle saddle
Selon grosseur (S.G.) according to size
Serpolet wild thyme
Sévigné garnished with mushrooms, roast potatoes, lettuce
Smitane sauce with sour cream, onions, white wine
Socca chickpea flour fritter
Soissons with white beans
Soja (pousse de) soy bean (soy bean sprout)
Soja (sauce de) soy sauce
Sole à la Dieppoise sole fillets, mussels, shrimps, wine, cream
Sole Cardinale poached fillets of sole in lobster sauce
Sole Dugléré sole with tomatoes, onions, shallots, butter
Sole Marguéry sole with mussels and prawns in rich egg sauce
Sole Walewska *mornay* sauce, truffles and prawns
Sorbet water ice
Soubise onion sauce
Soufflé(e) beaten egg whites, baked (with sweet or savoury ingredients)
Soupière soup tureen
Sourdon cockle
Souvaroff a game bird with *foie gras* and truffles
Spaghettis (de) thin strips (of)
Spoom frothy water ice
Strasbourgeoise (à la) Strasbourg style: *foie gras*, *choucroute*, bacon

Sucre sugar
Suppion small cuttlefish
Suprême sweet white sauce
Suprême boneless breast of
    poultry; also describes a fish
    fillet
Sureau (fleurs de) elder tree
    (flowers of); delicious liqueur
Tacaud type of cod
Talleyrand truffles, cheese, *foie
    gras*
Talmousse triangular cheese pastry
Tanche tench
Tapé(e) dried
Tartare raw minced beef
Tartare (sauce) sauce with
    mayonnaise, onions, capers,
    herbs
Tarte open flan
Tarte Tatin upside down tart of
    caramelised apples and pastry
Telline small clam
Tergoule Normandy rice pudding
    with cinnamon
Terrine container in which mixed
    meats/fish are baked; served
    cold
Tête de veau vinaigrette calf's
    head *vinaigrette*
Thé tea
Thermidor grilled lobster with
    browned *béchamel* sauce
Thon tunny fish
Thym thyme
Tiède mild or lukewarm
Tilleul lime tree
Timbale mould in which contents
    are steamed
Tomate tomatoe
Topinambour Jerusalem artichoke
Torte sweet-filled flan
Tortue turtle
Tortue sauce with various herbs,
    tomatoes, Madeira
Toulousaine (à la) Toulouse style:
    truffles, *foie gras*, sweetbreads,

kidneys
Tournedos fillet steak (small end)
Tournedos chasseur with shallots,
    mushrooms, tomatoes
Tournedos Dauphinoise with
    creamed mushrooms, *croûtons*
Tournedos Rossini with goose
    liver, truffles, port, *croûtons*
Touron a cake, pastry or loaf
    made from almond paste and
    filled with candied fruits and
    nuts; also see *ouillat*, a
    Pyrénées soup
Tourte (Tourtière) covered
    savoury tart
Tourteau large crab
Tourteau fromager goat's cheese
    gâteau
Tranche slice
Tranche de boeuf steak
Traver de porc spare rib of pork
Tripes à la mode de Caen beef
    tripe stew
Tripettes small sheep tripe
Tripoux stuffed mutton tripe
Trompettes de la mort fungi
Tronçon a cut of fish or meat
Trou water ice
Truffade a huge sautéed pancake,
    or *galette*, with bacon, garlic
    and Cantal cheese
Truffe truffle; black, exotic, tuber
Truffée with truffles
Truite trout
Truite (au bleu) trout poached in
    water and vinegar; turns blue
Truite saumonée salmon trout
Tuiles tiles (thin almond slices)
Turbot (turbotin) turbot
Vacherin ice cream, meringue,
    cream
Valenciennes (à la) rice, onions,
    red peppers, tomatoes, white
    wine
Vallée d'Auge veal or chicken;
    sautéed, flamed in Calvados and

served with cream and apples

Vapeur (à la) steamed

Varech seaweed

Veau veal

Veau à la Viennoise (escalope de) slice of veal coated with egg and breadcrumbs, fried

Veau Milanaise (escalope de) with macaroni, tomatoes, ham, mushrooms

Veau pané (escalope de) thin slice in flour, eggs and breadcrumbs

Velouté white sauce with *bouillon* and white *roux*

Velouté de volaille thick chicken soup

Venaison venison

Ventre belly or breast

Verdurette *vinaigrette* dressing with herbs

Vernis clam

Véronique grapes, wine, cream

Verte green mayonnaise with chervil, spinach, tarragon

Vert-pré thinly-sliced chips, *maître d'hôtel* butter, watercress

Verveine verbena

Vessie (en) cooked in a pig's bladder; usually chicken

Viande meat

Vichy glazed carrots

Vichyssoise creamy potato and leek soup, served cold

Viennoise coated with egg and breadcrumbs, fried (usually veal)

Vierge (sauce) olive oil sauce

Vierge literally virgin (best olive oil, the first pressing)

Vigneron vine-grower (wine-maker)

Vinaigre (de) wine vinegar or vinegar of named fruit

Vinaigre de Jerez sherry vinegar

Vinaigrette (à la) French dressing with wine vinegar, oil, etc.

Viroflay spinach as a garnish

Volaille poultry

Vol au vent puff pastry case

Xérès (vinaigre de) sherry (vinegar)

Yaourt yogurt

Zeste (d'orange) rubbing from (orange skin)

Regional Cuisine

In the notes which follow I examine first the French regions with Atlantic seaboards, starting in the north and finishing at the Spanish frontier; then the regions bordering Belgium, Germany, Switzerland, Italy and the Mediterranean; and, finally, the regions of inland France.

North Fish takes pride of place, freshly landed at the ports of Boulogne, Calais, and smaller ones like Le Crotoy. *Sole, turbot, maqueraux, barbue, lotte de mer, flétan, harengs, merlan, moules, crévettes*; all appear on menus. So do soups and stews, many with root vegetables: *waterzooï* – fish or chicken stew; *hochepot* – meat and vegetable *pot-au-feu*; *carbonnade* – beef stew with beer. Leeks are super; enjoy *flamiche aux poireaux* (*quiche*-like pastry). Seek out the *hortillonages* (water-gardens) of Amiens and their fine vegetables. Try *gaufres* (yeast waffles) and *ficelles* (variously stuffed pancakes). Beer, too, is good.

Normandy Land of cream, apples and the pig. Vallée d'Auge gives its name to many dishes, including chicken, veal and fish; the term means cream, apples or cider, or apple brandy (Calvados) have been added. Cider is first class. Pork products are everywhere: *andouilles* – smoked tripe sausages, eaten cold; *andouillettes* – small grilled tripe sausages. Fish are superb: *sole à la Normande, à la Dieppoise, à la Fécampoise, à la Havraise* (the last three are ports); *plats de fruits de mer*; shrimps; oysters; *bulots* (whelks); mussels. Enjoy tripe; *ficelles* – pancakes; cow's milk cheeses; rich cream; butters, both salty and sweet; salad produce and potatoes from Caux; exquisite apple tarts; *canard à la Rouennaise*; and fish stews.

Brittany Fish and shellfish are commonplace: lobsters, *huîtres, langoustes*, crabs, of varying sorts, *moules*, prawns, shrimps, *coquilles St-Jacques*; to name just a few. Enjoy *cotriade* – a Breton fish stew with potatoes and onions; *galettes* – buckwheat flour pancakes with savoury fillings; *crêpes de froment* – wheat flour pancakes with sweet fillings; *far Breton* – a batter mixture with raisins; *gâteau Breton* – a mouthwatering concoction; *agneau de pré-salé* – from the salt marshes near Mont-St-Michel (fine omelettes are also made there); and *poulet blanc Breton*. Brittany is one of France's market-gardens: enjoy artichokes, cauliflowers, cabbages, onions and strawberries.

Charentes/Vendée western half of Poitou-Charentes. La Rochelle is a famed fishing port; consequently fish predominates. Oysters are glorious (see *Huîtres* in Glossary). The port of La Cotinière, on the island of Oléron, is renowned for its shrimps. Challans, in the Vendée, is reputed for its quality ducks. Charentes is second to none for butter, goat's milk cheeses, Charentais melons, Cognac, cabbages, mussels, *mojette* (white beans) and salt-marsh lamb from the Marais Poitevin.

Southwest One of the great larders of France; can be divided into several distinct areas. From the countryside that lies in a semicircle to the north-west, west, south and south-east of Bordeaux comes: lamb from Pauillac; oysters (*gravettes*) from Arcachon; eels (*pibales*); beef (*entrecôte Bordelaise* is the bestknown); onions and shallots; *cèpes*; *alose* (shad); and *lamproie* – lamprey (eel-like fish). The Garonne Valley is one vast orchard: try prunes from Agen; peaches; pears and dessert grapes.

South of the Garonne is **Gascony**: famed for *foie gras* (duck and goose); *confit* (preserved meat from both birds); jams and fruits; and Armagnac. Try a *floc* (Armagnac and grape juice).

To the south and west of Gascony are **Béarn** and the **Landes**. From the latter came *palombes* and *ortolans*, ducks and chickens. Among traditional Béarn specialities are *garbue* – the most famous of vegetable soups; *poule au pot* – the chicken dish given its name by Henri IV; *tourin, ouliat* and *cousinette (cousinat)*. See the Southwest for further details.

West of Béarn is **Basque** country: tuna, anchovies, sardines and salmon (from Béarn also) are great; Bayonne ham, *piments* (peppers), *piperade, ttoro* (fish stew) and *gâteau Basque*.

Champagne-Ardenne & Ile de France Many of the specialities listed earlier in the North appear in the former, renowned for its potatoes and turkeys. In the Ardenne you'll enjoy smoked hams, sold in nets; *sanglier*; *marcassin*; and red and white cabbages. West of Verdun, at Ste-Menehould, try *pieds de cochon* (pig's trotters); *petits gris* (snails); and the many differing sweets and sugared almonds (Verdun is famous for them). Troyes is renowned for pork and *andouillettes*.

Regional specialities and produce are all but non-existent in the Ile de France. Look out for cherries from Poissy, beans from Arpajon and tomatoes from Montlhéry. Enjoy *pâtés* and *terrines* and tempting *pâtisseries* and *galettes*.

Alsace There is a strong German influence in much of the cooking; pork, game, goose and beer are common. *Foie gras* (fattened goose liver) is superb. So, too, is a range of tarts; *flammekuchen* – flamed open tart; and some with fruit (*linzertorte* – raspberry or bilberry open tart); jams, fruit liqueurs and *eaux-de-vie* (see Alsace wines). Stomach-filling *choucroute* and local sausages are on most menus; as are *kougelhopf*, *beckenoffe* and *lewerknepfle* (see Alsace specialities). Enjoy *tourte Alsacienne* – pork pie. Use *winstubs* (wine bars).

Lorraine on the north-west borders is known for its *madeleines* (tiny sponge cakes), *macarons*, mouthwatering *quiche Lorraine*, fruit tarts, omelettes and *potée*.

Jura This is dairy country; witness the numerous excellent cheeses encountered in the region. Try *Jésus de Morteau* – a fat pork sausage smoked over pine and juniper; *brési* – wafer-thin slices of dried beef; and many local hams. *Morilles* and other fungi are common; so are freshly-caught trout and other freshwater fish.

Savoie & Hautes-Alpes *Plat gratiné* applies to a wide variety of dishes; in the Alps this means cooked in breadcrumbs; *gratins* of all sorts show how well milk, cream and cheese can be combined together. Relish *fondue* and *gougère*. Freshwater lake fish are magnificent (see the regional specialities for Savoie). Walnuts, chestnuts, all sorts of fruits and marvellous wild mushrooms are other delights.

Côte d'Azur & Provence A head-spinning kaleidoscope of colours and textures fills the eyes: aubergines, peppers, beans, tomatoes, cauliflowers, asparagus, olives, garlic, artichokes, courgettes; the list is endless. Fruit, too, is just as appealing: melons from Cavaillon; strawberries from Monteux; cherries from Remoulins; glacé fruit from Apt; truffles from

Valréas and Aups. Fish from the Med are an extra bonus: *bar* and *loup de mer, daurade, St-Pierre*, monkfish and mullet; these are the best. Lamb from the foothills of the Alps near Sisteron; herbs of every type from the *département* of Var; nuts from Valensole; honey and olive oil; *ratatouille*; sardines; *saucisson d'Arles; bouillabaisse* and *bourride; soupe de poissons* and *soupe au pistou*; what memories are stirred as I write.

Corsica Savour game and charcuterie: *prisuttu* – raw ham, like Italian *prosciutto; figatelli* – grilled pig's liver sausage; *lonzu (lonza)* – slice of pork pickled in salt and herbs; *coopa (copa)* – pork sausage or shoulder of pork. Chestnut flour is used in many ways, particularly in desserts. Fine citrus fruits and, befitting the island of the *maquis*, superb herbs.

Languedoc-Roussillon & Cévennes The same products and dishes listed under Provence are available here. Also oysters and mussels (*les coquillages*) from the lagoons (particularly the Bassin de Thau; visit Mèze and Bouzigues). Excellent shellfish; cherries from Céret; anchovies; apricots and pumpkins. Enjoy *brandade de morue* (salt cod), *confit d'oie* (and *canard*), *cassoulet* and *saucisses de Toulouse*.

Loire The river and its many tributaries provide *alose, sandre, anguille*, carp, perch, pike, salmon and *friture*. A tasty *beurre blanc* is the usual sauce with fish. *Charcuterie* is marvellous: *rillettes, rillons, andouillettes, saucissons, jarretons* and other delights. Cultivated mushrooms come from the limestone caves near Saumur.

The **Sologne** is famous for asparagus, frogs, game, fungi, lake and river fish and wildfowl. You'll be offered, too, many a *pâté*, fruit tarts (it's the home of *tarte Tatin*) and pies.

Burgundy Refer to the often seen regional specialities. Many dishes are wine based: *coq au Chambertin* and *poulet au Meursault* are examples. Enjoy hams, freshwater fish, vegetables, *escargots*, mustard and gingerbread from Dijon and blackcurrants (used for *cassis*, the term for both the fruit and the liqueur made from them).

Lyonnais The culinary heart and stomach of France. There is a variety of top-class produce on hand: Bresse poultry (*chapons* – capons – are unforgettable treats); *grenouilles* and game from Les Dombes; Charolais cattle from the hills west of Beaujolais; fish from the rivers and pools (pike *quenelles* appear everywhere); *charcuterie* from Lyon, particularly sausages called *sabodet, rosette, saucisson en brioche* and *cervelas*; and chocolates and *pâtisseries* from Lyon.

Auvergne & Ardèche Both areas which keep alive old specialities. Refer to the regional lists but here are some of the best: *potée Auvergnate* – a stew of cabbage, vegetables, pork and sausage; *friand Sanflorin* – pork meat and herbs in pastry; *aligot* – a purée of potatoes, cheese, garlic and butter; *pounti* – a small egg-based savoury souffle with bacon or prunes; and delectable *charcuterie*, hams, *saucisson, saucisses sèches* (dried sausages), *pâtés* and so on. The quality and variety of cheeses are second to none. Cabbages, potatoes, bacon and cheese feature on menus. The area around Le Puy is famed for its lentils and Verveine du Velay – yellow and green liqueurs made from over 30 mountain plants. The Ardèche is renowned for its sweet chestnuts (relish *marrons glacés*).

Berry-Bourbonnais & Poitou – eastern half of Poitou-Charentes. The flat terrain of Berry-Bourbonnais is dull country, the granary of France. The area is renowned for beef, deer, wild boar, rabbits, hares, pheasants and partridge.

Much of Poitou lies in the deserted, wooded hills of Limousin (as do the western edges of Auvergne). Apart from the specialities listed look out for *mique* – a stew of dumplings; *farcidure* – a dumpling, either poached or sauteed; and *clafoutis* – pancake batter, poured over fruit (usually black cherries) and baked. Limousin is reputed for its *cèpes* – fine, delicate, flap mushrooms; and also for its reddish-coloured cattle.

Dordogne A land of truffles, geese, ducks, walnuts, *cèpes*, chestnuts, sunflowers and fruit. *Foie gras* (goose and duck) is obligatory on menus; as are *confits* of both birds (preserved in their own fat) and *magrets* (boned duck breasts which have become so popular in the last decade throughout France). *Pâtés* incorporating either poultry or game, and truffles, are common place. If you see *miques* (yeast dumplings) or *merveilles* (hot, sugar-covered pastry fritters) on menus, order them. In the south, in the Lot Valley and towards the Garonne, it's a land of orchards: plums, prunes, figs, peaches, pears and cherries.

Regional Specialities

ALSACE

Beckenoffe (Baeckeoffe) (Baeckaoffa) "baker's oven"; a stew, or hotpot, of potatoes, lamb, beef, pork and onions, cooked in a local wine
Choucroute garnie sauerkraut with peppercorns, boiled ham, pork, Strasbourg sausages and boiled potatoes. Try it with a beer (*bière*)
Chou farci stuffed cabbage
Flammekueche (Tarte flambée) bacon, onion and cream tart
Foie gras goose liver
Kougelhopf a round brioche with raisins and almonds
Krapfen fritters stuffed with jam
Lewerknepfle (Leber Knödel) liver dumpling (pork liver dumpling)

Matelote Alsacienne in Alsace made with stewed eels (in the past from the River Ill) – sometimes with freshwater fish
Pflutters Alsacienne potato puffs
Potage Lorraine potato, leek and onion soup
Schifela shoulder of pork with turnips
Tarte (aux mirabelles) golden plum tart. Also with other fruits
Tarte à l'oignon Alsacienne onion and cream tart

BERRY-BOURBONNAIS

Bignons small fritters
Bouquettes aux pommes de terre grated potato, mixed with flour, egg white and fried in small, thick pieces
Brayaude (gigot) lamb cooked in white wine, onions and herbs
Chargouère (Chergouère) pastry turnover of plums or prunes
Cousinat (Cousina) chestnut soup (*salée* – salted) with cream, butter and prunes; served with bread
Gargouillau a *clafoutis* of pears
Gouèron a cake of goat cheese and eggs
Gouerre (Gouère) a cake of potato purée, flour, eggs and *fromage blanc* (fresh cream cheese), cooked in an oven as a *tourtière*
Lièvre à la Duchambais hare cooked slowly in a sauce of cream, chopped-up shallots, vinegar and pepper
Milliard (Millat) (Milla) a *clafoutis* of cherries (see Poitou-Charentes)
Pâté de pommes de terre a tart of sliced potatoes, butter, bacon and chopped-up onions, baked in an oven. Cream added to hot centre
Poirat pear tart
Pompe aux grattons a cake, in the shape of a crown, made up of a mixture of small pieces of pork, flour, eggs and butter
Sanciau thick sweet or savoury pancake; made from buckwheat flour
Truffiat grated potato, mixed with flour, eggs and butter and baked

BRITTANY

Agneau de pré-salé leg of lamb, from animals pastured in the salt marshes and meadows of Brittany
Bardatte cabbage stuffed with hare, cooked in white wine and served with chestnuts and roast quail
Beurre blanc sauce for fish dishes; made from the reduction of shallots, wine vinegar and the finest butter (sometimes with dry white wine)
Cotriade fish soup with potatoes, onions, garlic and butter
Crêpes Bretonnes the thinnest of pancakes with a variety of sweet fillings; often called **Crêpes de froment** (wheat flour)
Far Breton batter mixture; vanilla-flavoured sugar, rum, dried prunes
Galette takes various forms: can be a biscuit, a cake or a pancake; the

latter is usually stuffed with fillings like mushrooms, ham, cheese or seafood and is called a **Galette de blé noir** (buckwheat flour)
Gâteau Breton rich cake with butter, flour, egg yolks and sugar
Gigot de pré-salé same as *agneau de pré-salé*
Kouign-amann crisp, flaky pastries of butter, sugar and yeast
Palourdes farcies clams in the shell, with a *gratiné* filling
Poulet blanc Breton free-range, fine quality white Breton chicken

BURGUNDY

Boeuf Bourguignon braised beef simmered in red wine-based sauce
Charolais (Pièce de) steak from the excellent Charolais cattle
Garbure heavy soup; mixture of pork, cabbage, beans and sausages
Gougère cheese pastry, based on Gruyère cheese
Jambon persillé parsley-flavoured ham, served cold in its jelly
Jambon en saupiquet, Jambon à la crème, Jambon à la Morvandelle ham with a piquant cream sauce, wine and wine vinegar
Matelote freshwater fish soup, usually based on a red wine sauce
Meurette red wine-based sauce with small onions. Accompanies fish or poached egg dishes
Pain d'épice spiced honeycake from Dijon
Pochouse (Pouchouse) stew of freshwater fish and garlic, usually white wine based. Rarely seen on restaurant menus
Potée see *Garbure*

CHAMPAGNE-ARDENNE

Flamiche aux Maroilles see *Tarte aux Maroilles*
Flamiche aux poireaux puff-pastry tart with cream and leeks
Goyère see *Tarte aux Maroilles*
Rabotte (Rabote) whole apple wrapped in pastry and baked
Tarte aux Maroilles a hot creamy tart based on the local cheese

COTE D'AZUR

Aïgo Bouido garlic and sage soup – with bread (or eggs and cheese)
Aïgo saou fish soup (no *rascasse* – scorpion fish) with *rouille*
Aïoli (ailloli) a mayonnaise sauce with garlic and olive oil
Anchoïade anchovy crust
Berlingueto chopped spinach and hard-boiled eggs
Bouillabaisse a dish of Mediterranean fish (including *rascasse, St-Pierre, baudroie, congre, chapon de mer, langoustes, langoustines, tourteaux, favouilles, merlan* and, believe it or not, many others) and a soup, served separately with *rouille, safran* and *aïoli*
Bourride a creamy fish soup (usually made with big white fish), thickened with *aïoli* and flavoured with crawfish

Brandade (de morue) à l'huile d'olive a mousse of salt cod with cream, olive oil and garlic
Capoum a large pink *rascasse* (scorpion fish)
Pain Bagna bread roll with olive oil, anchovies, olives, onions, etc.
Pieds et paquets small parcels of mutton tripe, cooked with sheep trotters and white wine
Pissaladière Provençal bread dough with onions, anchovies, olives, etc.
Pistou (Soupe au) vegetable soup bound with *pommade*
Pollo pépitora Provençal chicken *fricassée* thickened with lemon-flavoured mayonnaise
Pommade a thick paste of garlic, basil, cheese and olive oil
Ratatouille aubergines, courgettes, onion, garlic, red peppers and tomatoes in olive oil
Rouille orange-coloured sauce with hot peppers, garlic and saffron
Salade Niçoise tomatoes, beans, potatoes, black olives, anchovy, lettuce and olive oil. Sometimes tuna fish
Tapénade a purée of stoned black olives, anchovy fillets, capers, tuna fish and olive oil
Tarte (Tourte) aux blettes open-crust pastry with filling of Swiss chard (not unlike Chinese cabbage) and pine nuts
Tian Provençal earthenware dish

DORDOGNE

Bourrioles d'Aurillac sweet pancakes, made from buckwheat flour
Cèpes fine, delicate mushrooms. Sometimes dried
Chou farci stuffed cabbage. Sometimes *aux marrons* – with chestnuts
Confit de canard (d'oie) preserved duck (goose)
Cou d'oie neck of goose
Foie de canard (gras) duck liver (goose)
Friands de Bergerac small potato cakes
Merveilles hot, sugar-covered pastry fritters
Mique stew or soup with dumplings
Pommes à la Sarladaise potatoes, truffles, ham or *foie gras*
Rilletes d'oie soft, potted goose
Sobronade soup with pork, ham, beans and vegetables
Tourin Bordelais (Ouillat) onion soup
Tourin Périgourdine vegetable soup
Truffes truffles; black and exotic tubers or fungi, as large as walnuts, which grow on the roots of certain oak and hazelnut trees
Truffes sous les cendres truffles, wrapped in paper (or bacon) and cooked in ashes

HAUTES-ALPES

See those listed in the Savoie region

ILE DE FRANCE

Refer to these five regions: Normandy to the west; the North; Champagne-Ardenne to the east; and Burgundy and the Loire on the southern borders of the Ile de France.

JURA

Brési wafer-thin slices of dried beef
Gougère hot cheese pastry – based on Comté cheese
Jésus de Morteau fat pork sausage smoked over pine and juniper
Poulet au vin jaune chicken, cream and *morilles*, cooked in *vin jaune*

LANGUEDOC-ROUSSILLON

Aïgo Bouido garlic soup. A marvellous, aromatic dish; the garlic is boiled, so its impact is lessened. Served with bread
Boles de picoulat small balls of chopped-up beef and pork, garlic and eggs – served with tomatoes and parsley
Bouillinade a type of *bouillabaisse*; with potatoes, oil, garlic and onions
Boutifare a sausage-shaped pudding of bacon and herbs
Cargolade snails, stewed in wine
Millas cornmeal porridge
Ouillade heavy soup of bacon, *boutifare*, leeks, carrots and potatoes
Touron a pastry of almonds, pistachio nuts and fruit

LOIRE

Alose à l'oseille grilled shad with a sorrel sauce
Bardette stuffed cabbage
Beuchelle à la Tourangelle kidneys, sweetbreads, morels, truffles, cream
Bourdaines apples stuffed with jam and baked
Rillauds chauds strips of hot bacon
Rillettes potted pork
Sandre freshwater fish, like perch
Tarte à la citrouille pumpkin tart
Tarte Tatin *upside-down* tart of caramelised apples and pastry
Truffiat potato cake

LYONNAIS

Bresse (Poulet, Poularde, Volaille de) the best French poultry. Fed on corn and, when killed, bathed in milk. Flesh is white and delicate
Gras-double ox tripe, served with onions
Poulet demi-deuil *half-mourning*; called this because of the thin slices of truffle placed under the chicken breast; cooked in a *court-bouillon*

Poulet au vinaigre chicken, shallots, tomatoes, white wine, wine vinegar and a cream sauce
Rosette a large pork sausage;
Sabodet see *Glossary of Menu Terms*
Tablier de Sapeur *gras-double* coated with flour, egg-yolk, breadcrumbs

MASSIF CENTRAL (Auvergne, Ardèche and Cévennes)

Aligot purée of potatoes with Tomme de Cantal cheese, cream, garlic and butter
Bougnette a stuffing of pork, bread and eggs – wrapped in *crépine* (caul)
Bourriols d'Aurillac sweet pancakes, made from buckwheat flour
Brayaude (gigot) lamb cooked in white wine, onions and herbs
Cadet Mathieu pastry turnover filled with slices of apple
Clafoutis baked pancake batter, poured over fruit, usually cherries
Confidou Rouergat ragout of beef, red wine, tomatoes, garlic and onions
Cousinat (Cousina) chestnut soup (*salée* – salted) with cream, butter and prunes and served with bread
Criques grated potato, mixed with eggs and fried – in the form of pancakes. Related to the *truffiat* of Berry
Farçon large *galette* of sausage, sorrel, onions, eggs and white wine
Farinette buckwheat flour pancakes – meat and vegetable filling
Friand Sanflorin pork meat and herbs in pastry
Jambon d'Auvergne a tasty mountain ham
Manouls see *Trénels*
Milliard (Millat) (Milla) a *clafoutis* of cherries (see Poitou-Charentes)
Mourtayol a stew with beef, chicken, ham, vegetables and bread
Omelette Brayaude eggs, pork, cheese and potatoes
Perdrix à l'Auvergnate partridge stewed in white wine
Potée Auvergnate stew of vegetables, cabbage, pork and sausage
Pountari a mince of pork fat in cabbage leaves
Pounti small, egg-based savoury soufflé with bacon or prunes
Rouergat(e) Rouergue; the name of the area to the west of Millau
Salmis de colvert Cévenole wild duck, sautéed in red wine, onions, ham and mushrooms
Soupe aux choux soup with cabbage, ham, pork, bacon and turnips
Trénels mutton tripe, white wine and tomatoes
Tripoux stuffed sheep's feet
Truffade a huge *galette* of sautéed potatoes

NORMANDY

Andouillette de Vire small chitterling (tripe) sausage
Barbue au cidre brill cooked in cider and Calvados
Cauchoise (à la) with cream, Calvados and apple
Douillons de pommes à la Normande baked apples in pastry

Escalope (Vallée d'Auge) veal sautéed, flamed in Calvados and served with cream and apples

Ficelle Normande pancake with ham, mushrooms and cheese

Marmite Dieppoise a fish soup with some, or all of the following: sole, turbot, *rouget*, *moules*, *crevettes*, onions, white wine, butter and cream

Poulet (Vallée d'Auge) chicken cooked in the same way as *Escalope Vallee d'Auge*

Tripes à la mode de Caen stewed beef tripe with onions, carrots, leeks, garlic, cider and Calvados

Trou Normand Calvados – a "dram", drunk in one gulp, between courses; claimed to restore the appetite

NORTH

Carbonnade de Boeuf à la Flamande braised beef with beer, onions and bacon; if only more chefs would prepare this great dish

Caudière (Chaudière, Caudrée) versions of fish and potato soup

Ficelles Picardes ham pancakes with mushroom sauce

Flamiche aux Maroilles see *Tarte aux Maroilles*

Flamiche aux poireaux puff-pastry tart with cream and leeks

Gaufres yeast waffles

Goyère see *Tarte aux Maroilles*

Hochepot a *pot-au-feu* of the North (see *Pepperpot*)

Pepperpot stew of mutton, pork, beer and vegetables

Sanguette black pudding, made with rabbit's blood

Soupe courquignoise soup with white wine, fish, *moules*, leeks and Gruyère cheese

Tarte aux Maroilles a hot creamy tart based on Maroilles cheese

Waterzooï a cross between soup and stew, usually of fish or chicken (Don't bypass Serge Pérard's exhilarating fish restaurant at 67 rue de Metz in Le Touquet; his *soupe de poissons* is fabulous. Robin Yapp at Mere (my favourite wine supplier) stocks the soup (0747) 860423)

POITOU-CHARENTES

Bouilliture (Bouilleture) a freshwater eel stew with shallots and prunes in Sauvignon white wine

Boulaigou thick sweet or savoury pancake

Bréjaude cabbage, leek and bacon soup

Cagouilles (also called **Lumas**) snails from the Charentes

Casserons en matelote squid in red wine sauce with garlic and shallots

Cèpes fine, delicate, flap mushrooms; please do try them

Chaudrée a ragout of fish cooked in white wine, shallots and butter

Chevrettes local name for *crevettes* (shrimps)

Clafoutis pancake batter, poured over fruit (usually black cherries), and then baked; another treat you must not miss

Embeurrée de chou white-heart cabbage, cooked in salted water, crushed and served with butter

Farcidure a dumpling – either poached or sautéed

Farci Poitevin a *pâté* of cabbage, spinach and sorrel, encased by cabbage leaves and cooked in a *bouillon*

Migourée a sort of *chaudrée*

Mique a stew of dumplings

Mogette (Mojette) small pulse beans in butter and cream

Mouclade mussels cooked in wine, egg yolks and cream; can be served with some Pineau des Charentes

Oysters for an explanation of *les claires, belons, gravettes, marennes* and other terms see the *Glossary of Menu Terms* (under *Huîtres*)

Soupe aux fèves des Marais soup of crushed broad beans with bread, sorrel, chervil and butter

Soupe de moules à la Rochelaise soup of various fish, mussels, saffron, garlic, tomatoes, onions and red wine

Sourdons cockles from the Charentes

Tartisseaux fritters

Tourtou thick buckwheat flour pancake

PROVENCE

Please see the specialities listed in the Côte d'Azur

SAVOIE

Farcement (Farçon Savoyard) potatoes baked with cream, eggs, bacon, dried pears and prunes; a hearty stomach filler

Féra a freshwater lake fish

Fondue hot melted cheese and white wine

Gratin Dauphinois a classic potato dish with cream, cheese and garlic

Gratin Savoyard another classic potato dish with cheese and butter

Lavaret a freshwater lake fish, like salmon

Longeole a country sausage

Lotte a burbot, not unlike an eel

Omble chevalier a char, it looks like a large salmon trout

SOUTHWEST

Besugo *daurade* – sea-bream

Chorizos spicy sausages

Confit de canard (d'oie) preserved duck meat (goose)

Cousinette (Cousinat) vegetable soup

Echassier a wading bird of the Landes

Garbure (Garbue) vegetable soup with cabbage and ham bone

Gâteau Basque a shallow, custard pastry – often with fruit fillings

Grattons (Graisserons) a *mélange* of small pieces of rendered down duck, goose and pork fat; served as an appetiser – very filling

Hachua beef stew

Jambon de Bayonne raw ham, cured in salt. Served as paper-thin slices

Lamproie eel-like fish; with leeks, onions and red Bordeaux wine sauce

Lou-kenkas small, spicy sausages

Loubine (Louvine) grey mullet (like a sea-bass)

Ortolan a small bird (wheatear) from the Landes

Ouillat (Ouliat) Pyrénées soup; onions, tomatoes, goose fat, garlic

Palombes (Salmis de) wild doves and wood pigeons from the Landes and Béarn, sautéed in red wine, ham and mushrooms

Pastiza see *Gâteau Basque*

Ramereaux ring doves

Salda a thick cabbage and bean soup

Tourin (Tourain) see *Ouillat*. (*Touron*: see Languedoc-Roussillon)

Tourtière Landaise a sweet of Agen prunes, apples and Armagnac

Ttoro (Ttorro) a Basque fish stew

CORSICA

Aziminu the Corsican *bouillabaisse*. Large *rascasse* (called *capone* or *capoum*), red peppers and pimentos are among the local ingredients

Canistrelli an almond cake flavoured with *anis*

Cédrat a sour lemon-like fruit used in sweets and liqueurs

Falculelle (Falculella) a cheesecake using Broccio cheese

Fiadone an orange-flavoured flan made with Broccio cheese

Fritelle chestnut flour fritter

Panizze a fried cake made from chestnut flour (or cornmeal)

Piverunata (Pebronata) a stew of kid (young goat), or beef, or chicken – in a sauce of red peppers, garlic and tomatoes

Pulenta (Polenta) in Corsica this is usually made from chestnut flour – similar in appearance to the Italian boiled commercial version

Stufatu the Italian influence is strong in Corsican cooking – especially pasta. This dish is macaroni with mushrooms and onions

Torta castagina a tart covered with crushed almonds, *pignons*, *raisins secs* and a dash, or two, of rum

Ziminu a pimento and red pepper sauce for fish

FRENCH WINES & CHEESES

For details of one thousand or so French wines and cheeses I refer you to the regional introductions of my guide, *French Leave Encore*. Apart from providing details of the wines and cheeses the accompanying regional maps also show their respective birthplaces and, in addition, two invaluable indexes make tracking them all down child's play. Use the indexes both in France and at home.